COLLECTED WORKS OF

BERNARD LONERGAN

VOLUME 20

SHORTER PAPERS

GENERAL EDITORS

Frederick E. Crowe and Robert M. Doran

COLLECTED WORKS
OF BERNARD
LONERGAN

SHORTER PAPERS
edited by Robert C. Croken,
Robert M. Doran, and
H. Daniel Monsour

Published for Lonergan Research Institute
of Regis College, Toronto
by University of Toronto Press
Toronto Buffalo London

ISBN 978-0-8020-9753-8 (cloth)
ISBN 978-0-8020-9517-6 (paper)

Printed on acid-free paper

Library and Archives Canada Cataloguing in Publication Data

Lonergan, Bernard J.F. (Bernard Joseph Francis), 1904–1984
   Collected works of Bernard Lonergan / edited by Frederick E. Crowe
   and Robert M. Doran

   Contents: v. 20. Shorter papers / edited by Robert C. Croken, Robert M.
   Doran and H. Daniel Monsour
   ISBN 978-0-8020-9573-8 (v. 20: bound). – ISBN 978-0-8020-9517-6
   (v. 20: pbk.)

   1. Theology – 20th century.   2. Catholic Church.   I. Crowe, Frederick E.
   II. Doran, Robert M., 1939–   Lonergan Research Institute   IV. Title.

   BX891.L595 1988   230   c88-093328-3 rev

The Lonergan Research Institute gratefully acknowledges the generous
contribution of the MALLINER CHARITABLE FOUNDATION, which has made
possible the production of this entire series.

The Lonergan Research Institute gratefully acknowledges the contribution toward publication of this volume of the VASCO DE QUIROGA JESUIT
COMMUNITY, Mexico City.

University of Toronto Press acknowledges the financial support for its
publishing activities of the Government of Canada through the Book
Publishing Industry Development Program (BPIDP).

Contents

PART THREE: EARLY REVIEWS

PART FOUR: REVIEWS AND BOOK NOTICES
FROM THE ROMAN YEARS

PART FIVE: LATER SHORTER PAPERS, RESPONSES, REVIEWS

General Editors' Preface

At first blush, this volume will appear to some readers as a variegated collection of items that the editors could not place anywhere else. Even the title, 'Shorter Papers,' is not quite accurate, as several items (for example, 2, 3, and 65) are longer than some papers in other volumes. So what is the rationale behind this particular collection of materials, precisely as a collection? It is to provide access in one volume to writings of Bernard Lonergan that most people would not think of consulting if they wanted to ascertain Lonergan's mind on any given topic, and yet that provide a privileged access to that mind and to the person behind it precisely in some of his most personal qualities: his development, his religious commitment, his fairness to other authors, his loyalty and gratitude to some of his students.

The items extend from some of the earliest of Bernard Lonergan's writings – The *Blandyke Papers* are earlier than any other materials that will appear in the Collected Works – to some very late pieces. The order is almost entirely chronological, not only in the five parts but also in the individual items in each part. There are only a few overlappings between parts, from a chronological point of view, and these are exclusively between parts 2 and 3. The materials span nearly fifty years, and while it is true that for the most part they are writings that would not fit in another volume of the Collected Works, still there is something to be said for gathering in one volume what could almost be described as a series of glimpses rather than a collection of rigorous arguments demanding careful analysis. Perhaps only the first two items in the book would fit that latter description, and I dare say most readers will find these to be among the more difficult of Lonergan's papers.

My fellow General Editor Frederick Crowe[1] as well as Richard Liddy[2] and William Mathews[3] have all provided valuable commentaries on these difficult early works, and I refer readers to their commentaries and interpretations. What almost leaps off the page in both of these writings is the anticipation of insight into phantasm and the suspicion that there is something more fundamental than logic. This shows that, while Lonergan's work was cumulative, there is an amazing continuity in his intellectual trajectory from the late 1920s all the way to the early 1980s.

I wish to thank my fellow editors, Robert Croken and Daniel Monsour, for their work on this volume. All of the preparatory work and a good deal of the final work was done by Robert Croken. He is also responsible for the index. Daniel Monsour surely ranks among the academy's most creative and resourceful researchers. We are very fortunate to have at our disposal his skills at discovering rare but valuable bits of information that throw considerable light on texts and their meanings. He even discovered the twenty-nine libraries in the world that have a particular volume that was able to provide the answer to one of our questions! And one of those libraries is at Seton Hall University, where Richard Liddy did the research that we needed.

The editors all wish to thank Michael Shields for translating two of the pieces from Latin and for his advice on the lexicon of Latin and Greek words and phrases.

And all three of us, as editors of this particular volume, wish to acknowledge the continuing inspiration of my fellow General Editor, Frederick Crowe. In the contract that Fred signed with University of Toronto Press some twenty years ago for the publication of the Collected Works, he and I were named as Editors, and until the work on this particular volume we were both closely involved in the production of all the books that make up this series, even when we were not editors of a particular volume. It is only appropriate that Fred remain acknowledged as a General Editor until the entire series has been published. Bernard Lonergan would want this, and I want it as well. Fred's name will appear facing the title page of every subsequent volume in this series.

1 Frederick E. Crowe, *Lonergan* (London: Geoffrey Chapman, 1992).
2 Richard M. Liddy, *Transforming Light: Intellectual Conversion in the Early Lonergan* (Collegeville, MN: The Liturgical Press, 1993).
3 William A. Mathews, *Lonergan's Quest: A Study of Desire in the Authoring of* Insight (Toronto: University of Toronto Press, 2005).

One comment seems necessary. We are all creatures of our time, whether we like it or not, and nowhere is this more obvious than in our language. From the beginning of the Collected Works project, Frederick Crowe and I decided that we could not change Lonergan's fairly frequent use of exclusive language, which after all was the common practice at the time he was writing. We had no doubt that he would speak differently today, but he is not writing today. In the current volume, there appear two instances of terms that are racially inappropriate. Once again, the editors' decision was that we have to present the data on Bernard Lonergan as we find them in his writings. I can witness to his deep sensitivity to racial stereotypes and cultural imperialism, and I am certain that there was no intention on his part to be offensive. He spoke as the common sense of his people at his time had taught him to speak, and I hope that all readers will acknowledge how difficult it can be to move beyond such learned habits.

In keeping with our policy, we have used the *Oxford American Dictionary* and the *Chicago Manual of Style* as guides to editorial decisions, but we have not followed them slavishly. Translations from scripture are as Lonergan gave them in the original manuscripts. Brackets generally indicate editorial additions.

ROBERT M. DORAN
Marquette University

PART ONE

The *Blandyke Papers*

1

The Form of Mathematical Inference[1]

In the genesis of Greek philosophy three stages have been distinguished, the poetical, the dialectic, and the expository.[2] If this may be taken as representative of the natural development of thought on any subject, it would seem that mathematical inference cannot be considered to have yet reached

---

1 [The first five papers of this volume were written by Lonergan during his philosophical studies at Heythrop College, 1926–30. A series of papers, written by the students, were called the *Blandyke Papers*. 'These *Papers*, being extra-curricular and in a sense "holiday" work, are named from a village near Liège where the students had their weekly holiday in the years when English laws forced the Jesuit seminary across the English Channel. They were not published but handwritten in a notebook (after being duly refereed) which was left in the College reading-room.' Frederick E. Crowe, *Lonergan*, Outstanding Christian Thinkers Series (London: Geoffrey Chapman, 1992) 32, n. 33. Copies of Lonergan's handwritten *Papers* are in the library of the Lonergan Research Institute, Toronto, and were carefully transcribed to a typewritten text by Michael Shields in the 1980s. Both sources have been used in the current editing. The section headings are editorial additions.
      The present paper appeared in *Blandyke Papers* no. 283 (January 1928) 126–37. 'His (Lonergan's) very first article was called "The form of mathematical inference." This is not the one that appeared in *Thought* fifteen years later as "The form of inference," but a quite distinct treatment of the act that would become famous as "insight into phantasm."' Crowe, *Lonergan* 14. For a commentary on this paper in relation to John Henry Newman, see Richard M. Liddy, *Transforming Light: Intellectual Conversion in the Early Lonergan* (Collegeville, MN: The Liturgical Press, 1993) 20–22.]
2 E. Seymer Thompson, *The Meno of Plato*, ed. with introduction, notes, and excursuses (London, New York: Macmillan, 1901), in the Introduction.

exposition,[3] for we find a singularly complete disagreement on the question between Fr Joyce and Fr Coffey.[4] Examination and discussion of the data, therefore – a work which a tyro may undertake with benefit to himself and no harm to others – happens to be profitable at present; and this is my apology for venturing to point out a hypothesis without attempting to verify it with any scientific thoroughness.[5]

1   *Vis Cogitativa* and Concrete Inference

There seems to be a foundation for this hypothesis in St Thomas, who followed some of the Moors in adding *vis cogitativa* to Aristotle's account of cognitional faculties and functions. Fr Coffey states[6] that his [St Thomas's] doctrine on this point is not very clear, and this, though unfortunate for philosophy generally, frees me from the onerous duty of consulting the exegetes.[7] However he [St Thomas] does state quite clearly that the *syllogismus*

---

3 [In Thompson's discussion, the expository stage is reached when '[a] thinker having succeeded in framing a system that satisfies him, assuming the attitude of a teacher propounds it in a consecutive treatise.' *The Meno of Plato* x. For Thompson, in Greek philosophy this stage was reached with Aristotle.]

4 See George Hayward Joyce, *Principles of Logic* (London, New York: Longmans, Green & Co., 1908) 199–201; Peter Coffey, *The Science of Logic: An Inquiry into the Principles of Accurate Thought and Scientific Method*, vol. 1, *Conception, Judgment, and Inference* (London: Longmans, Green & Co., 1918) 385–95.

5 [In the pages cited, Joyce notes that some recent logicians have maintained that much of the reasoning employed in mathematics is not syllogistic, for frequently such reasoning does not involve a subject–attribute relation but a relation between two quantities. This view Joyce believes to be 'erroneous': his position is that the subject–attribute relation is involved in such reasoning, for that relation 'is inseparable from judgment,' and that, despite appearances, the inference in such arguments finds its ultimate justification in the *dictum de omni et nullo* and not in some axiom such as 'Things which are equal to the same thing are equal to each other.' Coffey, by contrast, argues that the examples of valid mathematical reasoning that Joyce cites are indeed based on the axiom just mentioned and not on the *dictum de omni et nullo*, and that even if one grants that such reasoning can be couched in syllogistic form by including the axiom as the major premise, the resulting syllogism 'can hardly be claimed to be an equivalent expression of the original argument.' It is this disagreement that provides the occasion for Lonergan to 'venture' and illustrate his own 'hypothesis' regarding mathematical inference, 'without attempting to verify it with any scientific thoroughness.']

6 Coffey, *The Science of Logic* 1, 394.

7 [In the later *Verbum* articles, Julien Peghaire is the exegete that Lonergan would draw upon to assist him in clarifying the doctrine of *vis cogitativa* in St Thomas. See Peghaire's article 'A Forgotten Sense: the Cogitative

expositorius is a *sensibilis demonstratio seu resolutio facta ad sensum*,[8] and accordingly it would seem that he held that there were two kinds of inference, one sensible, the other conceptual, which is quite sufficient for my purpose.

2   Universals of Sense, Generic Image, and Axioms

The next point to be made is that 'universal' and 'particular' do not constitute an adequate diagnostic between 'conceptual' and 'sensible' according

---

according to St. Thomas Aquinas,' *The Modern Schoolman* 20 (1943) 123–40, 210–29; and Bernard Lonergan, *Verbum: Word and Idea in Aquinas*, vol. 2 in Collected Works of Bernard Lonergan, ed. Frederick E. Crowe and Robert M. Doran (Toronto: University of Toronto Press, 1997) 43–44, n. 150. Peghaire remarks in his article (210) that Averroes [Ibn-Rushd] regarded the possible intellect as one for the entire human race and outside of the individual, and he identified Aristotle's corruptible passive intellect, indispensable for the act of understanding, as the formal constitutive difference of the human species, and characterized it as the cogitative. And he adds that St Thomas's views on the function of the cogitative in intellectual cognition 'are found in the context in which he is stating his case against Averroes.' This last fact, perhaps, explains Lonergan's references to St Thomas following 'some of the Moors ...' Interestingly, in *Lonergan*, Crowe remarks that at this time Lonergan 'does not seem to have read Thomas' (14). So it seems a plausible conjecture that his knowledge of Thomas's doctrine of *vis cogitativa* during this period was, for the most part, filtered either through his teachers at Heythrop, or through textbooks and other secondary sources he read, or through both.]

8 See Joyce, *Principles of Logic*, 190, note. [*De natura syllogismi*, a spurious work, is quoted: 'Syllogismus expositorius non est vere syllogismus, sed magis sensibilis demonstratio, seu resolutio facta ad sensum, ad hoc quod consequentia quae vera est secundum intellectualem cognitionem, declaretur in sensibili.' An expository syllogism is one that admits of singular terms and premises or, in a more restricted sense, one in which the middle term is singular. In *Formal Logic* (Oxford: Clarendon Press, 1955), A.N. Prior remarks that singular propositions, that is, propositions about some definite individual, 'are not much discussed by Aristotle ...' The Scholastics, by contrast, used singular propositions in 'their most characteristic examples' of syllogisms. He adds that the term *syllogismus expositorius* was taken from Aristotle's proof by *exposition* or *ekthesis* (see p. 157). For some representative texts in which Scholastic writers discuss syllogisms with singular terms, see I.M. Bochenski, *A History of Formal Logic*, trans. and ed. Ivo Thomas (Notre Dame: University of Notre Dame Press, 1961) 232–33.]

to Aristotle's statement.[9] Beside Fr Moncel's[10] abhorrence of the term 'universal' on the ground that it suggests a misleading notion of concepts, there is St Thomas's authority that a certain amount of universalization is done in sense perception.[11] Nor should Aristotle be pressed, for in this paragraph he is giving reasons why a general truth is better than a particular.[12] Now it would seem that the only kind of proposition which Aristotle recognized was the predication, of which this statement of his is perfectly true, while mathematical inference does not use subject–attribute relations such as 'The train is moving,' but relations between two discrete objects, for example, '*A* is north of *B*,' '*A* is taller than *B*.' On this point I quote Fr Coffey: 'The truth is that when the mind goes through this simple inference [namely, $A > B$, $B > C$, therefore $A > C$] it has *three* objects of thought before it, namely, *A*, *B*, and *C*; that in the three constituent judgments it relates these terms (in pairs), *not* by the logical copula "*is*," which would express a *subject-attribute* identity, but by a copula which expresses a directly and intuitively apprehended *relation of magnitude* between the terms of each pair – by the copula "*is greater than.*"'[13]

9   Joyce, *Principles of Logic* 186, note, where Aristotle is quoted and translated. [Joyce says that 'particular propositions always depend in the last resort on sensible experience.' Then he quotes Aristotle, *Posterior Analytics*, I, c. 24, § 11, as follows: 'The universal proposition is the object of intellectual intuition; the particular ends in sense experience.' In Bekker's numbers, the text is *Posterior Analytics*, I, 24, 86a 28–30. Mure's translation is: '… commensurately universal demonstration is through and through intelligible; particular demonstration issues in sense-perception.' See *The Basic Works of Aristotle*, ed. Richard McKeon (New York: Random House, 1941) 150.]

10   [Fr Victor Moncel, s.j. (1874–1954) was a professor of psychology, first at St Mary's Hall, Stonyhurst, and then at Heythrop College, until he retired from teaching in 1940. According to Crowe, *Lonergan* 13, Moncel was the lecturer on psychology and the history of philosophy in Lonergan's first year at Heythrop. We may be touching here on one largely unmentioned formative influence on Lonergan, for Moncel is clearly downplaying the importance of universals in knowing, or at least assigning them a lesser importance than what he calls 'Intuition,' taking the word perhaps from Thomas's usage (see his article 'Professor Spearman and Scholasticism,' *The Month* 143 [1924] 217–25; see also Lonergan, *Verbum* 25, note 52; note that Lonergan himself will speak here of 'an intuition of the *vis cogitativa*'). Some indication of Moncel's attitude to universals can be gleaned from his article.]

11   [A point to which Lonergan returns in *Verbum* precisely in the context of the *cogitativa*. See, for example, 43 and n. 150.]

12   Aristotle, *Posterior Analytics*, I, 24, 86a 22–30.

13   Coffey, *The Science of Logic* I, 387, emphasis his.

Assuming therefore the possibility of universals of sense, let us see if there are any such universals. The following inference is as likely as any to be admitted to be a *sensibilis demonstratio*. An egg is in a dish, the dish is in the warmer, therefore an egg is in the warmer. Now from this concrete inference can be extracted a relation of universal application which might be called an axiom; it is: 'whatever contains a container contains what is contained in the container.' How do we know the truth of this axiom? Kant might call it a synthetic a priori judgment. The Scholastics are not very illuminating when they explain that the predicate is *exegetive de ratione subjecti*. But it would seem highly probable, when one makes more gradual the change from concrete inference to universal proposition, that both inference and axiom are apprehensions of the *vis cogitativa*. For if we consider this argument a *resolutio facta ad sensum*, is there any difference in making it a *resolutio ad phantasma* and saying: '*A* is in *B*, *B* is in *C*, therefore *A* is in *C*?' It would seem not: for if *vis cogitativa* apprehends the implication in the first without any appeal to a higher principle, then it can so apprehend the implication of the second in virtue of a generic image[14] which represents satisfactorily the relation said to hold between the indeterminate *A*, *B*, *C*.

To bring this function of the generic image out more clearly, let us take a case somewhat more complicated and consequently requiring more noticeable visualization. This argument is as much a *sensibilis demonstratio* as

14 See diagrams at the end of this paper. [We may see in this 'generic image' a forerunner connected with what Lonergan will later refer to as free images, 'under the influence of the higher levels [of cognitional process] before they provide a basis for inquiry and reflection' (Bernard Lonergan, *Insight: A Study of Human Understanding*, vol. 3 in Collected Works of Bernard Lonergan, ed. Frederick E. Crowe and Robert M. Doran [Toronto: University of Toronto Press, 1992] 299). It approximates as well to what he will later refer to occasionally as schematic images, that set of aspects in the data necessary for the occurrence of a particular insight or set of insights (ibid. 55, 379). On free images under the influence of intelligence, see also the reference in *Verbum* 44, note 50, to 'a sensitive potency under the influence of intellect ...' And on schematic images see also 'An Interview with Fr. Bernard Lonergan, S.J.,' in *A Second Collection: Papers by Bernard J.F. Lonergan, S.J.*, ed. William F.J. Ryan and Bernard J. Tyrrell (Toronto: University of Toronto Press, 1974) 223, and *Method in Theology* (Toronto: University of Toronto Press, 2003) 86. Nor would we be wide of the mark if we took Lonergan as referring to the generic or schematic image when he remarks in *Phenomenology and Logic: The Boston College Lectures on Mathematical Logic and Existentialism*, vol. 18 in Collected Works of Bernard Lonergan, ed. Philip J. McShane (Toronto: University of Toronto Press, 2001) 26: 'The tutor whom I had in mathematics in England, Fr O'Hara, said that to do mathematics you need an X-ray mind. You want to see the skeleton.']

the preceding: 'London is east of Bristol, Bristol is south of Liverpool, therefore London is southeast of Liverpool.' Here the visualization is of a particular right-angled triangle. If we say, '*A* is east of *B*, *B* is south of *C*, therefore *A* is southeast of *C*,' we have as it were a generalization of the above inference, and it depends upon a somewhat different (generic) image. For if we ask ourselves what is meant by saying '*A* is southeast of *C*' we find we cannot mean it as due southeast, or southeast in the particular way London is southeast of Liverpool, but only that *A* is somewhere within the quadrant limited by lines due east and due south of *C*. For *A* might be very nearly due east or due south, and in many positions which we would not ordinarily refer to as southeast. It would seem that the truth of this inference was apprehended by *vis cogitativa* from a generic image.

The next step then is to note the affinity between the inference, 'Because *A* is in *B* and *B* is in *C*, therefore *A* is in *C*,' and the universal proposition, 'If *A* is in *B* and *B* is in *C*, then *A* is in *C*.' The only difference between them is that in one the premises are categorical, in the other the same propositions are hypothetical, and on that account have their name changed from premise to antecedent. There is no reason therefore not to attribute both to *vis cogitativa* if one is due to it. Finally it is only a matter of paraphrase to substitute words for the symbols and say, 'Whatever contains a container contains what is contained in the container.'

Hence, besides the other objections against considering those inferences which are based upon a direct correlation of objects as being formally syllogistic – namely, that the reduction necessitates Procrustean procedure, that we are conscious of no subsumption of particular under general – it would seem that axiom and concrete inference are on the same level of thought, that both depend directly upon an intuition of the *vis cogitativa*, and therefore both are equally and *per se* valid. In no real sense, then, is the truth of the particular a consequence of the truth of the general: there seems to be the same relation between them – or at least a similar one – as is found between the scientific law and a fact of experience.

There is, however, another important implication of the above hypothesis. It makes invalid as a universal principle the retort, 'You think it impossible because you cannot imagine it.' For on the above theory we know two and two make four because a visualization of two units added to two units results in four units; we know the truth of axioms on the same grounds. Consequently, it is only by an inconsistency admitting some pronouncements of *vis cogitativa* to be correct and gratuitously setting others aside, that anyone could hold that parallel lines ever meet, that superposition is invalid in geometry,[15] that four lines all perpendicular to one another pass through the same point. Further, it gives a definite explanation of some propositions which Kant alleged to be synthetic a priori. It now remains for me to show how geometry and algebra belong to concrete and not abstract thought.

3   *Vis Cogitativa* and an Example of Concrete Inference in Geometry

That in geometry we use the figure in the diagram only as a help while the thought is concerned with *triangularitate ut sic*, or whatever it may be, is a ready and simple explanation of the universality of the conclusions in geometry. However, if we examine a simple proposition we shall see that this is not the sufficient nor the only explanation. Let us take the 32nd Proposition of Book I [of Euclid's *Elements*], 'If any side of a triangle be produced, the external angle is equal to the sum of the two internal nonadjacent angles':

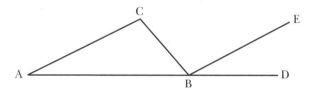

BE is drawn ‖ to AC; therefore $\angle ACB = \angle CBE$; $\angle CAB = \angle EBD$; therefore $\angle CBD = \angle CAB + \angle ACB$.

Now if we were dealing with *triangularitate ut sic*, we would expect a reason to be given why in all triangles BE would divide the external angle $\angle CBD$. The fact that Euclid does not give such a reason suggests that he dealt with the figure in the diagram in which BE does divide the external angle. The fact that such a reason can be found in Proposition I 17[16] is offset by the fact that nothing but a kinetic generic image (described below) will account for a similar line dividing a similar angle in Proposition I 16.[17]

---

15 [For an explanation of superposition (*epharmozein*) and a discussion of its role in geometric proofs, see Sir Thomas Heath's discussion of Common Notion (or Axiom) 4, 'Things which coincide with one another are equal to one another,' in *The Thirteen Books of Euclid's Elements*, trans. with introduction and commentary by Heath, 2nd rev. ed. (New York: Dover Publications, 1956), vol. 1: 224–28.]

16 [Euclid I 17: 'In any triangle two angles taken together in any manner are less than two right angles.']

17 [Euclid I 16: 'In any triangle, if one of the sides be produced, the exterior angle is greater than either of the interior and opposite angles.']

But suppose Euclid's proof only concerns this triangle; how can we know it will apply to all triangles? Visualize this triangle with all lines produced indefinitely. Then imagine the line *CB* swinging round as on a pivot at *B*. Every instant we see a different triangle and in the infinity of triangles seen while *CB* moves from coinciding with *AB* to coinciding with *BE*, *CB* is always a transversal of parallels, and therefore $\angle ACB = \angle CBE$ in all these instances. A few more infinities might be examined similarly by moving *AB*, or by moving *AC* with *BE* following in phase since it is by construction a parallel, and in all of these $\angle CAB = \angle EBD$. To the objection that no one ever goes through such a phantasmal gyration, I answer that this may happen due to intellectual passivity, but that some similar process is natural when we wish to find an exception to a geometrical conclusion, that it seems the only explanation of propositions where different cases are recognized, that if it was more common we would know there were four cases and not three in Euclid III 20,[18] that the fallacy of pseudographema[19] shows that the diagram is more important than it is ordinarily believed.

4   *Vis Cogitativa* and an Example of Concrete Inference in Algebra

I do not know what other solutions there are to the question, Why are symbols essential to algebra? On this hypothesis it is because they make ideas suitable objective-matter for the operations of *vis cogitativa*. However, conventions are the chief source of the algebraic economy of thought (which symbolic logicians are endeavoring to bring into philosophy). By a convention I mean the transference of an axiom into a rule: this involves the substitution of a habit for an act of reason; for example, a mathematician cancels the common factors, multiplies across, or transfers quantities from one side to the other, not from any reference to the four axioms about equals or because of a direct intuition of *vis cogitativa*, but simply from memory and habit.

---

18 [Euclid III 20: 'In a circle the angle at the centre is double of the angle at the circumference, when the angles have the same circumference as base.' See also Heath's comments on the proof of this proposition in *The Thirteen Books of Euclid's Elements*, vol. 2: 47–49; see 275–76.]

19 See H.W.B. Joseph, *An Introduction to Logic* (London: Oxford, Clarendon Press, 1906) 530 note. [By *pseudographma*, Aristotle meant erroneous inferences in geometry based on 'false construction.' Examples are given in Joseph.]

To show algebra may be concrete inference we take the following problem. 'A dealer buys a number of horses for £280. If he bought 4 less he
would have paid £8 more for each. How many did he buy?' *Vis cogitativa* may
approach this concrete case in two ways: first, by guessing the number of
horses and with the guidance of arithmetical conventions verifying this
guess: for example, let the guess be 10 horses, then the price of each horse
was £28, then 6 horses at £36 each should have cost £280 – guess again; secondly, by making a sophisticated guess: let x be the number of horses, then

$$\frac{280}{x}$$

is the price of each horse, then

$$\frac{280}{x} + 8$$

is the hypothetical price of each horse, but

$$\frac{280}{x - 4}$$

is also the hypothetical price. Therefore

$$\frac{280}{x} + 8 = \frac{280}{x - 4}$$

The equation is the result of a simple concrete inference. The rest of the
work is the application of methods to get x on one side of the equation and
alone. Multiplying across, [we get]

$$280x - 4 \times 280 + 8x(x - 4) = 280x.$$

Subtracting equals, [we get]

$$- 4 \times 280 + 8x(x - 4) = 0.$$

Removing common factors, [we get]

$$- 140 + x^2 - 4x = 0.$$

Factoring by hit and miss, [we get]

$$(x - 14)(x + 10) = 0,$$

Therefore

$$x = 14.^{[20]}$$

I do not think Cardinal Newman's illative sense is specifically the same as
these concrete inferences, but that question requires separate treatment.

20 [Lonergan does not mention the other solution to the equation, – 10, for
obviously a negative number has no application to the stated concrete
problem.]

Appendix

I have appended a few generic images to illustrate some of the examples.

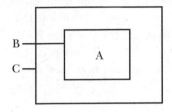

If *A* is in *B* and *B* is in *C* then *A* is in *C.*

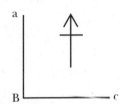

If *B* is south of *A* and *C* is east of *B* then ...;

A is any point on '*aB*,' *C* any point on '*cB*.'

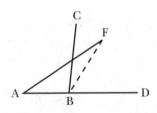

To illustrate Euclid I 16. *F* will always lie between *C* and *D* so that *FB* divides ∠*CBD*, because if we visualize, say, *AF* moving with pivot at *A*, as long as it crosses *CB* (construction) *F* always lies between *C* and *D.*

2

The Syllogism[1]

As it is a fallacy to introduce the standards of one's own time into the interpretation of a thinker of the past, it would seem more accurate to say that Aristotle invented the syllogism rather than that he propounded a theory of inference. That the modern notion of the aim of logic, namely, to give distinctness to mental acts in respect of their content by discussion and classification, was evolved rather than emerged, is evidenced by the Scholastic conception of the end of logic proposed by Fr Frick in this manner: '*Finis* logicae est: tutam et expeditam reddere rationem ad *recte* cogitandum itaque *veritatem* certo inve-

---

1 [*Blandyke Papers* no. 285 (March 1928) 33–64. In the autograph, Lonergan has in brackets, 'Paper read before the Philosophical and Literary Society,' and in an unnumbered footnote he writes, 'The conclusion has been modified and some minor changes have been made elsewhere.' Frederick E. Crowe situates the paper in Lonergan's early writings: 'This is a paper he had given before the Philosophical and Literary Society, and would some years later revise and publish in *Thought*. It probably represents an interest in his first year of philosophy (we remember that the professor spent a good deal of the year on logic, and gave short shrift to epistemology). But it gives clear signs of a mind that was already transcending logic toward the intellectualist position of the *verbum* articles.' Crowe, *Lonergan* 16. The revised paper published later was 'The Form of Inference,' *Thought* 18 (1943) 277–92; republished in *Collection*, vol. 4 in Collected Works of Bernard Lonergan, ed. Frederick E. Crowe and Robert M. Doran (Toronto: University of Toronto Press, 1988, 1993) 3–16; for further information on the relation of 'The Syllogism' to 'The Form of Inference,' see the introductory note in *Collection* 256–57. For continued commentary on this Blandyke Paper and Newman, see Liddy, *Transforming Light* 22–24. The section headings are editorial additions.]

niendam.'[2] If we take the *Prior Analytics* as presenting a method of drawing conclusions with certainty, we shall be more just to Aristotle than if we choose to believe he was giving what we call a theory of inference. To insist on the latter is to invite criticism of the putative theory. For in the first place, Aristotle's definition of the syllogism is faulty inasmuch as it includes forms to which his doctrine cannot be applied.[3] Again, he speaks at times of hypothetical procedure and gives the rules governing it,[4] but apparently he did not conceive the hypothetical argument as the distinct form we know today. The question, Why did Aristotle reduce Figures 2 and 3 to Figure 1? also bears on the point.[5] For if he was mistaken in denying evident validity to those figures – and the consensus of opinion seems to be that he was mistaken[6] – then we are led to

2   ['The aim of logic is to present a sure and expeditious way of thinking correctly and arriving at truth with certitude.'] Carolus Frick, *Logica: in usum scholarum*, ed. 6 emendata (Friburg Brisgoviae: Herder, 1925) 8.

3   Joseph, *An Introduction to Logic* 225. [Joseph presents two definitions of the syllogism from Aristotle: 'A syllogism is discourse in which, certain things being stated, something other than what is stated follows of necessity from their being so' (*Prior Analytics*, I, 1, 24b 18); and 'Reasoning is an argument in which, certain things being laid down, something other than these necessarily comes about through them' (*Topics*, I, 1, 100a 25).]

4   Ibid. 316–17 note.

5   [The placement of the middle term in the premises of a syllogism and the consequent way it functions in a syllogistic argument determines to which figure (*schēma*) the syllogism belongs. There are four figures: (1) the middle term is in the subject position of the major and in the predicate position of the minor; (2) the middle term is in the predicate position in both the major and the minor; (3) the middle term is in the subject position in both the major and the minor; (4) the middle term is in the predicate position in the major and in the subject position in the minor. The fourth figure is also referred to as an indirect first-figure syllogism. Reduction, as explained by Joseph (*Introduction to Logic* 264) is '[t]he process of exhibiting by the help of the first figure the validity of syllogisms in the other two (or three) [figures].']

6   [Aristotle regarded syllogisms in the first figure as 'the most scientific' (see *Posterior Analytics*, I, 14, 79a 17–32). In this paper, however, the more prominently emphasized characteristic of first-figure syllogisms is their perfection. Aristotle distinguished 'perfect' (*teleioi*) syllogisms in the first figure and 'incomplete' or 'unfinished' syllogisms in the other figures. Joseph (264) mentions a commonly held interpretation that for Aristotle a syllogism was perfect when 'the necessity of the inference appeared sufficiently from the premisses as they stand,' and that syllogisms in the second and third figures required supplementing for the necessity to appear in this way. For a brief account of the debate among interpreters, see Günther Patzig, *Aristotle's Theory of the Syllogism: A Logico-Philological Study of Book A of the* Prior Analytics, 2nd ed., trans. Jonathan Barnes (Dordrecht, Neth.: D. Reidel Publishing Co., 1963) 69–83. In 'The Form of Inference' 3, Lonergan reports Joseph's position that 'the second and third figure ... conclude in their own right' and that 'their reduction ... is always superfluous.']

suspect that there was some fundamental error in his theory of inference which brought about that mistake. Consequently, even if one should hold that Aristotle was presenting a theory, the question of inference would be open, for when one considers that logic is an inductive science setting up types of mental acts in virtue of careful but never exhaustive examinations of varied instances, and that inductive conclusions are ever obnoxious to[7] restatement, it becomes evidently legitimate to inquire into a doctrine which appears to have so questionable an origin.

1   Types of Inference

I have seen in a textbook of logic the following startling statement: 'The transition from the mental acts, which constitute the major and minor premises, to the conclusion is spontaneous, immediate and necessary.'[8] Would not this be a misleading account of any inference? The same might be said, but I think more exactly, of the consequence of the conjunction of the right proportions of hydrogen and oxygen, plus an electrical disturbance, or even of a slot machine: 'Put in a penny, pull the trigger, and the transition to the appearance of a box of matches is spontaneous, immediate and necessary.' It would seem to be more reasonable to consider the major and minor not as mental acts, but as items of knowledge – to take the reason as acting only because of a reason, rather than to posit a necessary succession of a third act upon two previous ones.[9]

As Fr Moncel says, the act of inference is a judgment differentiated from other judgments in this, that while the latter follow upon experience, inferential judgment is the apprehension of the implication of a previous judgment.[10]

1.1 Syllogistic and Non-syllogistic Inference

Now just as other judgments may be a priori or a posteriori, so in inference the mind may immediately and intuitively know the implication of the

---

7   [In an earlier usage, 'obnoxious' meant 'liable to, subject to, exposed to, open to.' Lonergan is using the word in this sense here.]

8   [The statement, misquoted slightly by Lonergan, is found on p. 189 of Joyce's *Principles of Logic*: 'The transition from the mental acts which constitute the premises, to the conclusion, is spontaneous, immediate, and necessary.']

9   [This is perhaps the earliest allusion in Lonergan's corpus to the reality that, following St Thomas, he will later refer to as *emanatio intelligibilis.*]

10 [Lonergan does not tell us where Fr Moncel said this, but it seems likely that his audience would have known the location.]

premise, or it may not. This gives a division of inference based on a fundamental characteristic, for there are inferences in which one premise does
no more than state the implication of the other premise, and there are
other inferences in which this is not the case. For example,

All organisms are mortal.	Whatever is organic is mortal.
Men are organisms.	Men are organic.
Therefore, men are mortal.	Therefore, men are mortal.

It would seem that in both of these inferences, which are materially the same,
the function of the major premise is to bring out the implication of the middle term: it tells what it is to be an organism. If we knew things in their
essences so that our knowledge of the attribute 'organic' included all that
that attribute implied, it would be sufficient to be given the minor premise,
'Men are organic,' and we would immediately infer, 'Men are mortal'; but
since the implication of being organic is known to us otherwise, it is necessary in formal reasoning to make a second premise (the major) express the
implication of what should be the only premise (the minor). This explains
why the syllogism seems ultimately to be either useless or a *petitio principii*, and
gives the reason for Mr Joseph's final answer to Mill: 'The subsumption in syllogism belongs ... to thinking which has not complete insight into the
grounds of all its premises at once.'[11] Clearly, if we knew that 'being organic'
meant 'being liable to death,' it would be impossible to know the minor without *eo ipso* knowing the conclusion; on the other hand, if we were unaware of
this implication, we would have no major premise, and consequently we
could not arrive at the conclusion from a formal inference. This is why we syl-
logize only when examining or defending a logical position, and live the rest
of our no less rational lives on the plane of apperception.[12] For inference is

11 Joseph, *Introduction to Logic* 307 [correcting Lonergan's slightly inaccurate quo-
    tation. The sentence in the second edition of Joseph's book (1916, repr. 1925)
    reads (311), 'The subsumption in syllogism belongs ... to thinking which has
    not complete insight into the necessity of all the facts in its premises at once.']
12 [The 'plane of apperception' is contrasted both with the general procedure of
    inferring one judgment from another and with the method of drawing conclu-
    sions in syllogistic reasoning. It refers to the process of making judgments
    following upon experience. What Lonergan here calls 'apperception' is what he
    later spoke about in other terms in *Insight*'s discussions of commonsense proce-
    dures. See, for example, his simple and well-known example of the worker's
    judgment, 'Something happened' (Lonergan, *Insight* 306–308). The judgment
    is not the result of syllogistic reasoning nor is it an inferential judgment, that is,
    a judgment apprehending the implications of a previous judgment.]

not the highest manifestation of the intelligence of man: for him to know yet dispense with inference is for him to resemble more closely the angel, who knows, yet, I am told on good authority, never infers.

As an example of an inference of the other type, we have the following:

$$A > B, B > C, \text{ Therefore } A > C.$$

Here the premises give accidental relations. To say '$A > B$' is not telling the meaning of being B; neither premise is subsumed, both being of equal importance. In this case it would seem that the mind, in virtue of a perceptual scheme or a visualization, correlates A and C and draws a conclusion parallel to the intuition of the a priori axiom.[13] Many arguments can be urged against the opinion that this inference is not in virtue of a special intuition but in virtue of a subsumption under an axiom. For one presentation of them I refer anyone who disagrees to Fr Coffey's refutation.[14] However, it seems sufficiently plain that it is the same act in the affirmation:

$$\text{If } A = B \text{ and } B = C, \text{ then } A = C,$$

which is the symbolic equivalent of the axiom of equals, and in the inference:

$$\text{Because } A = B \text{ and } B = C, \text{ therefore } A = C.$$

This type of inference is manifold; its essence seems to be that a single fact admits different specifications. For example, 'A is north of B,' 'B is south of A,' are two statements of the relative position of A and B, which may be represented to the mind independent of either of these propositions by a perceptual scheme, a visualization of A in the north and B in the south; the meaning either of the propositions has for us is found in the perceptual scheme; and if we say one proposition implies the other, it is

---

13 [For a clarification of this, see the discussion of the *vis cogitativa*, concrete inference, and axioms in the previous paper. Given the context, and in view of Lonergan's reference to Coffey a few sentences on, it seems likely that the a priori axiom Lonergan has in mind is the one mentioned by Coffey: 'A magnitude which is greater than another is greater than all magnitudes than which this latter is itself greater' (*The Science of Logic* I, 387).]

14 Coffey, *The Science of Logic* I, 389–90. [See also 'The Form of Mathematical Inference' 4, n. 5.]

only because they both mean the same thing. That the meaning is found in the perceptual scheme is borne out by the fact that one proposition does not necessarily imply the other, as might hastily be asserted, for in the case wherein the north pole lies between A and B, then though A is north of B, B is also north of A. An example which exhibits a development of the principle just illustrated (inasmuch as here a complex relation, making up a single fact, is adequately defined while certain of the constituent relations are omitted) is: A is north of B, B is an equal distance west of C. The complex relation here specified may be represented by a perceptual scheme in which A, B, and C are at the angles of a right-angled isosceles triangle; one draws the conclusion by forming the perceptual scheme and then literally seeing that A is northwest of C.

The diagnostic between this form of inference and syllogism is that this form involves an apprehension of the implication of the premise (or premises), and this apprehension may always be expressed either in an axiom or by prefixing 'if' to the premises and replacing 'therefore' by 'then' (for example, if '$A = B$, $B = C$, then $A = C$' is the canon of the inference '$A = B$, $B = C$, therefore $A = C$'), while in the syllogism this apprehension is already contained in the major premise and accordingly to introduce any reason for the inference beyond the meaning of the major is to confuse the two distinct forms of inference.

The rules of the syllogism betray such a confusion.[15] They concern themselves with the valid ways of relating one class to another, directing their whole attention to the requisite distribution of the right number of terms. In consequence they are perfectly obvious, ensure perfect validity, and also are entirely beside the point: they pay no heed to meaning but furnish a formal test quite extrinsic to the thought of an argument. Reduction appears in no better plight, inasmuch as visualizations are more apt to profit by transposition of terms than meanings are. That Aristotle transposed not merely to bring the middle term into relief but also to make the validity evident is attested, first by his parallel use of *reductio ad impossibile*, which can hardly claim to be other than proof, secondly by his statement, 'I say a syllogism is perfect when it requires nothing beyond the premises as they stand for the necessary consequence to be evident, but an unfinished syllogism

---

15 [For a formulation of the eight syllogistic rules for testing or preserving validity in syllogisms that Lonergan was no doubt familiar with, see Joseph, *Introduction to Logic* 247–54. For another discussion of the rules that Lonergan was probably aware of, see Coffey, *The Science of Logic* I, 305–18.]

one which requires one or more alterations.'[16] How there can be an inference when the necessary consequence is not evident is not apparent, yet some logicians presume that Aristotle admitted the self-evidence of Figures 2 and 3.

2   Predication, Logical Whole and Part, and the Hypothetical Argument in Inference

2.1 Objective Identity of Object and Attribute

Logical whole and part is a very misty conception, and as Aristotle speaks of wholes and implies parts we must find out a precise meaning for the terms.[17] This involves an account of predication, and as predication will come up again it will be necessary to be quite explicit. A predication expresses the objective identity of an object and an attribute. The loose definition of a judgment as the identification of two concepts is rejected on other grounds, and particularly by Fr Moncel on psychological grounds which cannot be entered into here.[18] The point is that this definition

16 Aristotle, *Prior Analytics*, I, 1.7 [*The Basic Works of Aristotle*, ed. Richard McKeon (New York: Random House, 1941) I, 1, 24b 23–26: 'I call that a perfect syllogism which needs nothing other than what has been stated to make plain what necessarily follows; a syllogism is imperfect, if it needs either one or more propositions, which are indeed the necessary consequences of the terms set down, but have not been expressly stated as premisses.']

17 [Lonergan will refer in n. 20 below to two texts in Aristotle's *Prior Analytics*, one of which is behind the pseudo-classical *dictum de omni et nullo*. It is useful to cite them here to throw light on what he is referring to when he speaks of 'logical whole and part.' *Prior Analytics*, I, 1, 24b 26–30: 'That one term should be included in another as in a whole is the same as for the other to be predicated of all of the first. And we say that one term is predicated of all of another, whenever no instance of the subject can be found of which the other term cannot be asserted: "to be predicated of none" must be understood in the same way.' Ibid. I, 4, 25b 32 – 26a 1: 'Whenever three terms are so related to one another that the last is contained in the middle as in a whole, and the middle is either contained in, or excluded from, the first as in or from a whole, the extremes must be related by a perfect syllogism. I call that term middle which is itself contained in another and contains another in itself: in position also this comes in the middle. By extremes I mean both that term which is itself contained in another and that in which another is contained. If *A* is predicated of all *B*, and *B* of all *C*, *A* must be predicated of all *C* ... Similarly, also, if *A* is predicated of no *B*, and *B* of all *C*, it is necessary that no *C* will be *A*.']

18 [Again, we are not told where Moncel rejected the 'loose definition' of a judgment, but Lonergan's remark provides another indication that Moncel may have exercised some influence on his thought during this period.]

implies that we think of concepts, not of things, and obviates the distinction between object and attribute. Aristotle was defining an object when he spoke of the *sensibile per accidens*; in modern phraseology it is a unity in a sensational continuum. An attribute is primarily a *sensibile per se*,[19] and then any

19 [Lonergan gives no reference in Aristotle for this, but we may refer to *De anima*, II, 6, 418a 20–25: 'We speak of an incidental object of sense where e.g. the white object which we see is the son of Diares; here because "being the son of Diares" is incidental to the directly visible white patch we speak of the son of Diares as being (incidentally) perceived or seen by us. Because this is only incidentally an object of sense, it in no way as such affects the senses ... [S]pecial objects of the several senses ... constitute the objects of sense in the strictest sense of the term ...' If one recalls Lonergan's discussion in 'The Form of Mathematical Inference' of St Thomas's *vis cogitativa* and the 'universals of sense,' this passage acquires an even greater significance and interest. For it occasioned a commentary by St Thomas (*In II De anima*, lect. 13, §§387–98) that goes well beyond Aristotle's text to launch into a discussion of the role of the *vis cogitativa* in human knowing: '... for an object to be a sense-object incidentally it must first be connected accidentally with an *essential* sense-object; as a man, for instance, may happen to be white ... Secondly, it must be perceived by the one who is sensing; if it were connected with the sense-object without itself being perceived, it could not be said to be sensed incidentally. But this implies that with respect to *some* cognitive faculty of the one sensing it, it is known, not incidentally, but absolutely. Now this latter faculty must be either another sense-faculty, or the intellect, or the cogitative faculty [*vis cogitativa*], or natural instinct [*vis aestimativa*] ... But if this apprehension is of something *individual*, as when, seeing this particular coloured thing, I perceive this particular man or beast, then the cogitative faculty (in the case of man at least) is at work, the power which is also called the "particular reason" because it correlates individualised notions, just as the "universal reason" correlates universal ideas. Nevertheless, this faculty belongs to sensitivity; for the sensitive power at its highest – in man, in whom sensitivity is joined to intelligence – has some share in the life of the intellect ...' From the translation by Kenelm Foster and Silvester Humphries (London: Routledge and Kegan Paul, 1951) 257–58. While it would be fanciful to suppose that what Lonergan says on predication and on the distinction between object and attribute in this very early paper coincides in every detail with his later thought, we can at least note some lines of continuity. Thus, there is a line of continuity from what he refers to here as 'a unity in a sensational continuum,' the *sensibile per accidens*, through the universal in the particular as distinct from the abstract universal (*Verbum* 43–44 and n. 150), to the thing as a unity-identity-whole in data, grasped by considering data, not from any abstractive viewpoint but by taking data in their concrete individuality and in the totality of their aspects (*Insight* 271). Again, if one confines one's consideration to experiential conjugates, there is a line of continuity from the distinction in this paper between object and primary attribute (the *sensibile per se*) and the account of predication as expressing the objective identity of an object and an attribute, to the distinction in *Insight* (271–72) between a thing and its experiential conjugates and to the account there of the relation named attribution.]

objective or interpretative aspect or feature of the object, for example, 'The mountain is precipitous, blue in the distance, majestic'; here 'mountain' denotes an object, while the predicates give aspects with varying degrees of objectivity. Besides this concrete object, there is also the abstract object; this is had by considering an attribute as an object, personifying it so to speak, or making out that it is quasi self-subsistent. For example, 'Men intend to do things'; the intending is here an attribute, but when we speak of 'intentions' we speak of abstract merely putative objects. Hence it is that the psychologist apologizes for speaking of instincts and purposes, and when strictly accurate limits himself to 'instinctive and purposive agents.' It is impossible for an abstract term to be derived from a concrete term qua concrete; the object is known to us only as a unification of attributes: such apparent exceptions as 'manhood,' 'triangularity' are solved by the simple question, 'What did I mean by manhood or triangularity?' I find that I mean no more than the more notable characteristics of a man or the properties of a triangle. However, not every term derived from an attribute is abstract, but only those which denote the attribute qua object; compare 'green' with its derivative 'greenness' (abstract) and 'organic' with its derivative 'organism' (concrete).

2.2 *Objective Relations among Attributes and among Objects*

Now objective relations are not limited to the affirmation or negation of the identity of objects and attributes. An attribute may be related to another attribute as ground to consequence: 'If an object is lighter than air, it tends to rise'; 'lighter than air' is an attribute which implies in the object a second attribute, 'a tendency to rise.' This ground–consequence relation may also be expressed by an indefinite relative or a conditioning adjectival relative, 'whatever is lighter than air,' or 'all objects which are lighter than air tend to rise.' Object may also be related to object (1) as ground to consequence, and (2) in any of the manifold of visualized relations.

What is commonly called an immediate inference might be thought to be an inference from a predication, but this does not seem to be so. I do not infer that 'some green objects are grass' from the predication 'grass is green' but from the object–object relation or class-inclusion 'grass is among green objects.' As the artificiality of the permutations of immediate inference would suggest, this form seems based to a great extent on a perceptual scheme; it neglects the meaning of the predicate as denoting an attribute and substitutes as an equivalent the class of objects to which the attribute belongs.

This perversion of predication is one way in which the subject may be said to be in the whole of the predicate. If, instead of taking the predicate in extension, we take both terms in connotation, there are cases in which the predicate is in the whole of the subject, that is, when the predicate is part of the connotation of the subject; but as it cannot be urged in accidental predication that the predicate is thus in the whole of the subject, this view does not seem adequate to explain Aristotle's metaphor.[20]

However connotation, no more than extension, is not the meaning of a term, or rather if the argument is because the predicate or the subject is a whole, then a perceptual scheme is introduced, and it makes no difference whether this be Porphyry's tree or Euler's circles. One might as well argue because the egg is in the dish and the dish is in the warmer, therefore the egg is in the warmer.[21] Aristotle as an elucidation or confirmation of his statement about wholes in a syllogism[22] adds, 'For if A is predicated of all of B and B is predicated of all of C, then A must be predicated of all of C.'[23] Now if we substitute for the word 'predicate' what the word stands for, this will not be so self-evident as might be supposed. We get:

A is an attribute of the object B
B is an attribute of the object C.

Unless we are prepared to admit that B can somehow be an attribute and an object and yet retain one identity, we have to say that, because an object can be named from its attribute, B denotes in the major an object, not because the object is B but because some object has B as attribute. But thus there is only one object referred to in the premises (C); as B is primarily an attribute, to say that A is an attribute of the object B is only a makeshift; and what would seem to be the real meaning is that if any object has the attribute B it must also have the attribute A: for while no conclusion seems to follow from

20 See Aristotle, *Prior Analytics*, 1.1.8 [McKeon 1, 1, 24b 28–33], 1.4.2 (especially 1.4.2 [McKeon 1, 4, 25b 32 – 26a 1] where *eschaton* suggests that Aristotle meant *S* in *P*). [For this text see above, n. 17.]
21 [The same example is used in 'The Form of Mathematical Inference' as an example of a *sensibilis demonstratio*. See above, p. 7.]
22 Aristotle, *Prior Analytics*, 1.4.2 [see above, nn. 17 and 20].
23 Ibid. 1.4.3 [McKeon 1, 4, 25b 39 – 26a 2: 'If *A* is predicated of all *B*, and *B* of all *C*, *A* must be predicated of all *C*.']

A is an attribute of the object B

B is an attribute of the object C

we have an obvious reason for concluding when

B is an attribute of the object C,

an object with attribute B must have attribute A.[24]

The hypothetical seems the necessary way of avoiding the anomaly of *Nota notae*, which, while it does better justice to the intentional force of the thought than does the *dictum*, implies that a note is related to another note the same way as a note is related to the *res ipsa*.[25] The *dictum de omni* claims our attention as an explanation of mediate predicative reasoning. In it the major premise is the core of the argument. Aristotle defined universal predication[26] as that in which no part of the subject (in extension, *mēden labein tōn tou hypokeimenou*) was to be denied (or if negative, admitted) the predicate; the *dictum* finds in its four moods of the first figure that[27] the major premise

24 [Lonergan wrote '... must have attribute C,' but that does not make sense. Just a few lines earlier he had written, 'it must also have the attribute C,' and by hand corrected 'C' to 'A.' Clearly, that is what he means here as well.]

25 [The principle is *Nota notae est rei ipsius*, translated by William and Martha Kneale as 'What qualifies an attribute qualifies a thing possessing it.' *The Development of Logic* (Oxford: Clarendon Press, 1962) 79. Later in the same work it is said that Kant 'tried to defend the view that all syllogistic reasoning depends on the single principle *Nota notae est rei ipsius*.']

26 Aristotle, *Prior Analytics*, 1.1.8 [McKeon 1, 1, 24b 28–30: '... one term is predicated of all of another, whenever no instance of the subject can be found of which the other term cannot be asserted.']

27 [Traditionally, propositions are said to differ with respect to quality (an affirmation or a negation) and quantity (a universal or a particular). Four propositional forms can then be distinguished: A propositions, that is, propositions that are affirmations as to quality and universal as to quantity; I propositions, that is, propositions that are affirmations as to quality and particular as to quantity; E propositions, that is, propositions that are negations as to quality and universal as to quantity; and O propositions, that is, propositions that are negations as to quality and particular as to quantity. The mood of a syllogism is determined by the disposition of its premises according to quality and quantity. Keeping in mind the distinction between major and minor premises, and placing the major premise first, there are sixteen possible ordered combinations of premises for syllogisms: AA, AI, AE, AO, IA, II, IE, IO, EA, EI, EE, EO, OA, OI, OE, OO. Each of these may be found in each of the four figures. It follows that the total number of possible combinations is sixty-four. Of these, nineteen are traditionally recognized as yielding valid conclusions: four for the first figure, four for the second figure, six for the third figure, and five for

is a predication; it finds all minors affirming that *S* is part of the subject of the major; it concludes because universal predication means that no part of the subject is to be denied the predicate; hence the first figure is the ideal figure, and it is based on the nature of universal predication. A first objection is that the minor does not tell us immediately that 'the *A*'s are among or part of the *B*'s'; this is not predication, which would give that '*B* was an attribute of the object *A*'; the *dictum* seems to safeguard predication in the major only to do away with it in the minor. The second objection is that it justifies reduction and makes the rules of the syllogism intrinsic to the thought, while it would seem that reduction of Figures 2 and 3 to Figure 1 is mostly a distortion, and the rules are extrinsic and merely formal. Again, it leaves unexplained the transition from informal to formal inference, making the major premise instead of a formality the basis of the argument. Lastly, to argue from the general to the particular seems far more like an inference in

------

the fourth or indirect first figure. The four valid moods of first-figure syllogisms are indicated by the mnemonic expressions 'Barbara,' 'Celarent,' 'Darii,' and 'Ferio,' with the three vowels in each expression serving to indicate, in order, the quality and quantity of the major premise, the minor premise, and the conclusion. Boldface type is used here to indicate how each expression serves to indicate which of the A, I, O, E propositions make up the valid moods in each syllogistic figure and the order in which those propositions occur. The three vowels in each of the mnemonic expressions for the valid moods of second-figure syllogisms, 'Cesare,' 'Camestres,' 'Festino,' 'Baroco,' again indicate, in order, the quantity and quality of the major premise, the minor premise, and the conclusion. The same rules apply for the mnemonic expression for the valid moods of third-figure syllogisms, 'Darapti,' 'Felapton,' 'Disamis,' 'Datisi,' 'Bocardo,' 'Ferison,' and for the first three vowels of the mnemonic expressions for the valid moods of fourth-figure or indirect first-figure syllogisms, 'Baralipton,' 'Celantes,' 'Dabitis,' 'Fapesmo,' 'Frisesomorum.' In addition, the initial consonant in each mnemonic expression for the valid moods of second-, third-, and fourth-figure syllogisms pairs the syllogism to the mood of the first-figure syllogism to which it can be reduced. The procedure for the reduction is indicated by the following consonants, when placed immediately after a mnemonically significant vowel: 's' (= *simpliciter*), indicating the proposition symbolized by the preceding vowel is to be converted simply; 'p' (= *per accidens*), indicating that the proposition symbolized by the preceding vowel is to be converted *per accidens*; 'm' (= *muta*), indicating that the premises must be transposed; and 'c' (= *per contradictionem*), indicating that the reduction is indirect or *per impossibile*. The remaining consonants, 'b,' 'd,' 'l,' 'n,' 'r,' and 't' have no logical significance and merely serve to form expressions that can come together to form an easily memorized rhythmic formula.]

virtue of a *resolutio facta ad sensum*[28] than one from the meaning; it is more probable that the major is introduced to give the implication of the minor, than that the minor is introduced to show the extension of the major.

To explain the major premise as a ground–consequence relation is not new. Kant identified the syllogism and the hypothetical but on this account reduced hypotheticals to the syllogism. Mr Joseph, though rejecting the reduction of the hypothetical, admits Kant's analysis of the first figure, as putting more clearly than the *dictum* the nerve of the inference.[29] The fact that he does not discuss the reduction of the syllogism to the hypothetical may in part be accounted for on the ground that logicians have been occupied curbing the absorptive tendencies of the syllogism.

3   Syllogism and the Reduction to the Hypothetical

The syllogism presents no formal characteristic by which it might be distinguished from the hypothetical. The name 'hypothetical' may occasion a doubt, which passes when we realize that the truth of the major is not conditional but as categorical a truth as any predication. The syllogism can hardly be said to consist of predications unless some explanation be found of the anomaly of the middle term; this anomaly runs through the other figures. In the second we have *P* is *M*, in the third we have *M* is *S*, in the fourth *M* is *S* and *P* is *M*, all of which disregard the fundamental notion of predication, namely, the identity of an object and an attribute. The hypothetical brings out fully that emphasized characteristic of Figure 1 as the scientific figure. It is clear that the middle term designates the *ratio essendi* as much in one form as in another. But in the hypothetical there is not merely a designation, which may be brought to consciousness in an afterthought but plays no part in the reasoning itself, but, besides being *ratio essendi*, the middle is also *ratio ratiocinandi*: the cause of the attribute belonging to the object in the real order is the reason why the mind attributes the predicate to the subject in an act of inference. In the real order man is liable to death because he is organic; in the inference we learn from the major, 'Whatever is organic is mortal,' the attribute 'organic' necessarily implies the attribute 'mortal,' in the minor we see that the object 'man' has the attribute 'organic.' On the other hand, the *dictum* draws the conclusion not because 'man is organic,' but because 'all organisms are mortal.' The inferiority of

28 See Fr Joyce's quotation from St Thomas, *Principles of Logic* 190. [See above, p. 5, n. 8.]

29 Joseph, *Introduction to Logic* 286–87.

this appears still more when we consider that science does not inform us that 'all organisms are mortal' or that 'all objects lighter than air tend to rise,' but it does give the necessary implication of one attribute in another, that 'whatever is organic is also mortal,' or 'whatever is lighter than air tends to rise.' To transfer precipitously this necessary correlation of attributes to a universal statement of the nature of objects is but inviting a Mill to bring the charge of a *petitio principii.*

First-figure arguments are of two kinds: in Barbara and Darii, the presence of one attribute in a subject (its distribution is immaterial to the inference) establishes the presence of a second, for example, 'whatever is organic is mortal'; in Celarent and Ferio, the presence of an attribute in the subject excludes a second attribute, for example, 'whatever is proverbial is not true.' The typical forms of these are, therefore:

If S is M, it is P
S is M
Therefore S is P

If S is M, it is not P
S is M
Therefore S is not P

The second figure does not differ essentially from the first. Taking this example in Camestres:

All true roses bloom in summer
The Christmas rose does not bloom in summer
Therefore the Christmas rose is not a true rose[30]

we can tell at once that the conclusion follows. We do not have to transpose major and minor, convert the new major, infer, convert the conclusion, before we can know its validity. Nor need we even with Aristotle suppose the contradictory of what we know from the minor to be true.[31] But we

30 [The example is taken from Joseph, *Introduction to Logic* 290. Lonergan then mentions how Camestres is reduced to a syllogism in Celarent. First, the premises are transposed, and then the original minor is converted simply. This yields a conclusion that is then converted simply to correspond with the original conclusion.]
31 [This is indirect reduction or reduction *per impossibile.*]

immediately see that the absence of the attribute 'blooming in summer' proves the absence of the second attribute 'being a true rose.' The true form of the argument thus becomes:

> If the Christmas rose does not bloom in summer, it is not a true rose
> It does not ...
> Therefore it is not ...

Baroco is the same argument with the subject undistributed. The form

> If S is not M, it is not P
> S is not M
> Therefore S is not P

is the exact opposite of that of Barbara and Darii which is, 'If S is M, it is P.'[32] This explains the peculiar difficulty of reducing Camestres and Baroco (Faksoko)[33] to the first figure. These moods have no equivalent in the first figure, which never draws a negative conclusion from an affirmative major. The other two moods of Figure 2 [Cesare and Festino] are of the same form as Celarent and Ferio: they argue from the presence of an attribute in the subject to the absence of a second attribute, and are a justification of Aristotelian reduction:

32 [An example of a syllogism in Baroco is the following: Every fool (P) is annoying (M). But some chatterbox (S) is not annoying (M). Therefore some chatterbox (S) is not a fool (P). Reduced to the hypothetical form, then, it would be: If some chatterbox (S) is not annoying (M), some chatterbox (S) is not a fool (P). But some chatterbox (S) is not annoying (M). Therefore, some chatterbox (S) is not a fool (P).]

33 ['Faksoso' is an obscure, less frequently mentioned mnemonic for logical reduction. John Neville Keynes remarks on p. 185 of the first edition of his *Studies and Exercises in Formal Logic* (London: Macmillan and Co., 1884) that George Croom Robertson (1842–92), who was professor of mind and logic at University College, London, from 1866 till a few months before his death in 1892, and the editor of *Mind* from 1876 to 1891, was the first to suggest 'Faksoko' to represent the method of direct reduction by contrapositing the major premise and obverting the minor premise. The 'k' denotes obversion, and the 'ks' obversion followed by conversion, that is, contraposition. Thus, in the reduction of Baroco to Ferio we go from 'All P is M, Some S is not M, therefore Some S is not P' to 'No non-M is P, Some S is non-M, therefore Some S is not P.' Aristotle did not use this procedure. In Aristotle's procedure for reduction to the first figure, Baroco, like Bocardo in the third figure, can only be reduced using indirect reduction or reduction *per impossibile*, with use of Barbara.]

No fish has lungs
Whales have lungs
Therefore whales are not fish[34]

This is Cesare; if we replace 'whales' by 'some whales,' we have Festino. The eight moods of the first two figures give us three of the four possible relations between attributes, namely:

If S is M, it is P
If S is M, it is not P
If S is not M, it is not P

The fourth possibility,

If S is not M, it is P

is usually expressed in the *modus tollendo ponens* of the disjunctive, for example,

He is either a knave, or a fool
He is not a knave
Therefore he is a fool

S is not M
Therefore S is P

This analysis leads one to believe that the syllogism separates the first and second figures in a wholly arbitrary and incongruous fashion, and that the second figure is as self-evident as the first though neither is done justice in syllogistic expression.

The third figure is quite different from the preceding two. In them we argue from the presence or absence of one attribute in an object to the presence or absence of a second attribute. In Figure 3 we deal instead with two objects and one attribute, and the inference is from the presence or absence of an attribute in one object, either

(1) to the possibility of finding or not finding that attribute in the species or genus of the object; for example,

34 [The example is taken from Joseph, *Introduction to Logic* 290–91.]

Queen Elizabeth was a great ruler; therefore a woman may be ...
If M is P, S may be P.
If Theaetetus was not beautiful, a young Athenian may [not] be ...
If M is not P, S may not be P

or (2) to the factual presence or absence of the attribute in part of the species or genus; for example, If amoebae need never die, some organisms need never die.

(a) If M is P, some S is P.
(b) If M is not P, some S is not P.

(a) = Darapti, Disamis, Datisi; (b) = Felapton, Bocardo, Ferison.

When the middle in this second case (2) is a singular term we have the *syllogismus expositorius*, which consists in substituting an alias of some sort for the subject of the minor.[35]

Socrates was virtuous
Therefore a wise man was virtuous

This inference was rightly made *sui generis* by the Scholastics, but it does not invalidate the use of a singular term as middle in (1); for example,

If Socrates was wise and virtuous, a man may be both wise and virtuous.

It appears therefore that the major in Figure 3 is much more of a formality than in Figures 1 and 2; in the latter the major gives the implication of having a certain attribute, in the former the process is reversed and we ascend from the particular to the species. Generally it is far easier to presuppose a knowledge of the classification language makes of objects than a knowledge of the implication of an attribute. We pass more readily from

---

35 [See the discussion of the *syllogismus expositorius* in 'The Form of Mathematical Inference' at pp. 4–5. In *Introduction to Logic* 296, Joseph remarks: 'Aristotle called the production of an instance by the name *ekthesis* or Exposition. He conceived that the proper mode of validating a syllogism in the third figure was by direct reduction, but added that it was possible to validate it *per impossibile* or by "exposition": "if all S is both P and R, we may take some particular S, say N; this will be both P and R, so that there will be some R that is P."' (He adds in a footnote a reference to *Prior Analytics*, I, 6, 28a 24–26.)]

Potassium floats in water
to
A metal may float
than from
Grains are nitrogenous
to
Grains are a flesh-forming food[36]

The syllogistic major of the third figure, apart from the fact that it expresses a relation between objects (*M* and *S*) as though it were a predication, does not offer any real reason for drawing the conclusion. We have Aristotle's word that it is not self-evident, and we have other reasons for not reducing it to Figure 1 to give it self-evidence. The fact that 'potassium is a metal' is in some way connected with the inference, but I think remotely, inasmuch as it contains the material basis of the proposition, 'If potassium floats, a metal may float,' which is a satisfactory major.

4   Concluding Reflections

4.1 Phenomenal Predication

As this is something of a second edition, I may as well profit by a criticism made at the reading of this paper and here append a conclusion somewhat different from the original one. The discussion which follows is for me *de quibusdam aliis*, and for anyone who also finds it such, I would recommend Fr Cardwell's article, *Blandyke Papers* 184,[37] which bears that title and puts the fundamental point of this sketch of predication very lucidly. There is obviously a difference between our knowledge and God's: God knows the thing-in-itself, we know it through its phenomena. Knowledge of the phenomena gives (more exactly, is) knowledge of the existence of the thing-in-itself and grounds for distinguishing and relating validly and accurately the things-in-themselves. Hence the concrete object is a unification of attributes (certain phenomena are attributed to one thing-in-itself), and predication (phenomenal) consists in saying that a thing-in-itself

36 [The example is taken from Joseph, *Introduction to Logic* 301.]
37 [According to Thomas McCoog, s.j., Archivist in the British Jesuit Province, *Blandyke Papers* 184 is not by Fr Cardwell. Fr Laurence William Cardwell (1889–1968) lectured in mathematics and physics at St Mary's Hall, Stonyhurst, from 1924 to 1926, and then moved to Heythrop, where he would have been on faculty when Lonergan was there.]

distinguished and denoted by the presence of certain phenomena also presents some other phenomenon.[38] For example, 'This flower is yellow': 'this flower' means a thing-in-itself designated by means of the phenomena common to all flowers and by the gesture 'this'; 'is yellow' means that this flower, the subject, has, besides the phenomena indicated by its name, a further phenomenon indicated by the word 'yellow.' It makes no difference whether we say that 'as a matter of fact' or 'by nature' 'this flower is yellow,' for 'by nature' only adds that all the flowers similar to this flower in the phenomena in virtue of which I call this flower this flower also have the phenomenon [of] yellowness. Phenomenal predication therefore only expresses a conjunction: $Xabc + d$ not $Xabc$ is d, where X denotes the thing-in-itself, abc the phenomena which distinguish it, d the phenomenon assigned to the subject by the predication. This may illustrate the abstract term: if I take d as an attribute I have the attributive term ('organic'); if I take it as marking a thing-in-itself, then it becomes a concrete term Xd ('organism'); but if I take the phenomenon d as a something-in-itself then I have the abstract xd (to coin a word 'organicity' or, to change the examples, virtue, intention, greenness).[39]

4.2 Noumenal Predication

To turn to what I venture to call noumenal predication: the phenomena cannot be conceived[40] as independent of the thing-in-itself, else they could not give us valid distinctions and classifications; every phenomenon therefore has an analogue in the thing-in-itself, and accordingly, while if we interpret 'this flower is yellow'[41] phenomenally, we merely state a conjunction; yet when we take these phenomena as standing for their analogues, we tell in part *what it is to be* this flower. But because we do not know the analogues, and the *to ti ēn einei* may be but our best analogy for conceiving God's knowledge, this predication is noumenal. Aristotle emphasized the

38 [Lonergan is returning here to the distinction introduced earlier (above, pp. 20–21) between the 'unity in a sensational continuum,' the *sensibile per accidens*, and an attribute as primarily a *sensibile per se*, and to the account of predication that follows upon this distinction.]

39 [Here Lonergan adds a sentence in the autograph, later crossed out: 'Incidentally this calls up Aristotle's statement, *Categ.* 5, that the accident (*en hypokeimenō*) may be at times predicated of the subject but never the definition of the accident: Priscian is a grammarian but not therefore a science.']

40 [In the autograph copy, 'conceived' is written above 'considered.']

41 [Here Lonergan provides his own note: '"yellow" does not do here, read "a buttercup."']

distinction between essential and accidental predication: if you say 'Socrates is a man,' you tell what Socrates *is*, for to be man is *what it is to be* Socrates, but if you say 'Socrates is snub-nosed,' you give merely an accident, and do not tell the what it is to be (of) Socrates. Now this is of importance to metaphysics, but to anything else it is a barren tautology. To say Socrates is a man is *Xabcd + ab*; it is as much by phenomena that you know 'Socrates is a man' as it is that you know 'Socrates is snub-nosed.'[42] It was the discovery of Descartes to make the work of science the resolution of complex and obscure phenomena to simple and familiar ones (the clear and distinct ideas).[43] But not only do the positive sciences give conjunctions of phenomena, for example, 'If notes produce beats they are unharmonious,' but they tell the nature of the phenomenon, they give its *to* [*ti ēn einai*][44] (using the expression analogously) for to produce beats is *what it is to be* unharmonious.[45] Now this appears to justify the syllogism and to be

42   Consider Fr Moncel's example of the waxwork attendant at Madame Tussaud's. [Again, Lonergan does not tell us where in Moncel's writings the example occurs, if indeed it does occur somewhere in his writings and was not mentioned, say, in the course of a lecture or discussion that Lonergan and his confrères attended. And without knowing what exactly Moncel said, and the context in which he said it, it is virtually impossible to know with any surety what precisely his example was meant to exemplify. Of course, one could conjecture that his example has something to do with certain similarities between the phenomenal characteristics of the wax figures and the attendant that, at first glance, do not enable one to distinguish the live attendant from the wax figures.]

43   See Louis Liard, *Descartes* 70. [The third edition was available to the editors – Paris: Lacan, 1911. Actually, what Liard says is, 'L'originalité de Descartes, ce qui le sépare des métaphysiciens du passé et le fait l'ancêtre des savants de nos jours, est d'avoir cherché et découvert l'unité des phénomènes au sein des phénomènes eux-mêmes.' Ibid. 70–71.]

44   [In the autograph, Lonergan abbreviates the Greek here, giving only the first letters of *ti ēn einai*.]

45   [The example is drawn from Joseph, *Introduction to Logic* 291: '*Notes that produce beats are not harmonious: The fourth and fifth produce beats; Therefore they are not harmonious.* This argument might be set forth in the second figure: *Harmonious notes do not produce beats: The fourth and fifth produce beats; Therefore they are not harmonious:* but here undoubtedly the syllogism in Barbara is better than the syllogism in Cesare; and any one who knew that concord was dependent on regular coincidence in vibrations and discord on the absence thereof, would extricate from the major premiss of the latter syllogism the major of the former, and think in Barbara. Nevertheless it is only this knowledge which makes him do so; and without it he might perfectly well validate to himself his conclusion by considering that if those notes were harmonious, they would not produce the beats they do. If the middle term gives a *ratio essendi*, we naturally put our reasoning into the first figure.']

the explanation of reduction. For from the premises '*A* is *B*,' '*B* is *C*,' because 'to be *C* is what it is to be *B*, and *A* is *B*, therefore *A* is *C*.' But this is not so satisfactory in Celarent [and] Ferio, where '*B* is not *C*,' since 'not *C*' is hardly 'what it is to be *B*.' To return therefore to Barbara [and] Darii, it must be noted that the argument above (on *ABC*) does not hold of '*Xabc* is *d*, *Xd* is *e*, therefore *Xabc* is *e*,' which is the usual form of these moods, nor is it '*Xabc* is *Xd*, *Xd* is *e*, therefore *Xabc* is *e*,' which would avoid the hiatus between *d* and *Xd*, at the expense of predication (which admits only attributes as predicates), and inaccurately states '*Xd* is *e*' when it is not *Xd* but *d* which *is e*;[46] but [the argument above on *ABC* holds that] '*Xabc* is *d*, to be *d* is to be *e*, therefore *Xabc* is *e*,' a form which has hitherto been unknown to the syllogism. Of the two majors 'to be *d* is to be *e*' and 'if *X* … is *d*, it is *e*' the predicative is preferable to the hypothetical; but excepting the *ratio essendi* forms of Barbara and Darii, which, unless we see fit to explain away the hiatus between the concrete and attributive middle (*d* and *Xd*), must be modified in expression as above noted, it still seems reasonable to deny any other syllogism[47] a right to be considered distinct from the hypothetical argument. *Kai mēn kai egō hōs ouk eidōs legō alla eikazōn.*[48]

46 [The emphasis in 'is' is Lonergan's.]
47 At least of Figs. 1 & 2. Neither the syllogistic nor the hypothetical form of Fig. 3 is satisfactory; but the discussion must be postponed.
48 [And I too speak as one not knowing but conjecturing.]

3

True Judgment and Science[1]

1 True Judgment as Consciously True

Truth may be attained by a scientific investigation or again by a judgment which may be anything from a guess to an intuition. The difference is that by science truth is not only known but also known to be known, while as there is no ready criterion between true and false judgments, one may judge truly but cannot know one has done so. For this reason certitude is restricted to scientific conclusions. However, if true judgment may be consciously true, then science ceases to be the one measure of evidence for certitude. That true judgment may be consciously true is the contention of the *Essay in Aid of a Grammar of Assent*,[2] and the principle of the reflex knowledge

1 [*Blandyke Papers* no. 291 (3 February 1929) 195–216. A footnote on p. 195 of the handwritten autograph text adds, 'A paper read before the Phil. & Lit. Society, Feb. 3, 1929. It has been compressed.' Frederick E. Crowe relates this paper to Lonergan's two previous papers and indicates how it advances his thinking: 'More important is Lonergan's third contribution, the "separate treatment" called for in his first article [see above, p. 11], for it is largely a study of Newman's illative sense, and thus the forerunner of his own theory of rational consciousness; there is more than a hint also of the next step, rational self-consciousness, so we have the third and fourth levels of the later intentional structure.' Crowe, *Lonergan* 16. For further commentary on this paper vis-à-vis Newman, see Liddy, *Transforming Light* 24–32. The section headings are editorial additions.]

2 [John Henry Cardinal Newman's book *An Essay in Aid of a Grammar of Assent* was first published in London in 1870 by Burns, Oates & Co. In this paper, Lonergan is using the 1891 edition, published in London by Longmans, Green and Co. The latter edition is used in editing as well.]

is the illative sense. On the analogy of the names 'moral sense,' [and] 'sense of the beautiful,' which designate the mind judging morality or beauty, the name 'illative sense' was given to designate mind in the function of judging inferences. According to logic, which is the form of demonstrative science, the only certain conclusions are deductions from self-evident propositions; hypotheses, theories, views may have any degree of probability but cannot be certainties, for absolute verification is logically impossible. The illative sense is just such an absolute verification. The mind in a given case may be able to determine the limit of converging probabilities and so discard as nugatory the nebulous possibilities which prevent an inference from being logically valid. In this action the illative sense is not supplying from nonintellectual sources a defect in the evidence; the logical defect is counted merely theoretical, and the mind by an *epieikeia* of reasoning meets a question in the spirit though not in the letter of rationality. It concludes a process which is too manifold in its data, too elusive in its procedure, too intimate in its discernment for adequate analysis to be possible or for a criterion of the abstractly self-evident to be fair. Thus we know the truth and know we know it, but prove it we cannot.[3] I am certain there is a country called Tibet, for it is impossible for all who have been to Tibet to conspire and to succeed in a conspiracy to deceive all men who have not travelled thither. It is impossible for them to conspire, for there is no adequate motive; it is impossible for them to succeed, for conspirators, if numerous enough, are bound to be betrayed. But if I may not appeal to my illative sense, I cannot be certain that there is no adequate motive or that in this particular instance the conspirators would be betrayed. My certitude, and the certitude of anyone with no better grounds than I have, is simply irrational, unless science is not the sole criterion of certitude. Further, it seems fair to say that the certitudes entertained by men who know nothing of deduction from self-evident premises are irrational if they admit no demonstration and even of doubtful rationality if they do.

3   [In the *Grammar of Assent*, Newman connects knowing a truth, knowing that we know that truth, and certitude with respect to that truth, as follows: '… let the proposition to which the assent is given be as absolutely true as the reflex act pronounces it to be, that is, objectively true as well as subjectively: – then the assent may be called a *perception*, the conviction a *certitude*, the proposition or truth a *certainty*, or thing known, or a matter of *knowledge*, and to assent to it is to *know*' (195–96). 'Certitude … is the perception of a truth with the perception that it is a truth, or the consciousness of knowing, as expressed in the phrase, "I know that I know," or "I know that I know that I know," – or simply "I know"; for one reflex assertion of the mind about self sums up the series of self-consciousnesses without the need of any actual evolution of them' (197).]

2   Formal Inference, and the Reasonableness of Informal and Natural Inference

Fr Thomas Harper in *The Month* attacks the very conception of informal inference. 'Either my inference is formally valid, or it is not. If it be formally valid, it is *ipso facto* moulded by logical law; if it is not, it is no inference at all.'[4] Newman presumed that informal inference is the rule and formal inference an afterthought – an analysis or a test of the ordinary procedure. ' … our reasoning ordinarily presents itself to our mind as a simple act, not a process or series of acts. We apprehend the antecedent and then apprehend the consequent, without explicit recognition of the medium connecting the two, as if by a sort of direct association of the first thought with the second. We proceed by a sort of instinctive perception, from premiss to conclusion … We perceive external objects, and we remember past events, without knowing how we do so; and in like manner we reason without effort and intention, or any necessary consciousness of the path which the mind takes in passing from antecedent to conclusion.'[5] In this passage I take Newman to be describing a judgment made upon the significance of any concrete proposition, for example, 'There will be a European war, for Greece is audaciously defying Turkey.' Such a prediction is an inference. The suppressed premise is 'any such defiance will involve Europe in war.' Fr Harper's argument is met, if it is granted that such a premise is logically implied in the conclusion, and that a reasoner commits himself to it in drawing the conclusion. However, this does not determine the way in which the individual did as a matter of fact reach the conclusion. The psychological process seems to me to be similar to that by which one intuits self-evident propositions, namely, by the comparison of the terms – in this case 'a defiance' and 'a European war.' It cannot be argued that the subject term was 'this defiance' and not 'such a defiance'; accordingly there is a syllogism in the thought.

> Any such defiance involves war.
> This defiance is such a defiance.
> Therefore …

4 [Rev. Thomas Harper, 'Dr. Newman's Essay in Aid of a Grammar of Assent. Part II,' *The Month*, new series 1 (12) (January–June 1870) 667–92, at 688.]
5 Newman, *An Essay in Aid of a Grammar of Assent* 259–60.

If this is the actual process of thought, then natural inference does differ from formal inference, for in formal inference the major would not be a simple definitive judgment but would be proved by a series of syllogisms (which would have self-evident propositions for the ultimate premises). Newman's contention is that we should be satisfied with the simple judgment because we cannot analyze all our grounds for making the judgment. If formal expression does not do justice to our real grounds, then formal expression is not the natural criterion of our real grounds. Thus we are left with the illative sense, and the work of analysis becomes supererogatory. This view is at once explained and plausibly justified in the passage: 'Common sense, chance, moral perception, genius, the great discoverers of principles do not reason. They have no arguments, no grounds, they see the truth, but they do not know how they see it; and if at any time they attempt to prove it, it is as much a matter of *experiment* with them, as if they had to find a road to a distant mountain, which they see with the eye; and they get entangled, embarrassed, and perchance overthrown in the *superfluous* endeavour.'[6]

I shall now endeavor to develop this point. The first condition of a scientific conclusion is methodic doubt or suspension of judgment; no attention is to be given any consideration which does not form part of the proof: 'Let language have a monopoly of thought; and thought go for only so much as it can show itself to be worth in language. Let every prompting of the intellect be ignored, every *momentum* of argument be disowned, which is unprovided with an equivalent wording as its ticket for sharing in the common search after truth. Let the authority of nature, common-sense, experience, genius, go for nothing.'[7] Opposed to this intransigence is our ordinary procedure. It is based on the principle that whatever is held, is held in virtue of its truth apparent, partial, or complete. Instead of pronouncing all our assents untrustworthy from a nervous fear of error, we take ourselves as we find ourselves, wrong perhaps in not a few opinions but for the most part right. By the digestion of these views and by the assimilation of new ones which come to us as the mind develops and experience increases, error is automatically purged away. 'This is the secret of the influence, by which the Church draws to herself converts from such various and conflicting religions ... it is by the light of those particular truths, contained

6 Ibid. 380. [The emphases are Lonergan's.]
7 Ibid. 263. [In this passage, Newman is discussing the 'method of logical inference' as 'a contrivance ... for interpreting the world.']

respectively in the various religions of men ... that we pick our way, slowly perhaps, but surely, into the One Religion which God has given, taking our certitudes with us, not to lose, but to keep them more securely, and to understand and love their objects more perfectly.'[8] 'Of the two, I would rather have to maintain that we ought to begin with believing everything that is offered to our acceptance, than that it is our duty to doubt of everything ... we soon discover and discard what is contradictory to itself; and error having always some portion of truth in it, and the truth having a reality which error has not, we may expect, that when there is an honest purpose and fair talents, we shall somehow make our way forward, the error falling off from the mind, and the truth developing and occupying it.'[9] In fact there is not the alternative of complete acceptance or complete doubt. A middle course is advocated, which is not to be determined by a priori rules. General and rigid rules are particularly without warrant in a world where, contrasted with the absoluteness of truth – what is true in one case being neither more nor less true than what is true in another – is the relativity of evidence, which varies from such strength that doubt seems extravagant to such tenuity that any decision will have the appearance of a guess. To lay it down that truth cannot be known unless directly or deductively self-evident seems mistaken, not only because presumably the illative sense does posit truth without self-evidence, but also because such a canon is at odds both with the mental constitution, for mind judges rather than syllogizes, and with the evidence at our disposal, which is far too manifold for us a priori to limit ourselves to the self-evident and burke the remainder. Again, it is fallacious to urge that assent must be proportionate to evidence, for evidence is the mark of truth, not the measure of assent, and truth once known is to be assented to unconditionally.[10]

The ideal, and perhaps the inspiration, of the syllogistic method is geometry. By syllogism geometrical rigor can be imposed on any subject, but at a price, for this imposition involves an assimilation of the data of experience to the elements of geometry. There is a marvelous simplicity about quantity. However complex the composition of various quantities, there is no degradation of the objectivity. Ideal conclusions are readily adjusted to reality, and any margin of error can be reduced to negligibility. When we would have the terms of another inquiry as univocal and precise, we must substitute notional for real apprehension. 'In Geometry again, the subjects of

8 Ibid. 249.
9 Ibid. 377.
10 See ibid. 172.

argument ... are precise creations of the mind, suggested indeed by external objects, but meaning nothing but what they are defined to mean ... it will be the aim [of the syllogistic method] to circumscribe and stint [the import of words] as much as possible ... to make them ... the *calculi* of notions, which are in our absolute power, as meaning just what we choose them to mean, and as little as possible the tokens of real things ... which mean we do not know how much, but so much certainly as, (in proportion as we enter into them,) may run away with us beyond the range of scientific management.'[11] 'Words, which denote things, have innumerable implications ... [it is the triumph of the logician] to have stripped them of all these connatural senses, to have drained them of that depth and breadth of associations which constitute their poetry, their rhetoric, and their historical life, to have starved each term down till it has become the ghost of itself, and everywhere one and the same ghost ...'[12] The distinction of real and notional apprehension I take to be one of degree, not of kind. The real is not of reality as it is in itself – such is had only by God[13] – while the notional is not unreal in the sense that it is not representative, but only less real. It is the apprehension of a few definite aspects of a thing which is apprehended in all its aspects in real apprehension. A further difference is that in notional apprehension attention is directed to the aspects, while real apprehension concentrates upon the unit-whole with the aspects known implicitly. Real apprehension may be described as impressional, that of one who enters into the object by sympathy, intuition, unformulated interpretation, while notional apprehension stands over against the object, successively views its relations, analyzes, and formulates.[14] 'In processes of this kind [the process of apprehending notionally] we regard things, not as they are in themselves, but mainly as they stand in relation to each other ... "Man" is

11 Ibid. 266–67.
12 Ibid. 267. [The phrase in brackets, 'it is the triumph of the logician,' is Lonergan's abbreviation of the original, 'but in inferential exercises it is the very triumph of that clearness and hardness of head, which is the characteristic talent for the art, to have stripped them ...'] *
13 See ibid. 283. ['We are accustomed, indeed, and rightly, to speak of the Creator Himself as incomprehensible; and, indeed, He is so by an incommunicable attribute; but in a certain sense each of His creatures is incomprehensible to us also, in the sense that no one has a perfect understanding of them but He.']
14 Herbert Wildon Carr, *Henri Bergson: The Philosophy of Change*, People's Books, vol. 26 (London & Edinburgh: T.C. & E.C. Jack, 1911) 64. [The autograph seems to have '64' but it is unlikely that that is the page Lonergan meant to refer to. Page 44 seems more likely.]

no longer what he really is, an individual presented to us by our senses, but as we read him in the light of those comparisons and contrasts which we have made him suggest to us. He is attenuated into an aspect, or relegated to his place in a classification ... all that fulness of meaning which I have described as accruing to language from experience, now that experience is absent, necessarily becomes to the multitude of men nothing but a heap of notions, little more intelligible than the beauties of a prospect to the short-sighted, or the music of a great master to a listener who has no ear.'[15] 'On only few subjects have any of us the opportunity of realizing in our minds what we speak and hear about; and we fancy that we are doing justice to individual men and things by making them a mere *synthesis* of qualities, as if any number whatever of abstractions would, by being fused together, be equivalent to one concrete.'[16] (The difficulty of integration of abstractions is *per accidens*; if the concrete could be perfectly analyzed into abstractions, there would be no difficulty in integration.)

Noting the effect of this distinction on Newman's style, Bertram Newman writes: 'Newman's ever-present sense of the inadequacy of words to represent things led him to employ words freely in his effort at an approximation. "It is as easy to create as to define," he says somewhere. It was not within the resources of any language to present more than a faint and broken reflection of realities, especially of those realities among which he himself lived.'[17] The effect on his thought is more pertinent. Abbé Bremond quotes the *Lectures on Justification*: 'I aim at contemplating things as they are and must be in their embodied form ... When I speak of faith, I am not speaking of a definition, or creation of the mind, but of something existing. I wish to deal with things, not with words ... I would treat of faith as it is actually found in the soul; and I say it is as little an isolated grace as a man is a picture. It has a depth, a breadth, and a thickness; it has an inward life which is something over and above itself; it has a heart, and blood, and pulses, and nerves, though not upon the surface.'[18]

15 Newman, *Grammar* 31–32.
16 Ibid. 33.
17 Bertram Newman, *Cardinal Newman: A Biographical and Literary Study* (London: G. Bell and Sons Ltd., 1925) 203–204.
18 Henri Bremond, *The Mystery of Newman*, trans. H.C. Corrance (London: Williams & Norgate, 1907) 125. [Bremond indicates that he is quoting from pp. 302–303 of the 1838 edition of Newman's *Lectures on Justification*, published in London by J.G. & F. Rivingtons, and in Oxford by J.H. Parker. (In later editions, the title became *Lectures on the Doctrine of Justification*.) The text Bremond cites is from Lecture 11, part 4. The lecture bears the title 'The Nature of Justifying Faith.']

The Abbé's commentary is: 'To abandon the abstract definition for the object defined, the portrait for its living original, is one of the essential principles of the method ... but [this] sheds on religious problems a special light, which the light of abstractions neither eclipses nor replaces. Life alone can judge life; only a theology which is concrete, real, and full of religious feeling can discern the untruth and unreality of a doctrine which calls itself religious, but which is not. The touchstone used by such living theology is not the abstract possibility, the logical coherence, but the moral richness, of a system.'[19] Again, '... [Newman] is of opinion that, in drawing such distinctions (between the reasonings of the intelligence and the exercises of living piety), intelligence suffers at least as much as piety.'[20] That the distinction between notional and real apprehension has a foundation in fact is beyond doubt. What that foundation is may be disputed. It seems, however, to be one of degree and not coincident with the Scholastic distinction of intellectual and sensible apprehension, inasmuch as its *differentiae* are quantity of content, direction of attention, and the presence or absence of a sense of reality or value. I am not aware of the impossibility of a distinction being made upon such grounds between different intellectual apprehensions of the same object. The imputation of nominalism may be thus explained away, especially as Newman was not a professional philosopher and intellectual apprehensions are a theory and not an experience.[21]

To sum up the argument, nature does not fail us in necessaries, a criterion of evidence is necessary, [and] science, the syllogistic method, shows itself to be inadequate and unfair (that is, not the natural criterion) in its preliminary clearing the field by methodic doubt or suspension of judgment, in the confinement of its attention to the abstractly self-evident, in its emptying out the content of our knowledge and its barren definitions of the things, the full meaning of which we are only more or less aware. The alternative criterion is the mind itself, 'far higher, wider, more certain, subtler, than logical inference,' which can use all our knowledge, evaluate evidence in the concrete, and remain in harmony with natural procedure neither a priori doubting everything or accepting anything.

19 Ibid. 125.
20 Ibid. 127 [words in parentheses added by Lonergan].
21 See F. Aveling, 'Universals and the "Illative Sense,"' *The Dublin Review* 275 (October 1905) 236–71.

3   The Illative Sense: A Way to Truth through Our Intellectual and Our Moral Being

The illative sense has been said to be a subjective criterion. It is subjective first in the sense that it provides no simple device for the elimination of the subjective. Science has such a simple device – methodic doubt. However, as has been already urged, simple devices are out of place in a complex world, and accordingly it is sophistical to find fault with a method for lacking what it should not have. But it is subjective in another sense. 'Shall we say that there is no such thing as truth and error, but that anything is truth to a man which he troweth? and not rather, as the solution of a great mystery, that truth there is, and attainable it is, but that its rays stream in upon us through the medium of our moral as well as our intellectual being; and that in consequence that perception of its first principles which is natural to us is enfeebled, obstructed, perverted, by the allurements of sense and the supremacy of self, and, on the other hand, quickened by aspirations after the supernatural.'[22] This is the way truth is to be reached by an individual. The evolution of thought in which truth gains the upper hand and error is purged away is to be accompanied and supplemented by a growth in moral character. Not science so much as wisdom is to be the individual's aim, and not the conditions of knowledge, but the conditions of wisdom are to be the basis of his implicit transcendental deduction. Before science was discovered and philosophers appeared, true judgment (that is, informal inference and the illative sense) constituted the sole way to truth. Proportionate to the development of science was the degradation of judgment till a climax was reached in the Eleatic Monism which more than any previous theory put the plain man's views at nought. A reaction quickly followed in the pragmatism of Protagoras who held some opinions better but none truer than others. Socrates and Plato, I venture to suggest, while they did not admit the impossible denial of objective truth, were at one with Protagoras in the appeal to wisdom. Socrates, a man subject to trances, with a mysterious inner voice, of noble character, was rather inspired by the loftiness than compelled by the dubious logic of the ideal theory. For Plato the basis of science, the absolute premise (*anhypothetos archē*), was the Good, and Plato refused to put down this fundamental doctrine in writing simply because it

22 Newman, *Grammar* 311.

could not be adequately expressed.[23] Aristotle defined science, but he was not a strict rationalist, apparently refusing to consider such questions as 'how do we know we are not dreaming when we think we are awake?' and remarking of the Eleatic doctrine 'that nothing could move,' that 'we are better off than to need to refute it.'[24] Newman quotes from the *Nicomachean Ethics* 6.11: 'We are bound to give heed to the undemonstrated sayings and opinions of the experienced and aged, *not less than to demonstrations*.'[25] The origin of the rationalism which the *Grammar* attacks seems to have been an unconscious assumption, made by post-Aristotelian skeptics who from a denial of a priori knowledge concluded the irrationality of certitude. Thus was implicitly set up the 'pretentious axiom' that science is the criterion of certitude.[26] Because the defenders of certitude also happened to be partisans of science, this assumption was left undisputed. There is a certain dramatic fitness that Newman, of whom Mark Pattison said, 'All the grand development of human reason from Aristotle down to Hegel was a sealed book to him,'[27] should point out to the rationalists that this superiority was based upon a mere assumption, that the 'plain man' was not so much a puppet after all. It has been the contention that this assumption is contradicted by our natural procedure. Science, anyway, is but a luxury of the few, certitude a prerogative of man, and wisdom the obligatory complement of

---

23 See John Burnet, *Greek Philosophy*, Part 1, *Thales to Plato* (London: Macmillan, 1914) 221 [the reference to 'a first principle which is no longer a postulate, namely, the Form of the Good,' occurs on p. 230]; and see Newman, *University Sermons* 275 [more fully: Sermon XIII, 'Implicit and Explicit Reason' (preached on St Peter's Day, 1840) in John Henry Newman, *Fifteen Sermons Preached before the University of Oxford between 1826 and 1843* (London: S.P.C.K., 1970) 275 – a reprint of the definitive third edition (1871), with the original pagination] and *The Arians of the Fourth Century* (London: Longmans, Green and Co., 1919) 137, for a similar attitude; also the *disciplina arcani* of the Early Church, and the 'economy.'

24 Eduard Zeller, *Aristotle and the Earlier Peripatetics*, vol. 1, trans. B.F.C. Costelloe and J.H. Muirhead (London: Longmans, Green and Co., 1897) 210.

25 Newman, *Grammar* 341 [emphasis added by Lonergan].

26 Ibid. 160: ['There are many truths in concrete matters, which no one can demonstrate, yet every one unconditionally accepts; and though of course there are innumerable propositions to which it would be absurd to give an absolute assent, still the absurdity lies in the circumstances of each particular case, as it is taken by itself, not in their common violation of the pretentious axiom that probable reasoning can never lead to certitude.']

27 [Mark Pattison (1813–84) was Rector of Lincoln College, Oxford, from 1861 till 1884. The remark about Newman is found in Mark Pattison, *Memoirs* (London: Macmillan, 1885) 210.]

his being. To make science the criterion of certitude despite its limitation is wantonly to tempt man (who, Newman somewhere says, does not wish to know the truth) to give up the quest for wisdom, to make it possible for him to be complacently agnostic in the high name of reason, when reason hardly countenances his criterion. He will deny the existence of God because the proofs do not convince him, and then accept the first theory to hand to explain away the religions of the world (cf. Renan). To meet the issue more directly, the charge of subjectivism has this much foundation: that Newman's method utilizes evidence which may prove inconclusive when formally expressed in words. The distinction between notional and real apprehension, and that between mind as criterion and logic, the common measure of all minds, give a sufficient explanation of the apparently incriminating difference between the internal and the professed grounds; and this to the extent that subjective influence (insofar as it is illegitimate) may be said to be *per accidens* in the same way as errors in sense perception are *per accidens*. (The chapter on the 'Indefectibility of Certitude' confirms this view.)[28] The same person both judges and wills; if you ask such a segregation of these two activities that all the world may be assured there has been no confusion of their functions, you ask too much: God made man differently, and his providence is the guarantee of nature.[29] Finally, the power of logic to correct subjective influence is easily overestimated. 'I meet everywhere,' says Abbé Bremond, 'with nothing but "demonstrations" and "demonstrators" ... Each of them promises to conduct his enquiry according to the rules, each parades the logical outfit of his time. It is not he, miserable and passionate man no, it is the pure reason which speaks, and it wishes to meet only with reason ... to the majority of those, who have taken in hand the examination of any question and who plume themselves on their exact and pure reasoning, the truth could say: – You do not know how to demonstrate me, and, in any case, you would find it very difficult to do, if already you did not, very fortunately, possess me. As for those who read you and think that they are yielding to the evidence of your arguments, do not let your understanding be in such a hurry to claim them as its spoil. They would not have read you, they would not have understood you, they would not have yielded to your proofs if, already, in twenty ways, they had not thought as you do.'[30]

28 Newman, *Grammar*, chapter VII [§2, pp. 221–58].
29 Ibid. 411–12.
30 Bremond, *The Mystery of Newman* 87–88.

4

Infinite Multitude[1]

In a celebrated paradox, Zeno argued that Achilles would *never* catch the Tortoise, because the Tortoise would be making headway while Achilles ran the distance of the handicap, and as Achilles would inevitably take some time to overcome this headway, the Tortoise in that time would be making more headway, and so on indefinitely. Now, the *never* seems gratuitous. All Zeno is entitled to say is that the number of successive handicaps Achilles must overcome is infinite. (I take an infinite number to be a number greater than any number theoretically assignable by man. Such a number is not merely indefinite, for what is actual is definite.) Further, there is no difficulty in supposing that Achilles traversed an infinite number of distances, for added together they do not make an infinite distance. To make an infinite distance there would have to be some assignable distance smaller than any particular distance in the sum. For example,

$$1 \text{ inch} = \tfrac{1}{2} + \tfrac{1}{4} + \tfrac{1}{8} \ldots \tfrac{1}{2}^n \text{ inches.}$$

The infinite series has a finite limit because there is no assignable fraction of an inch smaller than $\tfrac{1}{2}^n$ where n has any value. Similarly a finite time can be divided infinitely into suitable intervals in which Achilles may traverse each of the infinite number of distances.

As to the distinction *per partes proportionales* and *aliquotas*, Achilles does not advance *per partes proportionales* if that means that he stops to set up a trophy at the end of each of the distances. If *per partes proportionales* means that we are

---

1 [*Blandyke Papers*, no. 291 (February, 1929) 217–20.]

to consider the race from the point of view of the distances Achilles is behind the Tortoise at defined instants, I completely fail to see any falsification of reality. The mere fact that a point of view is involved is nothing. *Per partes aliquotas* implies that we advert to the contact of Achilles's feet with the ground or something similar. The distances Achilles is behind the Tortoise are real, and again (what is absent in the division of a continuum) the infinity of them are designated *actu*, though successively, by the respective positions of Achilles and the Tortoise at the instants Achilles overcomes the headway the Tortoise had been making. Not only is there objectively an infinite multitude every time one moving object passes another but these infinities are knowable. An angel without reaction time, not subject to a limit of visibility, capable of perfect knowledge of the position of the competitors, would be able to know each distance and to count them. Further, as Fr Hontheim[2] would admit,

2 [Lonergan is referring to the text found on pp. 713–14 of Joseph Hontheim's book *Institutiones theodicaeae sive theologiae naturalis secundum principia S. Thomae Aquinatis ad usum scholasticum* (Friburgi Brisgoviae: Sumptibus Herder, 1893). A translation by Michael G. Shields of that text follows: 'A successive multitude that is infinite in act is no less impossible than a simultaneous multitude. For there is nothing that would absolutely prevent the individual members of a successive series from being kept with the accretion of new ones, and so successive infinity, in the supposition that it is possible, becomes infinite. If, therefore, successive infinity is possible, so is simultaneous infinity; and if the latter is impossible, so is the former. For example, if from eternity an infinite number of days had passed, on each day God could have created a stone, just as he created each of those days by his power. Then today we should have an infinite number of stones. And so it appears again that a successive infinite multitude is no less impossible than a simultaneous multitude, because the former involves the latter. I do not see what reply could sensibly be made to these arguments. If you should say that God could not have so created and conserved the stones, lest something infinite be produced, your argument is worthless and a *petitio principii*. For this is precisely what our argument proves, that if the world is eternal, then an infinity is possible. If, therefore, you deny with St Thomas that an infinity of things can be produced, you must deny that the world has existed from eternity; for otherwise an infinite number could well be produced, as our argument proves.'

Joseph Hontheim, a German Jesuit and Professor of Theology, died in Valkenburg, Germany, on 2 January 1929, just a month before the publication of this paper. Lonergan knew of Hontheim through his publications in theology, as is clear in the following Letter to the Editor of *Blandyke Papers* (see below, pp. 48–49), where he responds to part of the critique of Hontheim by Francis Courtney, s.j., on the question of creation from eternity. Note that the letter contains a reference to the stone example just cited.

For the biographical information on Hontheim, we are indebted to Rev. Dermot Preston, s.j., Socius to the Provincial, and Brother James Hodkinson, s.j., assistant archivist of the British Province of the Society of Jesus.]

God could create a stone as Achilles ran each distance. Man cannot know an infinite multitude because *nihil in intellectu nisi prius fuerit in sensu.* Objections against infinite number are often based on the unconscious assumption that infinite number is a particular number and not, as is finite number, a class of numbers. If the former assumption leads to absurdities, then we have a proof of the truth of the latter.

Mathematical Appendix

If we presuppose uniform motion, the race can be represented by elementary algebra.

Let Achilles's speed $= a$ Tortoise's speed $= b$ handicap $= c$.

Time taken by Achilles $c/a + bc/a^2 + b^2c/a^3 \dots$

Headway made by Tortoise $bc/a + b^2c/a^2 + b^3c/a^3 \dots$

We have two G.P.'s;[3] the sum to infinity $a/(1 - r)$ gives the total time and total distance from Achilles's starting point to [the] moment when Achilles reaches the tortoise.

$$\text{Time} = \frac{c/a}{1 - b/a} = \frac{c}{a - b}$$

$$\text{Distance} = \frac{c}{1 - b/a} = \frac{ac}{a - b}$$

$$\text{Distance to } n \text{ terms} = \frac{c(a^n - b^n)}{a^{n-1}(a - b)}$$

Let $c = 100$, $a = 10$, $b = 1$

Then $n = 3$	Distance	$= 111.0$
$n = 4$		$= 111.10$
$n = 6$		$= 111.1110$
$n = 10$		$= 111.11111110$
$n = \infty$		$= 111.\bar{1}$

3   [A geometric progression (G.P.) is a sequence of numbers in which each term, after the first, is obtained from the preceding one by multiplying that term by a fixed number called the common ratio.]

5

A Letter on 'Creation from Eternity'[1]

The Editor of *Blandyke Papers*
Dear Sir,

In a recent trenchant article, criticism is offered of Fr Hontheim's arguments against creation from eternity.[2] I wish to question the criticism of what is referred to as the 'stones' example (pp. 92, 93, 94, *Blandyke Papers*, February, 1929).[3]

Fr Hontheim undertakes to show that a successive infinite multitude involves the possibility of a simultaneous infinite multitude: on each of an infinite number of days, God could create and preserve some durable object such as a stone; the result, at the end of an infinite number of days, would be a simultaneous infinity of stones. Therefore, if a successive infinity (an infinite number of days) is possible, so a simultaneous infinity (an infinite number of stones) is also possible.[4]

---

1 [*Blandyke Papers*, no. 292 (Easter, 1929) 313–15.]
2 [Fr Joseph Hontheim's argument is found in *Institutiones theodicaeae sive theologiae naturalis* (see above, p. 46, note 2) 710–15: Articulus V, 'Num creatio ab aeterno esse potest,' Thesis LIX, 'Nulla creatura ab aeterno esse potest.']
3 [The criticism was offered by Francis Courtney, S.J., a philosophy student contemporary with Lonergan at Heythrop College, in a preceding article, 'Creation from Eternity Not Repugnant,' *Blandyke Papers*, no. 291 (February 1929) 89–100. Courtney was a British Jesuit, born in 1905, and the author of *Cardinal Robert Pullen: An English Theologian of the Twelfth Century* (Rome: Gregorian University Press, 1954).]
4 [See above, p. 46, n. 2.]

Against this, the critic seems to urge that an infinite number of days cannot have an end; in other words, an infinite number of days is possible only on the condition that it never is infinite. Such at least seems to be the point of the analogy of touching points in a line, and the meaning of the statement that an infinite number of perishable things is infinite only in potency and therefore possible. There would seem to be a difference between things that will perish (and are produced only at intervals) never being a simultaneous infinity, and such things past and present (and future) never amounting in number to infinity. One cannot both deny the last, and affirm the possibility of a successive infinity, for a successive infinity is plainly impossible if it never can be infinite in any sense but that in which it is not infinite (namely, infinite in potency).

I can find no transference of a predicate from the days in an infinite duration to the duration itself. There is a transference of a predicate which belongs to any day to all the days, and this, if not tautologous, at least seems licit.

That the action of God is one, eternal, and not successive tells equally against an infinite number of things that will perish and an infinite number of things that will not. To discriminate against the latter class would seem to involve a limitation of God by his creatures; of course arguments may be producible to the contrary.

An argument seems suggested to this effect; if not, then this paragraph forestalls a plausible objection. A successive infinity of things that pass away never results in a simultaneous infinity; hence it is possible. An infinity of durable things results in a simultaneous infinity; hence it is impossible. As a possibility cannot contain the possibility of an impossibility, so a successive infinity of things that perish cannot involve the possibility of a simultaneous infinity. A *petitio principii* is concealed in this: for a successive infinity to be possible, not only must it not result in, but also it must not involve the possibility of, a simultaneous infinity. The second condition is obviously necessary, and it is the conclusion as well as a premise of the argument.

In the present state of my knowledge, I do not think creation from eternity is to be defended by a distinction between successive and simultaneous infinities.

I am your obedient servant,

B. Lonergan, s.j.[5]

---

5 Courtney replied to Lonergan's criticisms on pp. 317–23 of *Blandyke Papers*, no. 292, the same issue in which Lonergan's letter appeared.

PART TWO

Early Short Papers and Devotional Works

6

Gilbert Keith Chesterton[1]

In a famous preface to a definitely poor play, Victor Hugo outlined his conception of a new drama that was to be as large as life. The old classical distinction between tragedy and comedy was to be effaced; the sublime and the ridiculous were to be set side by side, and their juxtaposition was to result in a species of compressed reality, if not beauty, which was termed the grotesque.[2] He had caught an idea from Chateaubriand,[3] and prominent in the array of arguments for his theory was the contention that a catholic unity in difference, a manifold complexity, should mark the native art of Christian civilization. In the execution of this plan Hugo never rose above fine melodrama. One reason of his failure was that he thought to produce Christian art without being a Christian. Now Mr Chesterton is not

---

1 [*Loyola College Review* 17 (1931) 7–10. At this time, Lonergan was teaching at Loyola College, Montreal. In addition to his teaching he had other chores, one of which was faculty moderator of the annual *Review*. See Crowe, *Lonergan* 17–19.]

2 [Lonergan would seem to be referring to Victor Hugo's famous 1827 preface to his play *Cromwell* (Paris: Nelson, 1932), which is said to have served as the manifesto of the romantic school in France. An English translation of Hugo's preface can be found in *Prefaces and Prologues to Famous Books, with Introductions, Notes and Illustrations*, The Harvard Classics 39, ed. Charles W. Eliot (New York: P.F. Collier & Son, 1910) 354–408.]

3 [François René de Chateaubriand (1768–1848) was a French writer and diplomat, and is credited with being the founder of Romanticism in French literature. He is also the author of *Le génie du Christianisme*, in which he emphasized the beauty of Christian doctrine and its capacity to inspire literature and the arts.]

a dramatist;[4] but without reducing him to a formula, or making the 'grotesque' the source of his inspiration or the key to his mind, it is possible to use this conception to indicate many dominant features and important aspects. Happily, if only analogically, it characterizes his wisdom, his thought, his imagination, and his style.[5]

He advocates standing on one's head to see things properly, and this not by way of a casual paradox but on so many occasions and in such varied forms, that topsy-turvydom might be exalted into a metaphorical definition of his philosophy of life. 'Moor Eeffoc' (read it backwards) is to him 'the masterpiece of the good realistic principle – the principle that the most fantastic thing of all is often the precise fact.'[6] To a confusion of fantasy and fact, he adds a confusion of wisdom and folly. 'Simply by going on being absurd a thing can become god-like; there is but one step from the ridiculous to the sublime.'[7] Such imaginative flights into the theories of knowledge and conduct might lead anywhere; but here imagination is but the dress of an understanding that seems akin to intuitive vision. When Mr Chesterton urges that the way to be great is to be a great fool, he is reminiscent of St Paul. When to find the true value of things he would turn

4 [Although he is not remembered especially as a dramatist, Chesterton did in fact write a number of plays, some of them very brief, and some surviving only in fragments. All of Chesterton's known plays have been published in *Plays and Chesterton on Shaw*, vol. 11 in The Collected Works of G.K. Chesterton, compiled and introduced by Denis J. Conlon (San Francisco: Ignatius Press, 1989).]

5 [Chesterton wrote the following about the grotesque: '... the element of the grotesque in art, like the element of the grotesque in nature, means, in the main, energy, the energy that takes its own forms and goes its own way.' G.K. Chesterton, *Robert Browning* (London: Macmillan, 1904) 149. Ibid. 151: 'To present a matter in a grotesque manner does certainly tend to touch the nerve of surprise and thus to draw attention to the intrinsically miraculous character of the object itself.' Again, in *Chesterton on Dickens*, vol. 15 in The Collected Works of G.K. Chesterton (San Francisco: Ignatius Press, 1989) 203: 'This sentiment of the grotesqueness of the universe ran through Dickens's brain and body like the mad blood of the elves. He saw all his streets in fantastic perspectives, he saw all his cockney villas as top heavy and wild, he saw every man's nose twice as big as it was, and every man's eyes like saucers. And this was the basis of his gaiety – the only real basis of any philosophical gaiety.' Ibid. 314: 'The grotesque is the natural expression of joy ... When real human beings have real delights they tend to express them entirely in grotesques.']

6 [Ibid. 65. Chesterton is drawing from Dickens's own reminiscence of his boyhood.]

7 [Ibid. 50.]

them upside down,[8] he recalls Aristotle's doctrine of the 'mean' and the advice that comes as a corollary: to avoid the extremes one had best journey in the opposite direction to the rest of men.

It is to criticism that he confines his original mind. Despite a full recognition of the unequivocal pronouncements of *G.K.'s Weekly*, distributism is not the outburst of a theorist with a vision of Utopia; it proceeds from a desire to emphasize directly and persistently an aspect of human nature that both capitalism and communism overlook.[9] It is doing on a large scale what he does incidentally when he flourishes his brief for beer, pillories the millionaire who elaborately leads the simple life, ridicules the fatuous lady who indulges some charlatan by experimenting on the proletariat. It is not that his criticism is negative. A negative attitude would be agony to him; it is the invention of a decadent age and runs counter to the straightforward simplicity of his mind. He exposes fallacy and inconsistency with exultation because he loves mental honesty and loathes sham. He attacks 'Fancies and Fads'[10] because he knows the elemental claims of human nature. He has raised these principles to the domain of politics, and in their light he has studied religion. Hugo argued from Christianity to the 'grotesque'; Chesterton found in Christianity the supreme complement to the 'grotesque' he had already recognized in life. More than critical acumen, it was a grasp of the conditions of healthy living that brought him to the Church. His ideal would seem the old ideal of the universal man – the man who lives and thinks, who finds nothing so small that it fails to give him pleasure, who finds nothing so great that he may not think about it, either to question or to adore.

It may be because he did not attend a university that Chesterton has not spent his life merely reading and investigating. Modern education with its pompous curricula has overemphasized the measurable part of cultural

---

8   [See Chesterston, *Robert Browning* 151.]

9   [*G.K.'s Weekly* was a weekly review of politics, the arts, and literature that was 'edited' by Chesterton and published from March 1925 through to December 1936. It championed as an alternative to both capitalism and socialism the social and economic doctrine that became known as distributism. Distributism advocated the widespread distribution of private property, small-scale private productive ownership, and economic and political decentralization. A selection of thirty complete issues of *G.K.'s Weekly* has been published as *G.K.'s Weekly: A Sampler*, ed. Lyle W. Dorsett (Chicago: Loyola Univesity Press, 1986).]

10   [*Fancies versus Fads* is the title of a collection of Chesterton's essays that was originally published in 1923.]

development to the neglect of purely intellectual training. The methods of physical inquiry have invaded letters in the name of scholarship to make letters not a preparation for life but a lifelong pastime. Of these tendencies, Chesterton is free. He runs against the modern worship of science and scholarship to be the champion of plain thinking. He vindicates the plain man's right to think, not that he may think with the poetical scientists but that he may think for himself. He has extensive learning but his learning is subordinate to, is marshaled and even snubbed by an intellect that knows its rights. When he speaks it is not with a mandate from science, such as so many popularizers arrogate; it is with an appeal to the lore of human experience and to the first principles latent in daily life.

Great mental clarity and a remarkable aptitude for pertinent illustration are demanded of a man who would attack high-sounding theory with elusive common sense. It is so easy to argue from a system with all its presumptions and implications, so hard to settle a question with scarcely any premises but the perennial truisms. The modern itch for originality makes the work at once imperative and difficult. Private judgment has come to mean the intellectual's right to say what he pleases and the average man's choice of what may chance to please him best. With a happy combination of circumstances, a generous allotment of luck, and an imposing tome of pseudo-science to his credit, any clever person may command the enthusiastic support of vast numbers of men. Karl Marx had German materialism, the industrial revolution, reasonable publicity, a wild theory of value, and an outrageous conception of history. That originator of a great experiment on civilization is not a unique example of noble sentiment and addled thought uniting to bring forth a monstrosity. Democracy is faced with the alternative of teaching thought or meeting its decline and fall. Chesterton would undertake this task. To gratify the insistence upon novelty, he has evolved a style of bewildering brilliance and prestidigital wordplay.

His imagination is bent on charging things with significance. In his own phrase, he turns 'patterns into pictures,' sees in the squares of a chessboard the romance of chivalry, in the decorative scheme of a wallpaper the man who designed and even perhaps liked it. Swift once meditated on a broomstick;[11] Chesterton seems always at it. And when the broomstick fails

11 [Lonergan is referring to Jonathan Swift's parody *A Meditation upon a Broomstick according to the Style and Manner of the Hon. Robert Boyle's Meditations*, written in 1704.]

to suggest in some striking way the evil of capitalism, a weak point in evolution, or an absurdity of the agnostics, then he will turn to fable and legend, see witches riding brooms across a dark November sky, and reflect on the wisdom of old wives' tales and nursery rhymes. There is a perplexing side to the vigor and vividness of his imagery that is closely allied to symbolism. He puts awe and mystery into common things, but treats the roof of the stars as familiarly as the roof of his house. He is fond of the phrase 'the end of the world,' and it usually occurs as unexpectedly as in this description: 'The castle blocked the end of the valley and looked like the end of the world.'[12] It would seem that he envies the men of earlier times who could be afraid of falling off the end of the world. Their sense of the mysteriousness of things, even though due to an error, seems to him preferable to a shallow cocksureness that denies there is any mystery at all. They had the power of wondering, and that is the root of thought; we have a rather insignificant certainty that puts an end to thought.

As the medieval painters held a picture incomplete unless a vision of heaven and a glimpse of hell were included, so Chesterton when not finding humorous illustrations for a serious topic is setting a solemn background for his frolics. We take the first as a matter of course; it is the recognized way for authors to recompense those who buy and read their books. But if humor is not out of place in a weighty discussion, it is very rare that an ulterior purpose obtrudes on our frivolities. Our sweetest songs may be those that tell of saddest thought, but who would say that our maddest pranks are to be marked by a concern for the four last things? We like our fun unadulterated; when Chesterton refuses this seemingly reasonable request, there is food for thought. 'The Song of Quoodle' is of a piece with the fantasy and satire of 'The Flying Inn.' It begins with a cavalier scorn of grammar that touches a chord in the boisterous spirits of all.

> They haven't got no noses
> The fallen sons of Eve;
> Even the smell of roses
> Is not what they supposes;

12 [Lonergan is recalling the beginning of Chesterton's story 'The Honour of Israel Gow,' from *The Innocence of Father Brown*. The quote is not exact. See *The Father Brown Stories, Part I*, vol. 12 in The Collected Works of G.K. Chesterton, with introduction and notes by John Peterson (San Francisco: Ignatius Press, 2005) 120.]

But more than mind discloses
And more than men believe.[13]

The initial double negative disarms suspicion, wins sympathy and confidence, promises a lowbrow revel. For a bit, one is carried along by the rhyme and rhythm, then feels one is losing contact and begins again. Why 'The fallen sons of Eve'? Chesterton surely could have said 'mankind' in six syllables without bringing in that unhappy woman and the Fall. Again 'mind' cannot be a clumsy synonym for 'human nose'; it is, one is forced to admit, a gratuitous reminder that our minds are as weak as our sense of smell is poor. Now there is a novelty and audacity about this form of preaching that makes us forget our dislike of preaching. Under cover of casually baiting those who disagree with him, he is also raising the thoughts of those who do agree. Basically he is revealing the grand confusion of great and small, of important and trifling, that comes of seeing in the light of eternity.

Similarly in his detective stories, the grotesque emerges in Father Brown, the queer little priest, with his huge friend Flambeau, a reformed criminal.[14] It is apparent in the disconcerting habit of stimulating interest in the crime and then introducing a sturdy little lesson in logic, a disquisition on St Thomas Aquinas, or a cryptic allusion to the mystery of the Holy Trinity. To Chesterton a digression never seems out of place. His essays begin anywhere, find a central image, and then build up a closely reasoned and plainly intelligible attack on some aberration of the day.

His style jolts the indolent reader to attention or leaves him lost in a maze of words. He exults in playing with words, but his play is seldom child's play; more often does it recall the resourceful hero of Western fiction playing with a revolver. Delightful or annoying, it certainly is exceedingly incisive and effective. It would be hard to find a view presented and refuted as

13 ['The Song of Quoodle' (Quoodle is a dog) is a poem in Chesterton's novel *The Flying Inn*, one of three novels (the others being *The Ball and the Cross* and *Manalive*) now included in vol. 7 in The Collected Works of G.K. Chesterton, with introduction and notes by Iain T. Benson (San Francisco: Ignatius Press, 2004). The poem appears on p. 556. Benson writes (introduction, 29–30) that '[t]he target in the novel is the pervasiveness of political corruption, which left unchecked, can affect every aspect of the common man's life ...']
14 [The first two collections of Father Brown stories, *The Innocence of Father Brown* (orig. 1911) and *The Wisdom of Father Brown* (1915), are published in vol. 12 in The Collected Works of G.K. Chesterton. The remaining three, *The Incredulity of Father Brown* (1926), *The Secret of Father Brown* (1927), and *The Scandal of Father Brown* (1935), and the stories 'The Vampire of the Village' and 'The Mask of Midas,' are published in *The Father Brown Stories, Part II*, vol. 13 in The Collected Works of G.K. Chesterton, ed. John Peterson (San Francisco: Ignatius Press, 2006).]

briefly and convincingly as this. 'To me this old English world (early days of Dickens) seems infinitely less hard and cruel than the world described in Gissing's own novels. Coarse external customs are merely relative, and easily assimilated. A man soon learnt to harden his hands and harden his head. Faced with the world of Gissing, he can do little but harden his heart.'[15]

This power of succinct argument makes Chesterton a masterful essayist, but it also makes his books seem collected essays. In his hands, a long discussion becomes a series of discussions, each with a vitality of its own and contributing as a unit to the general effect. Again the bulk of his work is inextricably bound up with the present. He has written of Charles Dickens with penetration and appreciation, noticing what passes unobserved and illuminating what time has obscured. His study is relative to present needs; it does not attempt objective biography but aims at setting right mistaken contemporary opinion. This means that much of his work will not survive. But the point I would make is that the greater part is the more important. Literature is only a section of valuable writing; its two excellent functions, education and refined relaxation, are far from exhausting all the worthy purposes a writer can entertain. Within the province of journalism falls not only the external activity of the day, but as well the fermenting mass of crude ideas that constantly emanate from ambitious original thinkers. There is a singular detachment and nobility in making issue with ephemeral aberrations, in hoping to benefit posterity not by exquisite composition but by an endeavor to improve the present. To this work for some thirty years in verse and poetry, in stories, articles, and books, he has devoted the intellectual vigor and alertness that brought him to the Catholic Church.[16]

His reputation would stand higher did he not write so much, for a distinctive and exceptional style palls in the long run. To many it would seem that he has become content to be characteristically himself, to go through the familiar gymnastics and then hurry off the stage. Any single performance is by itself striking, but by now we have learned what to expect. This takes the edge off paradox and makes the fantastic commonplace. He is still the master of his conversational method, direct, entertaining, and when not convincing at least stimulating. But the blossoms of his prime with their bright tints and exotic scent have given way to the solidity and uniformity of grown fruit. He was not to be only a flower. A more robust purposiveness stamps his work, makes it not so much an ornament as an instrument of civilization.

15 [*Chesterton on Dickens* 41. George Robert Gissing (1857–1903) was an English realist novelist and journalist and the author of *The New Grub Street* and *Critical Studies of the Works of Charles Dickens*.]
16 [Chesterton was received into the Catholic Church on Sunday, 30 July 1922.]

7

The College Chapel[1]

It is again the privilege of the *Review* to record Loyola's acquisition of another building. Flanking the front building and linked to it by a closed-in cloister now stands the college chapel. A broad, steeply slanting copper roof between Flemish gables, with a lofty flèche, also copper-covered, near the western end where the incipient transepts cut across; windows, rectangular in the nave with buttresses between them, circular in the transepts and apse; a facade, well back from the street, that rises somewhat abruptly above the broad perron and challenges by its plain stretches of brickwork over the stone-framed doors and around the large gallery window: such in outline, or enumeration, is the new chapel. With differences that will be interesting to future amateurs of architecture, and economics, it matches the other buildings. Similar in its general lines and in material, it has the delightful quality of eliciting a perhaps confused satisfaction without being what one expects after familiarity with the rectilineal sweep of stone mullions in the front building's facade or the high-arched cloister and terra-cotta facings of the back buildings.

---

1 [*Loyola College Review* 19 (1933) 1–3. An unsigned editorial, this was Lonergan's second contribution to the *Review* during his three years of teaching at Loyola College, Montreal (see above, p. 53, n. 1). Frederick Crowe characterizes the editorial: 'This latter is true to his developing form in its easy passage from the concrete details of architecture to the sweep of world history, but it is quite unexpected in its mastery of the architecture itself.' Crowe, *Lonergan* 18–19. The new chapel of which Lonergan writes was called St Ignatius of Loyola College Chapel.]

Such preoccupations of matching the new piece with the old cloth do not interfere with one's impressions of the interior. A high-vaulted ceiling supported only by the side walls, and an abundance of light pouring through the amber windows give an air of spacious compactness that characterizes the whole arrangement. Ingenious contrivances for ventilation, heating, and acoustics, all successful be it said, are skillfully lost in the ribbed ceiling and the 'birnut' panelling[2] that runs around the walls. The sanctuary floor, level with the tops of the pews, is cut across by a wall in which is pierced a great arch framing the wide recess for the main altar. In front of this wall on either side of the recess are the side altars and, behind, sacristies with tribunes above; on the left side and harmoniously fitting in with the general scheme is an exceptionally fine pulpit. Unless accustomed to the strictly liturgical, one at first finds the main altar novel yet quickly comes to appreciate its peculiar charm. The tester, supported behind by the wall and in front by two chains from the ceiling, covers a space in which the central piece is a large bronze crucifix. Six massive bronze candlesticks stand on the altar itself; in the centre is the cylindrical cone-capped tabernacle in bronze but with a silver door. The symbolic inscriptions worked in the dossal and antependium associate this arresting simplicity with the early church when Greek was the language of the elite and of the slaves of Rome.

The bewilderment and the universal questioning that marks the present time make it natural to rise to the wider significance of the chapel and to point out that it is the concretion of a living tradition, something at once old and new. The frank utilization of materials that belong distinctively to the machine age and the subordination of all parts to their need make the chapel a child of the time, as does the fusion of styles to take advantage of modern structural simplifications. Yet how strikingly does this square with the Periclean epigram, 'We love beauty without expense.'[3] Gables that might rise above the canals of Ghent, round windows that might belong to a Gothic cathedral, a nave that suggests the romanesque, an altar to recall Byzantium and Rome – these blend not only in the skillful design of the

2 [The editors were unable to find the meaning of '"birnut" panelling,' but a Google search for 'birnut' yielded one hit: the phrase '"birnut" in flooring panel' with a link to John R. Cosgrove, 'Report on the Uses of Various Empire Woods ...' *Forestry* 7:1 (1933) 50–54. The editors thank John St James for this reference.]

3 [The reference is to the Funeral Oration of Pericles after the first year of the Peloponnesian War (430 B.C.), as recorded by Thucydides: 'Our love of what is beautiful does not lead to extravagance; our love of the things of the mind does not make us soft.']

architect but also in the spirit. For we are at one with the culture of the West and we deprive ourselves of none of its manifestations in three thousand years. We bring what we have of the Athenian's keen perception of measure, of the Roman's love of order, of the medieval passion for logic, of Renaissance enthusiasm for man, of the scientist's control of nature, and watch them cast off what they have of extravagance and crystallize into unity under the synthetic influence of the universal religion that comes from ancient Palestine and encircles the world.

Yet ancient as is the lineage and ecumenical the sources of the culture that is integrated in the chapel, it remains that we have no mere monument of times gone by. 'Your creeds are dead,' they say; but if so, what is alive? We hold no brief for sixteenth-century heretics, commended neither by valid thought nor winning characters; nor did we ever expect the naive Bible religion then foisted upon the populace with many a tirade against carnal knowledge to survive the inroads of sophists, or even the advance of science. But there is singularly lacking any evidence of life, of a power to unify and coordinate, in international leagues, in parliamentary government, in experts, in competition, in merchant prices, in nationalistic catch phrases, in technocracy – that brilliant product of practical education – or in Soviet Russia, the logical goal of dogmatic liberalism. On the other hand, there is patent an exuberance of vitality in the papal encyclicals that stand foursquare and eternally central against the shifting winds of opinion; there is magnificence and inspiration in a faith that possesses the loyalty of millions of hearts in every land without distinction of race or rank or attainment; there is perennial endurance in a philosophy too profound to be swept away by the dazzling dawn of new ideas in complacent minds, too accurate and rigorous to be assimilated by contemporary Pilates who ask, 'What is truth?' and do not stay for an answer, too realistic ever to be ignorant of what it is about or whither leads the intellectual mistiness of self-appointed oracles.

But it is not merely in historical associations nor in the impalpable realm of ideas that is to be found what constitutes the actuality of the chapel. The problem of education is not a problem of machinery, of devising curricula and securing professors, of buying libraries and getting the books read. That is all possible enough. But if the modern mind does not know what education should effect or how it should be effected – as it openly confesses it does not – we have no ground for surprise; such nebulosity marks its utterances on all questions that cannot, and not a few that can, be solved by the arts of exact measurement. But the real problem of education is the problem faced by the teacher who displays the heritage of civilization with what skill he masters, who watches and waits with conscious helplessness for the fecundation and blossoming and growth of that seed that can easily be sterile and easily be monstrous but not easily be fine and delicate, stout and sound. The mystery of individuality confronts him, and faced with it he can only quote: 'Paul plants, Apollos waters, but God grants the increase' (1 Corinthians 3.6). The course of life is enlightened and largely guided by its highest moments – moments when alone and reflective, man grasps how utterly alone he must be, he really is. How well, then, to be alone with Christ! And a chapel built from the estate of one who left all to follow him[4] is indeed a doubly sacred and doubly inspiring shrine.

4 [The reference is to Francis C. Smith, s.j., the son of a prominent Montreal family. Before pronouncing his final vows in the Society of Jesus on 2 February 1931, 'he disposed of his patrimony in favour of the construction at Loyola College of a new chapel and auditorium, named in his honour after his death, the F.C. Smith Auditorium.' *Dictionary of Jesuit Biography: Ministry to English Canada, 1842–1987* (Toronto: Canadian Institute of Jesuit Studies, 1991) 325–26.]

8

Secondary Patrons of Canada[1]

His Holiness Pope Pius xii has thought of Canada. By a formal act, rich in its profound significance, he has named as secondary patrons of our country the eight saints and martyrs who labored here and died as witnesses to Christ.[2] Nothing certainly could be more opportune at the present moment, when we are leagued in a terrible struggle against a power that would stamp out and destroy even the modern world's tepid love and secretive reverence for Christ. Nothing could be more inspiring for our future development, when we shall have to confront the economic problem and, by our honesty in facing it, work out our national destiny. But if we are to understand and to appreciate this gesture of the Sovereign Pontiff to us as a nation, we must pause and think; we must try to grasp what is a patron saint, and what ours mean to us.

There are many very simple things, like walking, or lacing a shoe, that can hardly be put in words. Similarly, it is much easier to accept and practice Catholic devotions to the saints than it is to distinguish and describe the many elements that enter into so spontaneous and so vital a movement. There is the very ordinary matter of projecting an ideal into some human embodiment: this one can witness in primitive literatures, in Homer's Achilles, the *Cid* of Spain, Roland of the *Chanson*, Siegfried of the *Nibelungenlied*;[3] it is no less apparent in nationalist history, in Livy's long

---

1 [*The Montreal Beacon* no. 33 (3 January 1941) 3.]
2 [See *Martyrs' Shrine Message* 5 (1941) 5–6.]
3 [A Middle High German epic of unknown authorship. Its themes are faithfulness and revenge.]

praise of Rome or in schoolbook accounts of Good Queen Bess and George Washington; and the same spontaneous impulse can be found in reflex, deliberate expression not only nobly as in Virgil's exquisite *Aeneid* but also degradingly in the apotheosis of a Lenin or a Hitler.

Obviously the Church has never wished, as have so many heresiarchs, to eliminate human nature. That men have ideals is a condition of human survival; that ideals be made palpable is a condition of their being effective. Symbols, then, of human greatness are not to be denied mankind, even though born again through baptism in Christ; and so we may observe in every age and culture the flowering emergence of saints and patrons to meet merely human exigencies and needs. The early centuries of persecution were glorious in their martyrs: the courageous dignity of Cyprian, the exuberant heroism of Laurence, the triumphant tenderness that has been transmitted in the recorded visions of Perpetua and Felicity. But the times changed, and to Christians who could live unmolested in a still thoroughly pagan world the evil of that contamination was vividly portrayed by St Antony in the Egyptian desert and by St Benedict in the mountains at Subiaco. When the dark ages ended and the modern Europe began to take shape, the northern songs of war and the southern songs of chivalry and courtly love not merely mingled but were merged in the higher synthesis of saintly knights and kings: St George for England, St Louis for France, St Wenceslas in Bohemia, St Stephen of Hungary, St Casimir of Poland belong to an age when warfare was limited by rules and when public opinion was marshaled by a more powerful agent than newspaper and radio. And if one wishes a modern instance, is there not something psychotherapeutic, a real balm for unreasoning fears, in St Thérèse's childlike confidence in God?

But not merely is the idea of the patron saint rooted in a profound exigence of human nature; also it passes in review the meaning of human life and reaches upward toward the throne of God. Christopher Dawson somewhere says – I fear I cannot quote exactly – that you can give men all the benefits of modern inventiveness, abundant food, pleasant dwellings, financial security, ever shorter hours of labor, ever growing facilities for recreation and entertainment, yet men will remain profoundly discontented; on the other hand, give them something to die for, and though they starve and sleep in ditches, though they endure the mounting strain of fatigue and pain, wounds and bereavement, still they will be happy.[4] This indeed is

---

4 [Perhaps an elaboration of: 'You can give men food and leisure and amusements and good conditions of work, and still they will remain unsatisfied. You

paradoxical, yet how can one deny its truth? There is an infinite longing in the heart of man which St Augustine diagnosed so long ago when he wrote: 'Thou has made us for Thyself, O Lord, and our hearts are restless till they rest in Thee.'[5] So exact is this, that all the efforts of the modern world to get along without God, to construct the family and the state, to conduct education and international relations, to orientate and develop our cultural heritage without any reference to God, have culminated only in the hideous nightmare of the fierce religions of hatred. This is not the place to analyze the revolutionary spirit, the bitter disillusionment and explosive discontent that surges forth in those who have penetrated to the hollowness and falsity that underlie the glamorous promise of Our Brave New World. To what lengths the spirit of revolution carries men we know in the countless horrors of the U.S.S.R. and of National Socialist Germany. And it is only a vapid incapacity for reflection that will fancy, 'Such things cannot happen here.' As intensely as any, Canadians desire a better world; as enthusiastically as any they will work for it; and the only question is, 'How hold from folly the helm of their hearts?'

I think we can find a lesson in Leon Trotsky's gospel of perpetual revolution. This visionary clearly saw that the only effect of Bolshevism was to create a new bourgeoisie, a new pattern of egoisms to be the real antitheses of an ideal world. But if revolution must be perpetual, it is not the revolution of violence and bloodshed, of terrorism, torture chambers, proscribed classes, and cultural nullity; it is the inner revolution in the heart of men that must be constant; it is the illumination of his understanding and the purification of his will that must ever be effected.[6] 'If any man will come after me, let him deny himself and take up his cross daily and follow me' (Luke 9.23). There is indeed an immediate and imperious necessity to rid the world of Hitler and all he stands for; but there is a deeper and more long-standing need for an inner victory, for the dethronement of the petty Hitlers in the hearts of us all.

---

can deny them all these things, and they will not complain so long as they feel that they have something to die for.' From Christopher Dawson, *The Modern Dilemma: The Problem of European Unity*. Essays in Order, no. 8 (London and New York: Sheed & Ward, 1932) 97.]

5 [Augustine of Hippo, *Confessions*, trans. Henry Chadwick (New York: Oxford University Press, 1991), book I, p. 3.]

6 [There is a handwritten marginal comment in a fragment on progress in the Lonergan archives (A23), the last words of which, unfortunately, are illegible: 'We preach perpetual revolution – but not in Trotskyist sense but in sense of ???']

The doctrine of renunciation taught by Christ is taught to us again by our Canadian Martyrs. They are the great figures in the heroic epoch, the pioneering days of our country. Before our lands were cleared or our cities built, they left the France of the Grand Siècle. And while merchants came for gain and soldiers for pay, while explorers and leaders came for adventure and fame, and colonizers to build homes, they came to live in the wigwams of savages, to learn their language, eat their food, share their lives, that by the double power of truth and example they might win human hearts to faith in Christ crucified. Nor was this enough. As though the renunciation enshrined in the daily routine of their labors did not suffice, the missions they had established were destroyed by fire and the tomahawks of the Iroquois, and they themselves died in cruel torment.

But the spirit of man knows not the short-lived barriers of space and time. To all Canadians they teach most unequivocally the greatest lesson in human life, the lesson of renunciation, of a renunciation complete, uncompromising, and without hope in this world. They teach it, not only externally through the historical accounts of what they did, but also and more potently by their intercessory power before the throne of God; for they will obtain for us the enlightenment that brings the necessity of self-denial, and the good will that makes intentions sincere and performance effective. This tremendous gift of God – the thought of it may well dismay the stoutest heart, but our strength is not in ourselves but in the Spirit of Christ – we must pray for. May our Martyrs intercede that we may have even the initial good will of willingness to pray.

A final thought. If I have succeeded in indicating in some poor way the profound significance to be attached to the Sovereign Pontiff's act in naming the Martyrs as secondary patrons of Canada, it is only right that I should end with an expression of appreciation for his thoughtfulness. The Vatican is a lonely place in these years of war, and, as has recently been reported, not only is the normal business of the Holy See impeded but even its relief work is meeting countless obstacles. May we not discern some special love for distant Canada in its past glories, in its present struggle, in its future needs, in the Pope's attention to our nation?

9

Savings Certificates and Catholic Action[1]

I wish to draw attention to the great significance of the government's 'Savings' campaign. The obligation it places on every loyal Canadian is manifest,

1 [This paper appeared originally in *The Montreal Beacon* (7 February 1941). Fifty-
one years later, Frederick E. Crowe edited the article for publication in the
Lonergan Studies Newsletter 13 (September 1992) 27–30, along with an Introduction and informative footnotes. Crowe's footnotes are incorporated here along
with additional comments by the present editors, all within brackets. Certain
words appeared in boldface in the *Beacon* publication, and are left that way here.
    The bulk of Crowe's introduction reads: 'Expecting the early appearance, as
volume 15 in the Collected Works, of Lonergan's economics study (*An Essay in
Circulation Analysis*), we thought it timely to publish here a little article he wrote
over fifty years ago in a very practical application of his economical principles.
    'The general context for the article was the Second World War which
Canada had entered on 10 September 1939. The major source the government found for financing war expenditures was a series of Victory Loans. At
the other end of the scale the children of the nation brought their nickels and
dimes to school for War Savings Stamps, which they stuck in special booklets
for post-war redemption. In between these extremes a War Savings Certificates program was launched; the certificates were issued in small denomina-
tions for the purpose of facilitating regular savings and contributions to the
war effort by persons of moderate means. During February 1941 this program
was vigorously promoted, and it was in this immediate context that Lonergan
wrote his little essay on savings. It appeared 7 February 1941 in *The Montreal
Beacon*, a Catholic weekly to which he often contributed.
    'There was a context as well in his personal studies. The economic depres-
sion had started him thinking back in 1930 on the problems involved, and
perhaps as early as 1939 – certainly a good while before 1944 – he had written
a draft of his views entitled "For a New Political Economy." Much revised, this
had turned by 1944 into the work that would become *An Essay in Circulation
Analysis*. The present article was not therefore the product of a whim, or

but what is not so obvious is the extraordinary opportunity it offers to Catholic Action.[2] May I develop the latter point?

Canada's war activities are generating approximately a 50% increase in the national turnover. Added to the ordinary volume of production for consumers, expenditure by consumers, and income from that expenditure, there is another volume which produces for war purposes, is financed by the government, and gives rise to a proportionate volume of income. Say, for the sake of argument, that the former is three thousand millions a year, and that the latter is one and a half thousand millions.

In that case the aggregate income of Canadians is roughly four and a half thousand millions a year. On the other hand, the goods and services for consumers are only equal to three thousand millions. It follows that there are one and a half thousand millions that cannot be spent for the very good reason that the goods and services are not there to be bought.

If Canadians attempt to live to the full extent of their present income, the only result will be that prices skyrocket. For production is rapidly approaching its maximum; when that is reached more spending will not mean more goods; it will mean only higher prices.

Such a rise in prices would be disastrous, both for those with money and those without any. It would be disastrous for those with money, for their money would be worth so much less. It would be disastrous for those without money, for either wages would follow the increase in prices or they would not; if they follow, then prices necessarily become so much higher again; if they do not follow, then present wage standards have to meet a higher cost of living.

---

simple propaganda for the war effort; not only did it have a decade of thought behind it, but it was written at the very time he was working out his views on economics; there are, in fact, evident links between the article and his earliest manuscript on that topic.']

2 [Catholic Action, understood as organized quasi-political activity on the part of the laity, praised and promoted by Pius XI, was a prominent theme in the thinking of the young Lonergan (who was very much oriented to social questions) during the reign of that pontiff. A certain ambiguity in the term led to its replacement under other popes by terms like 'lay apostolate'; Lonergan, however, continued to use it late in life, for example in his unpublished submission to the International Theological Commission, 'Moral Theology and the Human Sciences,' (1974, pp. 2 and 11–13 of the MS). The submission has been published as chapter 16 in *Philosophical and Theological Papers 1965–1980*, vol. 17 in Collected Works of Bernard Lonergan, ed. Robert C. Croken and Robert M. Doran (Toronto: University of Toronto Press, 2004); see pp. 302 and 308–309.]

The obvious and necessary solution is to make the one and a half thousand millions that cannot be spent on consumers' goods flow back to the treasury to pay for government and war enterprises. In that way the books balance, the circulation circulates. Ordinary activity generates three thousand millions in income; it can do so because the three thousand millions are spent to obtain goods and services. War activity generates another one and a half thousand millions in income; for it to do so continuously without causing a disastrous inflation, it too must flow back to its source.

But the problem is, how effect this return flow?

Taxes will account for part of it, but they cannot account for all. The reason is that taxes are general rules and no general rule or set of general rules can be devised that will cut exactly the right amount out of everyone's income. Further, the smaller the income, the greater the difficulty: to take 80% of an enormous income might not cause hardship; but to take 20% of a small income would be an intolerable burden in some cases while in others it would not be taking enough. It is easy to construct a big net to catch big fish but, when most of the fish are small, what is needed is a big net to catch little fish.

Now it is not impossible to make a big net to catch even the smallest fish; the Germans have had one for years in their 'guns not butter' program;[3] it enabled them to turn a major part of their industry to munitions and armaments without going bankrupt despite the prophecies of antiquated economists.[4]

But we do not want the German type of net, the totalitarian state; that is what we are fighting against.

Alternative then to force and terrorism, there only remains freedom and the responsible use of freedom. That is the approach to the problem taken by the Canadian government: it asks Canadians to be reasonable in their expenditure, not to increase unreasonably their demand for goods and services but to save, to save in a big way.

3 ['guns not butter' – A Nazi slogan coined in the mid-1930s and associated with the 1936 Nazi Four-Year Plan to make Germany economically self-sufficient and to prepare the country for war. Bartlett's *Familiar Quotations*, 13th ed. 1955, quotes from a speech given by Joseph Goebbels in Berlin, 17 January 1936, and reported in *Allgemeine Zeitung* on 18 January: 'We can do without butter, but, despite all our love of peace, not without arms. One cannot shoot with butter, but with guns.']

4 ['antiquated economists' – in this same article Lonergan will refer to the 'robot' of the old economists; repeatedly in his later writings he will refer to old views on 'the iron laws of economics' (for example, *A Second Collection* [Philadelphia: The Westminster Press, 1975; repr. Toronto: University of Toronto Press, 1996] 201, 234). See note 10 below.]

I leave to others to expound what precisely is expected of each individual. The point to which I wish to draw attention is the tremendous significance of the government program for all who are interested in Catholic social thought and Catholic Action.

Canadian Catholics are being asked, not to initiate, but to cooperate in the execution of their own social ideas.[5]

What Catholic social thought can effect has been shown in the concrete in the work done by Antigonish University[6] for Nova Scotia fishermen. More recently it has been again demonstrated by Fr Soucy[7] in the backwoods of Maine. Now we have an opportunity to contribute to action on a national scale. It is of vital importance that we make the most of it. Let us see how many Catholic ideas underlie the government campaign for saving.

First, there is the norm or measure of the savings the individual is to effect. It is **reasonableness**. According to St Thomas Aquinas,[8] reasonableness is the basic principle in human morality. We are asked to avoid all unreasonable increase of expenditure: what does that mean if not that we are asked to adopt the idea of **status**,[9] of a standard of living fitting for various walks of life, of balanced living according to that standard. What is this if not that the old economists' robot, motivated only by self-interest and living on the animal level of pleasure and pain, is supplanted by our idea of reasonable men living rational lives?[10] To drive home this idea, first in our

5   [This whole paragraph was printed in capital letters. If this was Lonergan's own decision (and that is our presumption) he probably meant to show the emphasis that now we more often show by using italics. There are other instances of this in his early writings.]

6   [St Francis Xavier University, Antigonish, Nova Scotia, home of the cooperative movement initiated by Monsignor M.M. Coady. Three months later, in this same Catholic weekly (2 May 1941, p. 3), Lonergan will review Coady's book *Masters of Their Own Destiny* (see below, paper 22).]

7   [D. Wilfrid Soucy, priest of the diocese of Portland, Maine. Both *The Catholic Periodical Index* (1939–43) and *Readers' Guide to Periodical Literature* (1939–41) list articles by or about him as a crusader for cooperation in the St John River valley of Maine. He died on Monday, 4 December 2000, at the ripe age of 97.]

8   [*Summa theologiae*, 2-2, q. 129, a. 3: 'bonum rationis ... est proprium hominis bonum'; ibid., 1-2, q. 55, a. 4, ad 2m: 'bonum animae est secundum rationem esse.']

9   [Lonergan's use of 'status' is no doubt related to that of the sociologists, but the emphasis, as he makes clear at once, is on living reasonably in one's state, not on any prestige attached to the state.]

10 [This contrast between the robot and the person acting according to reason runs through Lonergan's thinking on the human sciences. A good short exposition in the economics context is found in the 1958 lectures on *Insight*, published as *Understanding and Being* (vol. 5 in Collected Works of Bernard

study clubs, then throughout the Catholic community, is not only the first step but even the whole battle in our contribution to a restoration of economic health. For either the economic machine is controlled by a group of commissars as in Russia, or it is controlled by the purchases of consumers as in the democratic states; in the latter case consumers either live and buy according to rational planning, and then the economic machine can function properly; or else the consumers are simply a herd of hand-to-mouth automata shepherded about by screaming advertisements, gambling on the stock market to augment their putative pleasures, and doing everything possible to make the economic machine expand in the wrong directions and eventually explode.

Second, what is the motive for saving? It is our principle of **superflua status**,[11] surplus income. Such surplus is income beyond one's reasonable requirements for his standard of life. But plainly the one and a half thousand millions generated by our war effort are surplus income: they are in excess of the three thousand millions generated by the ordinary economy; they cannot be spent on consumers' goods; they cannot belong to any individual's standard of living. They happen to come to individuals, because that is the nature of the exchange system. But their function is to pay for the war effort, for that is the nature of the circulation. Catholic social thought affirms obedience to function: things have to be used as their nature dictates. The government's war budget and taxes, its appeals for the purchase of saving certificates, and the encouragement it gives to

---

Lonergan, ed. Elizabeth A. Morelli and Mark D. Morelli [Toronto: University of Toronto Press, 1990]): There was a theory that economics 'could be just as accurate and just as infallible in its predictions in a few years as Newtonian astronomy became ... This economics was determinist, materialist, and so on. But de facto what nineteenth-century economics did was issue precepts to free men ... Those precepts resulted in an enormous development of parliamentary democracy throughout Europe, and in an enormous economic development. While that economics and its precepts are inadequate, nevertheless they serve to illustrate the difference between a human science as uttering precepts and a human science as predictive, as imitating what the physicist or the chemist does. In the one case, the human sciences ... tell free people something that free people can do for themselves. But in the other case ... what can they produce? They can produce consultants to central governments; the central governments can only carry out the advice of the consultants by obtaining more power; and there results what is called creeping socialism' (194–95).]

11 [The grammar of this phrase is puzzling, but 'superflua' seems to be a neuter plural adjective used as a noun, so that the sense is 'the status of those who have more than they need for their way of life' – in any case Lonergan uses it for those with surplus income to spend.]

voluntary contributions, are three elements in an elastic plan to put into practice the principle of surplus income. Since that principle is ours, we must cooperate perfectly.

Now it requires only a little imagination and intelligence to grasp the significance of this situation for Catholic Action. We are asked to cooperate in a plan to execute our own principles. We are bound to cooperate as loyal citizens. But we have a very special interest in making a very great effort. For if we succeed in convincing ourselves and in teaching others to accept and practice the two fundamental points of balanced living and surplus income, then we shall learn to combine theory with practice, to understand the theory because of the practice, to spread and establish the theory through practice. It is what we have been looking for.

This is not all. If we take this opportunity seriously and make the most of it, we are making here and now the greatest possible contribution we can to the development of a democratic technique that can confront and solve any economic problem. Thus we prepare ourselves for the difficulties that will follow the end of the war, and, incidentally, we win the war on its ideological plane, for the totalitarians boast that democracy cannot meet the modern economic problem.

10

The Queen's Canadian Fund[1]

I was preaching a retreat to a community of nuns in the southcoast town of Worthing, some miles west of Brighton, when the theory of the blitzkrieg was first put to the test on the Poles. The matter of preparing and delivering three longish talks every day left me little time to read the disquisitions in *The Times* on the strategic significance of the Vistula and the Bug[2] and, in a last resort, the Pripet marshes.[3] Anyway, it was more important to get a gas mask – there was a fine of ten shillings if one failed to carry one about –, to devise ways and means to darken my window at night, and, by way of extra zeal, to observe the position of the pails of sand and the long-handled shovels with which one was to deal with the expected incendiary bombs. For, of course, we were still in the dark on the plans of the German High Command and, having nothing but imagination to draw on, were encouraged to prepare continuously against air raids that did not take place.

What did take place was the evacuation of the children. For two whole days they completely monopolized the railways and moved in schools with their teachers from congested cities to what were esteemed safer zones. Worthing was a reception area, and I heard a firsthand story from a nun

---

1 [*The Montreal Beacon* (11 April 1941) 2. At this time Lonergan was teaching theology at L'Immaculée Conception in Montreal, but here clearly draws upon an experience during the early stages of the Second World War.]
2 [The Vistula is the chief river of Poland, flowing from the Carpathians to the Baltic Sea. The (Western) Bug is a river flowing from west Ukraine, forming part of the Soviet-Polish border and flowing across east Poland to the Vistula.]
3 [The marshes of the Pripet, a river rising in the northwest Ukraine and curving east through Byelorussia to join the Dnieper north of Kiev.]

who had come with a flock from a rather tough section of London. She was utterly played out. For weeks the plan of evacuation had been in the air, and all the time there were interviews with hesitant parents who wanted teacher to decide whether or not they should send their children away. They would come and ask advice, decide one thing, and then go home to decide the opposite. Names of children kept moving off and on the lists over and over again, a motion that weakly symbolized the inner struggle of heart and head, of affection and prudence, upon a problem that admitted no solution satisfactory to both.

At last the time for deciding was over. Only if you sometime or other have attempted to organize, say, a picnic with an estimated attendance, can you form some idea of the complexity of the task of transferring thousands and thousands of children from one area to another. It was impossible to tell in advance who was going where. It was a great deal merely to send to each receiving center approximately the number that could be received. So, ignorant of their destination, they started off in buses to concentrate in railway terminals and be dispersed by trains over the face of England, Scotland, and Wales.

It was late in the afternoon when Worthing was reached, and, very much like refugees, they sat down on their bundles in the courtyard of the town hall to wonder what would be next. The question did exist, for there were more children than billets. The only thing to do about the overflow was to undertake a house-to-house canvass, to ring bell after bell and ask, 'Can you take a child?' By nine o'clock all the charges of my informant had been disposed of except two. They were a wild pair of lads who had given the good sister so much trouble in class that she had not yet ventured to inflict them on anyone else. But obviously they had to be provided for, and so with a firm hand on each she started out again. Luckily at the first place she tried, she heard: 'Certainly, sister, come in, bring them in. No, no, we will take both of them; come right in.' Never before had the poor youngsters seen carpets on floors. They were tired and hungry, but also timid and suspicious, and in the presence of the gracious strangers their vocabulary shrank suddenly to abrupt repetitions of 'No.' The sister stayed awhile till they were more at their ease, and then left. Fortunately she had a billet for herself, for the Mother Superior of the local convent had been out – despite the retreat – and had discovered the wandering nuns who had no place to go.

I found the incident impressive, impressive as must be any that recalls the description of the Last Judgment to be read in St Matthew: 'For I was hungry and you gave me to eat; I was thirsty and you gave me to drink; I was a stranger and you took me in; naked, and you covered me; sick, and you visited me; I was in prison and you came to me. Then shall the just answer him, saying: Lord, when did we see thee hungry and fed thee, thirsty and gave thee to drink? And when did we see thee a stranger and took thee in? Or naked and covered thee? Or when did we see thee sick or in prison and came to thee? And the king answering shall say to them: Amen, I say to you, as long as you did it to one of these my least brethren, you did it to me' (Matthew 25.35–40).

Yet the practical charity of the evacuation of the children cannot but be small when compared to that which I have not witnessed, when families are broken not by heartrending decisions but by bombs, when parents as well as children migrate because the house in which they lived and named their home is a tumbled heap of shattered brick and splintered wood. When so casually and encouragingly the papers assure us that German air activity was light, only the military viewpoint is expressed. The trifle of a light raid over a few cities is a long list of old and young, healthy and infirm, rich and poor, who suddenly are more destitute than the foxes who have holes, the birds of the air who have nests. The mighty strokes of the Luftwaffe deal out destitution to larger numbers with a larger hand.

For them there has existed and still exists the munificent Lord Mayor's Fund.[4] But if charity begins at home, charity to Britain does not go abroad in coming to Canada. Under the exalted patronage of Her Majesty[5] – beloved symbol of our fellowship – the Queen's Canadian Fund for Air Raid Victims makes its appeal on behalf of the Lord Mayor's Fund. It is an appeal for those whose sustained courage still keeps the battle three thousand miles away, for those who are hungry yet must be fed, thirsty yet must be given to drink, robbed of their wardrobes yet to be clothed, and if not strangers, then all the more sadly homeless in their own land. 'As long as you did it to one of these, you did it to Me.'

---

4 [Lonergan may mean what was established in 1923 as the Lord Mayor's Fund for Metropolitan Hospitals and Charities, with the inspiration of Sir John Swanson, Lord Mayor of Melbourne. In 1930 an Act of Parliament incorporated the new body, defining the functions, scope, organization and guidelines of the Fund, based not only on the experience of the Fund but to a large extent on the King Edward VII Hospital Fund of London.]

5 [Queen Elizabeth, 1900–2002.]

11

The Mystical Body and the Sacraments[1]

Many unities bind men together besides their unity in Christ. The bond may be conspicuous as a country on the map, or inconspicuous as a cultural tradition. It may be quiet and practical like a trade union or a sodality; or noisy and mysterious like a break on the stock market. It may be a fine ideal as democratic justice and equality; a grandiose dream like the Fascist empire; the efficient madness of Germany's racial pride; or just the homely brutality of Joseph Stalin. But whatever their nature, such bonds are ever present. Weak or strong, manifest or unsuspected, localized or far-reaching, vile or inspiring, they are ever manifold, ever pressing upon us, ever molding our deeds, our statements, our thoughts, our judgments.

In the aggregate these mysterious bonds are termed human solidarity, and from their grip there is no escape. Think what the Soviet rule means to one hundred and eighty million Russians. Yet the heavy imprint of that rule on the external way of life, on the inward thoughts, on the eternal destiny of every Russian is but a striking example a more general law. Because that regime is planned and organized, because it is dramatic in bloodshed and ruthlessness, because under the shadow of terrorism it fans out through the press, the radio, the school, the factory, the farm, the market, from the Polish marshes to the Pacific, from the Arctic to the Caspian, this giant octopus seizes the imagination and drives home the helplessness of the Russians in their solidarity.

1 [An article published in *The Canadian League* (March 1941) 8–10, 32. This magazine is a quarterly publication of the Catholic Women's League of Canada.]

But if only we reflect, we come to realize that a similar though far from identical helplessness is the lot of all men. Indeed we have free will, but the field in which our responsible choices are made, that is not of our doing. We were not asked whether we cared to be born, to select our parents or their ancestors, to choose our country, or the ideals and principles taught us in our youth. Our occupation and marriage – or lack of these – we attribute more to ourselves. Yet who can measure the role played by temperament and chance circumstance in these most serious decisions? If in them we are not too notably the unconditioned masters, then how much less in the daily routine on which we seldom reflect, which we leave to the control of custom and fashion? Finally, when we turn to broader issues, to prosperity and slumps, to the whims of dictators or of democratic public opinion, to peace and war, to national ambitions and enmities, to the historical forces immovably rooted in the past yet powerfully operative in the present, then we must confess that even we are no more than atoms, each indeed autonomous within his narrow orbit, for each is free, yet together swept in a swirling mass down the cataract of life to the serene pool of a green churchyard.

Examine that cataract. At first one is struck with a love of its beauties, its amazing progress, its splendid virtues, its courageous smile and lambent laughter. Draw nearer: one grows indignant at vast injustice, loathes soul-destroying bestiality, hates the confusing cult of ever shifting errors. Yes, the stream is contaminated at its very source, and every atom in the torrential flow is the disabled veteran of a primitive battle that was lost. Men are truly men: they acknowledge a rule and a law above that of beasts; they distinguish right and wrong; they praise many a heroic deed; they abominate much evil. Yet in their very manhood they are cripples: at the best, the good they would they do not, and the evil they would not, that they do; and at worst? Let St Paul answer.

> As they liked not to have God in their knowledge, God delivered them up to a reprobate sense, to do those things which are not befitting. Being filled with all iniquity, malice, fornication, avarice, wickedness: full of envy, murder, contention, deceit, malignity: whisperers, detractors, hateful to God, contumelious, proud, haughty, inventors of evil things, disobedient to parents, foolish, dissolute; without affection, without fidelity, without mercy. (Romans 1.28–31)

That picture is not merely of ancient Rome. It is the inevitable goal of all merely human progress. Men can and will revolt against such monstrous evil, but to what avail? Neither revolution, nor liquidation, nor reform, nor the European new order, nor the Asiatic new order, nor the dynamic of events, nor muddling through, nor common sense, nor any other human plan can end it. For every human effort will be equally corrupt, will equally have its source in the heart of man and in Adam's sin.

There is but one hope, one refuge, one remedy. Only one man has overcome the world, and that man was God. There has been but one complete victory over sin, and that victory was death, a death wrought in midair by the agony of crucifixion. 'I,' he said, 'if I be lifted up, will draw all things to Me' [John 12.32]. Into that death of his we too must enter, if we are to share the glory of his resurrection. To share that glory we pray when we recite, 'Thy kingdom come.' Into that death we enter when we receive the sacraments.

> Know you not (wrote St Paul) that all we who are baptized in Christ Jesus are baptized in his death? For we are buried together with him by baptism into death: that as Christ is risen from the dead by the glory of the Father, so we also may walk in newness of life. For if we have been planted together in the likeness of his death, we shall be also in the likeness of his resurrection. Knowing this, that our old man is crucified with him, that the body of sin may be destroyed, to the end that we may serve sin no longer. (Romans 6.3–6)

Such is the efficacy of the death of Christ. It draws the attention and wins the allegiance of a sinful world. Through its symbol and representation, the sacrament of baptism, it destroys the reign of sin in each individual, the reign of the old Adam vitiating every noble aim and bringing every good beginning to an evil end. But not only does it destroy. It lays the foundations of a new humanity, walking in a newness of life, walking in the freshness of freedom liberated from the clutch of sin's solidarity. Just as food that enters into the body is disintegrated and refashioned to become new blood, new tissue, new flesh, new bone, new sinew, so too by baptism is the dominion of sin broken in Adam's children of wrath to rebuild them anew in Christ. 'Unless a man be born again of water and the Holy Ghost, he cannot enter into the kingdom of God' (John 3.5). Be convinced of the reality of that new birth. The human body is not nourished by patching here a piece of lettuce and there a bit of beef; neither is the mystical Christ built up by any mere agglomeration of men. But as food is transformed into human flesh, so also men are transformed into more than men, into children of God and temples of the Holy Spirit, that in Christ they be as Christ who is the Son of God on whom the Holy Spirit descended.

Still, profound as is this spiritual change, our bodies do not at once die to rise again as Christ rose from the tomb. Our liberation is not complete. Our sojourn is prolonged until nature's course makes us pay by death the forfeit of Adam's sin. Thus, besides the sacrament of baptism, there are six more to strengthen the bonds uniting us with Christ, lest we become entangled in the tentacles of human solidarity, lest we let charity grow cold and faith grow dim and our hope of heaven so faded that we barter our eternal heritage for place or pleasure in this Egypt of our souls.

There is confirmation. 'Everyone that shall confess me before men, I will also confess him before my Father who is in heaven. But he that shall deny me before men, I will also deny him before my Father who is in heaven' (Matthew 10.32–33). It is not enough to believe inwardly in Christ; we must also give others the example of belief. 'With the heart we believe unto justice; but with the mouth confession is made unto salvation' (Romans 10.10). This confession of Christ is not always an easy matter, as even St Peter showed when a froward maid embarrassed him into disclaiming Christ. Nor need we think of ancient martyrs. In modern Germany Nazi pressure has been so great that parents have fallen on their knees pleading with their children to leave the Catholic school and desert the organizations of Catholic youth. In modern France it was accounted a great thing that five thousand professional men in Paris were found ready, after much labor, to jeopardize their careers by making their Easter Communion. 'If you had been of the world, the world would love its own: because you are not of the world, but I have chosen you out of the world, therefore the world hateth you' (John 15.19).

Against this inevitable hatred, our souls must be steeled. To give them the temper needed, Christ ascended into heaven and on Pentecost sent the Holy Spirit on the apostles and disciples. It is a grace that we too receive in confirmation, and to know its efficacy we need only compare St Peter, first brazenly denying Christ in the courtyard of the high priest [Luke 22.55–61], and later brazenly telling the high priest to his face that God was to be obeyed rather than men [Acts 4.5-21]. The Spirit revealed in Christ from Gethsemane to Golgotha has also been revealed not only by the apostles but by the martyrs of every age, not only by martyrs but by every Catholic who has endured slights and sneers, discrimination and ostracism, calumny and hatred for his belief in Christ, whom the world will ever reject.

There is the most blessed sacrament of the Eucharist. 'I am the vine: you are the branches. He that abideth in me and I in him the same beareth much fruit: for without me you can do nothing. If anyone abide not in me, he shall be cast forth as a branch and shall wither: and they shall gather him and cast him into the fire' (John 15.5–6). Since we are born again in Christ unto a newness of life, we must be sustained by the life that is in Christ. The branch that is not sustained by the vine withers away. But the branch that is grafted on to it, that draws its life from it, is the channel and the tool by which the vine brings forth its fruit. That is clear and simple. 'Amen, amen, I say to you, except you eat the flesh of the Son of man and drink his blood, you shall not have life in you. He that eateth my flesh and drinketh my blood hath everlasting life; and I will raise him up on the last day' (John 6.53–54). The point cannot be made any plainer. Would you ward off the death of your immortal soul? Go to communion: 'without me you can do nothing.' Would you grow in Christ, would you become what Christ would have been had he your life to lead? Go to communion: 'as the living Father hath sent me and I live by the Father, so he that eateth me, the same also shall live by me' (John 6.57). Would you be more reverent in your communions? Would you make them occasions for increasing your determination to reject all sin? You have only to recall that communion represents and applies the passion and death of your Lord. 'For as often as you shall eat this bread and drink this chalice, you shall shew the death of the Lord' (1 Corinthians 11.26).

But we are still weaklings in Christ, barely weaned from the world, still subject to deceit and temptation. Like the vineyard on a hill in a fruitful place, fenced in and cleared of stones and planted with the choicest vines, we too have been renovated in baptism and confirmed in the Holy Spirit and nourished by the body of Christ. And as that vineyard brought forth grapes not sweet and full but sour and wizened, so too we bring forth not the fruits of Christ's example and of the indwelling Holy Spirit but the fruits of our not yet glorified bodies and of the worldliness that surrounds us and presses us down. We become diseased members of the mystical body, to the public disgrace of Christ and to the scandal of those outside who are led to say that Catholics are not a whit better than anyone else. For this reason the sacrament of penance exists, the tribunal of the confessional. As before the tribunal of Pilate Christ was unjustly condemned to death, so by this tribunal the unjust members of Christ may be allowed to go free. 'Whose sins you shall forgive, they are forgiven them; whose sins you shall retain they are retained' (John 20.23). The sinner must repent and resolve amendment, but to be restored fully to the living body of Christ, he must also confess and be forgiven.

The sacraments of matrimony and orders are concerned with the extension of the mystical body. Not only does Christ grow in each individual, but also would he reach out through them to others, that the Church be perpetuated in every age to the consummation of the world. Thus by orders bishops and priests are procured to replace the apostles in their mission of teaching all nations. Similarly the sacrament of matrimony elevates a natural function into a function of the mystical body. Christian marriage is not merely for the procreation and education of more human beings; it is for the procreation and education of more Christians. In this duty even Catholics can be led astray at a time when contraceptives are a $250,000,000 yearly business and, since they commonly are defective, the number of abortions is rivaling the number of births. Such is the world which the Christian must renounce, for no man can serve two masters. Of the standard of living the gospel says: 'Sufficient for the day is the evil thereof' [Matthew 6.34]. Of the standard of holiness, it says: 'Be ye therefore perfect as your heavenly Father is perfect' [Matthew 5.48]. Not only to James and John but to every member of the mystical body is the question put: 'Can you drink the chalice that I shall drink?' [Mark 10.38, Matthew 20.22] for the love of Christ crucified for his mystical body is the model and measure of married love and married sacrifice [see Ephesians 5.25–32].

Extreme unction,[2] finally, is a sacrament with a double effect: sometimes it communicates the efficacy with which Christ cured the sick of ancient Palestine; always, when properly received, it clears away the scars and remnants of sin to prepare the soul for its first interview with the Lord of us all. If only then he smiles on you and says to you, Well done, is not that smile, are not those two words from him worth a thousand lives of faithful gratitude and love? Think it over.

---

2 [The sacrament for the dying. Following the liturgical renewal of Vatican II, it is now called the sacrament of anointing, both for those who are sick and for those in danger of death.]

12

Quatercentenary[1]

As a pilot raises or dips his plane or turns to right or left, so too does God rule. He is master of the hearts of men. Slowly, even suddenly, the pleasure or success on which one's heart is set might lose the blush of beauty, the promise of joy. Into one's will might pour a fire that only sanctity could assuage. What would you do?

It is a real problem, not to be solved as readily as those fancy who have never given it a thought. Take the case of Ignatius of Loyola. His dreams had been of feats at arms and bright-eyed praise. But his dreams were changed. Bugle-clear through the silence of his soul rang the call of Christ to men, to be men enough to live for the kingdom of God. Ignatius could not resist the claims of the Crucified. Yet what precisely was he to do?

At first he leaped to all the outward, showy things. He left his home, his possessions, his hopes of a career. He gave his fine clothes to a beggar and put on sackcloth. He lived in a cave, praying interminably, fasting to emaciation, scourging himself violently, and finding diversion only in performing

1 [*Loyola College Review* 27 (1941) 22–55. The occasion for the article was the 400th anniversary of the founding of the Society of Jesus by St Ignatius Loyola in 1540, and its approval by Pope Paul III. To mark the anniversary, see the Apostolic Letter of Pope Pius XII to Very Rev. Wlodimir Ledochowski, General of the Society, *Acta Apostolicae Sedis* XXXII (6 August 1940) 289–96. Here Lonergan focuses on St Ignatius and his early companions, and the initial apostolic ventures of the early Society.

A byline read, 'By Bernard J.F. Lonergan, s.J, '24.' Lonergan was in the class of 1924 at Loyola, but had entered the Jesuit Novitiate, Guelph, in 1922. The article was reprinted in *Loyola Today* 10:2 (December 1990) 3–4.]

menial tasks in the primitive public hospital of a nearby town. Still, where did this lead to? So he went a pauper pilgrim to Jerusalem and devoutly visited the scenes hallowed by the presence of our Lord. But when he revealed his intention to remain and work for the conversion of the Saracens, promptly he was bundled off on the first ship. What was he to do?

The question bothered him. Thousands in every age have been as generous as he. Few, if any, have had his capacity for reflection, for introspective analysis. God led him on, but he kept his eyes wide open. Ever alert, he studied his strange experience. He would ask why he felt now overjoyed and again dismayed, now ready for anything and later overpowered merely by the thought of sticking to his new life for a lifetime. These cyclic states of serenity and anguish he observed, tabulated, compared. By dint of experiment – the terrific experiment of saying 'yes' to every good impulse – he came to know practically the answers which theoretical theology and psychology together could hardly formulate.[2]

Another thing struck him. Usually God gives his grace not by buckets but by drops. It comes into our souls, not a fully grown tree of sanctity but just a seed. It makes us thoughtful; seriously we utter a prayer; honestly we make a good resolution. But always there are the birds of the air, the rocks, the trodden wayside, the thorns. What came as a seed, remains merely a seed. It does not grow into a tree. Against this appalling waste Ignatius worked out a method of exploitation, a set of spiritual exercises, something for the soul like a coach for a football team. How much a team depends on its coach! But teamwork with God's grace is an infinitely more delicate affair, and to teach such cooperation Ignatius planned and wrote out directions to be imparted in a thirty-day workout (commonly misnamed a retreat). It is his masterpiece. The topflight critics in this field – the popes – have never given any single book such repeated and such wholehearted praise.[3]

One thing leads to another. To put his ideas across, Ignatius had to get an education. He was well over thirty, but that did not impede him. Off he went, first to a Latin school at Barcelona, then to the universities of Alcala

2 [Ignatius describes his experience in his autobiography. A recent edition is *The Autobiography of St. Ignatius Loyola, With Related Documents*, trans. Joseph F. O'Callaghan, ed., with introduction and notes, John C. Olin, reprint edition (New York: Fordham University Press, 1993). See pp. 23–24.]

3 [Lonergan is referring, of course, to St Ignatius's *Spiritual Exercises*. See *The Spiritual Exercises of St. Ignatius, Based on Studies in the Language of the Autograph*, Louis J. Puhl, reprint edition (Chicago: Loyola University Press, 1997), one of several contemporary editions.]

and Salamanca, in which he did not get along with the inquisitors, and so finally for seven years to Paris. Of Paris he later affirmed that one learnt more there in one year than elsewhere in many. But as he was gathering in this human wisdom which competent masters can impart, he also gathered about him men. It was inevitable. He had something to give them. There was his roommate from the sheepcotes on Swiss mountain sides, who had kept his body pure and his soul in the high resolve to become, despite constricting poverty, a priest.[4] There was the idol of an intellectual elite, Xavier of Navarre, who if contemptuous of piety also was afraid of debauchery; he knew where it ended. These and some others found in Ignatius that rare combination: an incredibly intimate knowledge of the human soul in all its self-deceptions and unsatisfied, explosive aspirations; and simultaneously they found in him a decisiveness that belongs, not to introspective dreamers, but to the world's practical men and, most of all, to captains who lead troops in mobile warfare.

Strange fellowship of students! Their talent might have placed them in the forefront of any enterprise. But an elderly undergraduate, a former officer, was the focus of their intimacy. His spiritual exercises proved a blood transfusion in their lives. Together before the dawn [of the feast day] of our Lady's Assumption in 1534, seven of them went out towards high Montmartre and in the chapel of St Denis vowed poverty and chastity and their purpose to give their lives to the service of God and their neighbor. By 1539 they had done great apostolic work, and, to perpetuate their ideas and their spirit, they decided to found a new religious order. To this project Pope Paul III gave official approbation on September 27, 1540. It is the quatercentenary of this scholastic year.

What is, then, this Society of Jesus that came into existence four hundred years ago? Basically it is simply a matter of men: men from every social class; men laboring in every quarter of the globe; men devoted to a single cause, the service of Christ the King. But if you ask its special characteristics, these, I think, are three. They arise from the influence of Ignatius the soldier, the influence of Ignatius the ascetic, and the influence of Ignatius the student at Paris.

Most obvious to a soldier is the difference between veterans and recruits. No amount of make believe can cover it. The Society attempts no make believe. It gives men in its central corps seventeen years of intense training before admitting them permanently to its ranks.

4 [Pierre Favre from the Savoy Alps, the first of the early companions to be ordained a priest, in May 1534.]

Clear-cut to a soldier is the difference between officers and men. To bridge the abyss between paper schemes and concrete reality, training alone does not suffice. There must be cohesion, coordination, the supple direction of a tank brigade. The Jesuit lives to obey: not the woodenheaded obedience of which Foch[5] said: 'To take orders literally is murder,' but the intelligent subordination and adaptiveness necessary to make group action possible.

Manifest to a soldier is the matter of strategy. Not every game is worth the candle. One must distinguish different objectives. One must select, sacrifice here and concentrate there; not everything can be done. Thus the activities of the nascent Society fell into three integrated fields. Outstanding was its work in pushing back the frontiers of heresy. You can draw a line across Europe through the Netherlands and Germany to the old Ottoman Empire; to this day, south of that line is Catholic and north of it the Protestant sects; Poland is a Catholic outpost beyond it, and Geneva a Calvinist center within it; but roughly that is the watershed. Still, the Society did not merely send men like Canisius to Germany, like Bobola to Poland, like Campion to England. It worked on the home front. It entered the vital field of education. It came to dominate in the secondary schools of Catholic Europe, turning out the audience if not all the writers of the Grand Siècle of French literature. Simultaneously it poured into the mission field, the new lands of then recent discovery. Xavier rushed through the whole east, from Goa to Japan. More systematic work followed his exploration. Astronomers went to live in the court at Peking to obtain free access for their fellows who taught Christ to the people. The culture of India was studied: some lived the lives of Brahmin ascetics while others were pariahs of the pariahs; and the famous Malabar rites tried to adapt Roman liturgy to the oriental milieu.[6] In the Americas the problem was not adaptation to a culture but the creation of civilization. Of this the first condition was the

---

5 [General Ferdinand Foch (1851–1929). One of the foremost French generals in the First World War, he led the French forces in several battles against the Germans. In April 1918, he assumed the unified command of the British, French, and American armies. In this capacity, he was in some historians' estimation more responsible than any other one man for the victory in 1918. See *The Columbia Encyclopedia*, 6th edition, 2001. The editors have been unable to locate the quotation.]

6 ['Malabar rites ... is the name given to a series of Hindu observances from which arose a controversy which had to do with inland districts of Madura, Mysore and the Carnatic and not with the Malabar coast. The Jesuits of the seventeenth and eighteenth centuries, following the example of Fr. De Nobili (1577–1656), permitted their converts to retain certain Brahmin and Hindu

segregation of the savages from the exploitation of traders and the violence of adventurers. Thus in Canada the great effort was made not near the settlements at Quebec or Montreal but around distant Lake Huron; and the brilliant results such a method could achieve are revealed in the Paraguay Reductions, acclaimed even by agnostics as man's nearest approach to an ideal republic.[7]

Plainly in all of this the soldier's strategy yields place to the broad influence of university training. It had been at Paris that the rationalism of ancient Greece and the rude vitality of northern Christianity had clashed and then fused in the hands of Aquinas to the thunderstruck amazement of his day. The antinomy of faith and reason had been resolved, but two centuries later Constantinople fell and Byzantine scholarship moved westward to precipitate a new cultural crisis. Alcaic stanzas, Corinthian capitals and sinuous Platonic dialogue won a pagan day in the warm south. Against this humanism, conservative theology was bleakly negative. Still more reactionary, really, was Erasmus who would deny theologians the medieval achievement with its basis in Aristotle, while the revolutionary Luther, to whom reason was a slut and free will a fiction, rejected not merely humanism but with it humanity. Into this convulsion of western culture, as explosive and far more profound than the modern crisis of men and machines, came Ignatius's men from Paris. Their solution was concrete; they opened schools

---

customs, which they alleged had no religious significance or had been adapted to Christianity, but which others said were superstitious and idolatrous. Among these customs was the observance of caste (at one time there were distinct Brahmin and pariah missionaries); the Jesuits themselves lived as natives; and their methods were exceedingly successful.' *The Catholic Encyclopaedic Dictionary,* ed. Donald Attwater (London: Cassell and Co. Ltd, 1931) 320.]

7 [Reductions (Spanish *Reducciones*) or Settlements were the Indian mission territories in Paraguay administered by the Spanish Jesuits from late in the first decade of the seventeenth century and lasting for 160 years. 'The Jesuit administration was based on the principle that they were the guardians and trustees of the welfare of the Indians, not as a subject or lower race, but as untutored children of God; they had no contempt for their civilization and life ... Their opposition to Spanish imperialism, to slavery by colonists, and to the Inquisition, wrought their downfall. In 1767 King Charles III suppressed the Jesuits in the Spanish dominions, and in the following year those of Paraguay unresistingly gave up their thirty missions ...' *The Catholic Encyclopaedic Dictionary* 446. Among those Lonergan may have had in mind when he speaks of the Reductions being 'acclaimed even by agnostics as man's nearest approach to an ideal republic' are Jean-Jacques Rousseau and Voltaire, neither of whom is known for his affection for Catholicism in general or for the Jesuits in particular.]

that were not merely models of efficiency but as well educational syntheses combining and intertwining the triple cord of Europe's heritage: the Gospel, articulated thought, and balanced humanism. Our own stricken day, in which apostasy, sloppy economic speculation, and mechanized barbarism are at last revealing their true nature, more than makes manifest the wisdom of that educational program.

But no less than in the educational field, the influence of university training appears in the transformation which the Society effected in the concept of the religious life. Three great movements had preceded it: the solitaries that once peopled the Egyptian desert; the monasteries organized in the east by St Basil, in the west by St Benedict; and the medieval friars of St Dominic and St Francis of Assisi. The Jesuits found it possible to strike out on still another line, the very modern line of organized action. That grasp of current history has made their rule directly or indirectly the model of innumerable congregations founded since. Most notably, it was their clean break with monastic ideals that opened the way for nuns to step beyond cloister walls, to teach school and conduct hospitals and go off on foreign missions. Today such a practice seems obvious. But four hundred years ago, as Mary Ward discovered, to suggest it was scandalous and to attempt it was to invite fools, that infinite chorus, to cry out in most righteous indignation.

Still the broadening influence of a great university, even of Paris, is far from accounting for Ignatius's achievement. Not only a student, not only a soldier, above all he was a master of asceticism. If there is any 'power and secret' of the Jesuits, it is his *Spiritual Exercises*, his method of coaching cooperation with the grace of God. They alone explain the Society's record of two doctors of the Church, twenty-four saints, one hundred and forty-one blessed, one hundred and forty-eight officially recognized martyrs, one hundred and eighty-five men revered with the title of venerable. They alone have enabled the Society to live and die, and live again through wave upon wave of slander, confiscation, expulsion, and persecution. They alone can infuse some measure of, some approximation to, a common way of thought and character into the novices that enter today in Tokyo and Melbourne, Madura and Madagascar, Warsaw and Berlin, Lyons and London, Bogota and Guelph. And if the Jesuits of the present succeed in making any contribution to the solution of present problems, then it will be, as in the past, because each man finds himself in a framework hoisting him to the level of his better self, the spiritual framework conceived by Ignatius.

13

Chesterton the Theologian[1]

When asked to write on Chesterton as theologian, naturally I was tempted to twist my terms of reference and switch to the more obvious and abundant themes of Chesterton as metaphysician or Chesterton as apologist. There is an unmistakable metaphysical strain to the man who explained the development of a puppy into a dog as a matter of becoming more doggy. There is an overwhelming apologist in the man who made enormous fun of the endless fallacies current from *Heretics* to *The Thing*.[2] But how can a theologian be made of a man who repeatedly implied and often affirmed he was not one?

Chesterton had the profoundest respect for the technicalities in which centuries of reflection on the faith had deposited and crystallized and tabulated their findings. He set upon the 'provincial stupidity of those who object to what they call "creeds and dogmas"'[3] as upon the absurdity that

---

1 [Published in *The Canadian Register* no. 42 (11 December 1943) 5. Here the article had the title 'Was G.K.C. a Theologian?' – presumably the choice of the editor. In 1943 Lonergan was Professor of Theology at L'Immaculée Conception, Montreal. This piece has recently appeared in *The Chesterton Review* 30:1, 2 (Spring–Summer 2004) 51–53.]

2 [*Heretics* was first published (London and New York: John Lane, The Bodley Head) in 1905. It is now part of vol. 1 in The Collected Works of G.K. Chesterson, ed. David Dooley (San Francisco: Ignatius Press, 1986). *The Thing: Why I Am a Catholic* was first published (London: Sheed and Ward) in 1929. It is now part of vol. 3 in The Collected Works of G.K. Chesterton, with introduction and notes by James J. Thompson, Jr (San Francisco: Ignatius Press, 1990).]

3 [This remark occurs in G.K. Chesterton, *St. Thomas Aquinas*, now part of vol. 2 in The Collected Works of G.K. Chesterton (San Francisco: Ignatius Press, 1986) 487, in the context of a discussion of Manicheanism and of Platonic love.]

'Love your neighbor' is all you really need to know. With trenchant exasperation and tumbling images he insisted on the complexity of things, on the fact that without fixed beliefs there are only passing moods, on the infinite dangers of religious emotion running to a destructive flood when without the dams and walls of intellectual content.

But it is, perhaps, a Chestertonian paradox that Chesterton himself never became an adept in these technicalities. When *Orthodoxy* appeared in 1908,[4] Father Joseph Keating in *The Month* ended an article on the interesting young man with the remark: 'Had we the power, we should banish him to Monte Cassino for a year, there to work through the *Summa* of St Thomas with Dante as his only relaxation. On his return, we fancy, he would astonish the world.'[5] Now Chesterton did astonish the world; he even studied St Thomas and wrote a book on him;[6] but the book proposed to deal mainly with the figure, briefly with the philosopher, and with the theologian hardly at all.

Still there is a sense in which Chesterton was a theologian. Suppose that he wrote in the eleventh century instead of the twentieth. Then he could be ranked with St Anselm, for of that age no one expects the intellectual elaborations later evolved. Then being a theologian was simply a matter of a cast of mind that seizes the fitness and coherence of the faith, that penetrates to its inner order and harmony and unity. Such penetration was the soul of Chesterton. Years before his conversion he could write:

> It may be, Heaven forgive me, that I did try to be original; but I only succeeded in inventing all by myself an inferior copy of the existing traditions of civilized religion … I did try to found a heresy of my own; and when I had put the last touches to it, I discovered it was orthodoxy … I was always rushing out of my architectural study with plans for a new turret, only to find it sitting up there in the sunlight, shining, and a thousand years old … there was a moment when I

4 [G.K. Chesterton, *Orthodoxy* (London and New York: John Lane, The Bodley Head, 1908), now part of vol. 1 in The Collected Works of G.K. Chesterton.]
5 [Joseph Keating, s.j., 'Faith Found in Fleet Street (Mr. Chesterton's "Orthodoxy"),' *The Month* (November 1908) 484–97, at 497.]
6 [G.K. Chesterton, *St. Thomas Aquinas* (London: Hodder and Stoughton Ltd, 1933); see n. 3 above for information on the Collected Works edition of this title.]

could have invented the marriage vow (as an institution) out of my own head; but I discovered, with a sigh, that it had been invented already.[7]

Such grasp of fitness and coherence is the essential object of the theologian at all times. But there is a further point in throwing Chesterton back upon the background of the medieval scene. More than any other modern man he shared the fresh and fearless vitality of medieval inquisitiveness. His questions go to the roots of things. The answers he demands must be right on the nail. He combined a wholehearted contempt for the irrelevant with an ability to appreciate enormously, one might say inordinately, what really was relevant. In his famous 'A Meditation on the Manichees,'[8] with an ingenuous profundity reminiscent of Aquinas, he sets up parallels and contrasts that seem hopeless oversimplifications until – until you get the point. He does not fear to assert that because Christ was risen, Aristotle too had to rise again. He does not hesitate to leap from Manichaeism to Calvinism and throw in fakirs and Albigensians on the way. He does not, in modern style, nicely trace the influences of Christian tradition, Greek thought, and Arabic culture on the mind of Aquinas; he sets up a cosmic background, names him St Thomas of the Creator, and contrasts him with the Buddha and Nietzsche.[9]

This medieval insistence on the relevant is to be found in anything but medieval dress. Perhaps his deepest theological intuition is to be found in the most bizarre of mystery yarns. *The Man Who Was Thursday*[10] is a labyrinth of double roles, of plots and counterplots, of aimless, painful quests, of buffoonery and high seriousness, that lures the unsuspecting reader face to face with God and the problem of evil. Chesterton now knows better, though not differently, the Man who was Sunday.

7   [Chesterton, *Orthodoxy*; in the Collected Works edition, p. 214 for the first two sentences of the quotation, and p. 327 for the remaining two.]
8   [Chapter 4 of *St. Thomas Aquinas*; in the Collected Works edition, pp. 478–94.]
9   ['There is a certain private audacity, in his communion, by which men add to their private names the tremendous titles of the Trinity and the Redemption; so that some nun may be called "of the Holy Ghost"; or a man bear such a burden as the title of St. John of the Cross. In this sense, the man we study may especially be called St. Thomas of the Creator.' Ibid. 494.]
10 [G.K. Chesterton, *The Man Who Was Thursday: A Nightmare* (London: Simpkin, Marshall, Hamilton, Kent and Co. Ltd, 1908); now part of vol. 6 in The Collected Works of G.K. Chesterton, compiled and introduced by Denis J. Conlon (San Francisco: Ignatius Press, 1991).]

14

The Mass and Man[1]

A few years ago a non-Catholic from Canada dropped into a Catholic
church in Washington on a Sunday morning. It was not that the architecture appealed to him. The statues and other ornaments he liked even less.
The place was filled, mainly by Negroes. Mass was going on, and the cele-
brant was a Negro. Still, there were present a very large number of people
from the neighboring embassies. That spectacle was food for thought; for,
if in Washington racial feeling is well under control, it is nonetheless very
real. 'What,' he exclaimed to himself, 'does it matter if the architecture is
in bad taste and the statues are worse! Here are men and women of different races, from different parts of the world, yet forgetting their differences
and worshipping God under a single roof and in a single prayer.'

Expand such thoughts to sweep over all the world. One reads of Communist warfare in China, of political unrest in Indo-China, in the Dutch
Colonies, in Burma, and in India, of the weight of an uncomfortable neighbor pressing down upon Persia and Turkey, of the agony of Palestine and of
Greece, of the death throes of liberty behind the Iron Curtain, of the several
plights of Western Germany, of Italy, of France, even of England, of the
strikes without end and the disclosed and undisclosed spy rings in America.
The human family is divided as the congregation in that church in Washington

1 [An article published in *The Canadian Messenger of the Sacred Heart* 57
(June 1947) 345–50. The *Messenger* is a publication of the Apostleship of
Prayer, Toronto. The same article was reprinted in *The Catholic Mind* 45
(September 1947) 571–76. Paragraphing and divisions were somewhat differ-
ent in the two versions, and the current edition draws on both.]

was not divided. Yet it is the spectacle of the vast and threatening divisions of all mankind that prompted our Holy Father Pius XII to make it the intention of our prayers in the month of June that 'from the Holy Sacrifice of the Mass be drawn the power of saving human society.'[2]

The Symbolism of Calvary

The Mass is our memorial of the passion and death of Our Lord. In His sufferings and in the malice that inflicted them one easily may discern the representative and the symbol of the evils that now afflict humanity. Greed, stooping even to treachery, is Judas. Lust, capable of murder, is Herod. Political opportunism then urged: 'Let one man die for the people!' Injustice then cried: 'What need have we of witnesses!' Mass propaganda evoked the roar: 'Away with Him!' The cowardice of a high official vainly washed its hands. Then the hardy flunkies, interested only in their daily wage, took over to flog, and crown with thorns, and mock, and crucify. To the starving of today, He can only say, 'I thirst.' To the destitute, He can only show His nakedness. To the persecuted, the enslaved, the imprisoned, the tortured, the dying, His wounds cry: 'I, too, have been through it.'

Yet the real significance of Calvary does not lie in these external events. Many a man has been condemned by an unjust court and tortured, and put to death, that the violence of the penalty might somehow hide the injustice of the verdict. But of none of them, nor of all together, do we think as we do of the unjust sufferings and merciless death of Our Lord. Is it then that His sufferings and His death so hold our hearts because of the virtue that He displayed? It is, indeed, true that we are drawn by the courage that foretold without fuss a bald, shocking tale of what was to be, a courage that in the privacy of the garden of Gethsemane could melt and dissolve, save for a single, unbroken fiber of acceptance of the Father's will; a courage that, brought to the test in the public gaze, spoke calmly and unerringly but, for the most part, met indignity with the dignity of silence.

As we are drawn by His courage, so we are touched by His considerateness. Other men, when they fear and when they suffer, turn in upon themselves; their minds lose breadth of vision; their hearts are embittered. Capable of thinking first only of themselves, in fear and in pain they think

2 [Each month, the pope recommends a general intention for prayers to the universal church. The intention here was the occasion and theme of this lead article of the June 1947 issue of the *Messenger.*]

of no one else. Loving most of all themselves, they face fear and endure pain by yielding to hatred. Yet Our Lord could point out to Pilate that Pilate's was not the greater sin. He could tell the lamenting women: 'Weep not for Me but for yourselves and for your children' (Luke 23.28). For His executioners he could pray: 'Father, forgive them for they know not what they do' (Luke 23.34). Suffering did not impair His balanced grip of truth, nor injustice close His heart.

The Meaning of Calvary

Yet even this splendor of moral virtue is not the real meaning of Calvary. We have been looking at merely human things with only human eyes. We have been thinking of virtue as a human accomplishment and perfection. We have been thinking of suffering as the greatest of evils. We have been thinking of sin as an injury to one's fellow men. But, if we care to know truly, if we wish to know things as really they are, if we desire to rise above the deception, usually the self-deception, of all partial and incomplete viewpoints, then we must look not with our own eyes but with the eyes of God. Yet how can that be done? How can we slip off our own knowing and put on the knowledge of God?

By our faith in the revealed word of God, by our belief in the certain truth of what He has taught us, not only we can but also we do know what God Himself knows. The penetration of an infinite mind, the impartiality of divine judgment, is within our easy reach, if only we can at once affirm and pray: 'I believe, Lord; help Thou my unbelief' (Mark 9.24). Still, is it not childish to believe? It is childlike; but, 'unless you become as little children, you shall not enter into the kingdom of heaven' (Luke 18.17). On the other hand, it is not childish. Where today is the learning, where is the wisdom, to do better than did the Galilean fisherman when he exclaimed: 'Lord, to whom shall we go? Thou hast the words of eternal life' (John 6.68).

The meaning of Calvary, then, is to be known only by faith; it is to be known, not by arguing nor by understanding, but mainly by praying to believe and by believing. One 'Hail Mary' can be more helpful than two big books, and fifteen minutes of prayerful reflection than many a long lecture, and most lectures are very long.

By faith we know, though we may not understand, that it is not suffering but sin that is the greatest evil; and that sin is the greatest evil, not because it is an injury to man, but because it is an affront to God. But, one may ask, why should God mind? Is He not beyond all possibility of harm? Hush, believing is not a matter of knowing why, but of taking God's word for it. Yet, once one believes, one can come to understand too, though only dimly as does a child. For it is worse to wrong one near to us – a mother, a sister, a wife, or a father, a brother, a husband – than one less near. It is worse to wrong one who loves us than one who does not care. But who is nearer to each of us than God? Parents beget and nurture us. But God creates and conserves us. Husband and wife share each other's lives. But the soul and God share life eternal. Who loves us more than God, Who is love itself, Who alone can love from an infinity of love, and so can love each one of us not a whit the less because He loves so many more besides?

God's Love

Nor is God's love for each of us something wholly different from human love. How could it be? For where does human love come from? whence the ardor of its self-surrender? whence the strength of its fidelity? whence its overpowering joy, and, when not befouled, its calm, enduring happiness? All that these are, are what they are, because they come from God, because they are, so to speak, a sample of Him and a sign of what He is. Man was made in the image and likeness of God, to show forth the goodness of God, to return the love of God. Sin is the refusal to return that love, and it is the greatest evil because it refuses just the best that man can do.

Yet all our striving yields but a poor understanding of the evil of sin; and, understanding it so poorly, we cannot repair it. To understand sin, one must be God; to repair it, one must be man. Our Lord is both God and Man – God to understand sin, Man to repair it. Such is our faith. Such is the true meaning of Calvary.

Sacrifice

To merely human judgment the passion and death of Our Lord is the symbol of human suffering caused by human wrong; it is the drama of human vice and the consummation of human virtue. But to faith it is the chief act of religious worship, the act of sacrifice. Common to all sacrifices is that they are outward signs, acts more charged with meaning than the outward acts of themselves possess. Behind the sacrifice, effecting it, giving it its excess of meaning, there is the sacrificial spirit.

It is the spirit of adoration, not merely 'lost, all lost, in wonder at the

God Thou art,'[3] not merely overcome with awe in the presence of Infinite Majesty, but more simply and more solidly recognizing His supreme dominion and surrendering to Him all that one is with all one's heart and all one's soul and all one's mind and all one's strength.

It is a spirit of propitiation, not only knowing what God is and giving Him His due, but also knowing what sin is and desiring to repair it.

It is a spirit of thanksgiving to the unfailing source of all the good things we can desire or possess, but especially a spirit of loving thanksgiving for the greatest of gifts, the gift of Himself, which has been begun in us by sanctifying grace and is to be completed in the intimacy of the beatific vision.

It is a spirit of impetration: a spirit that shouted in the blind beggar outside Jericho: 'Jesus of Nazareth, have mercy on me' (Mark 10.47 [and Luke 18.35]); a spirit that bowed in the centurion: 'Lord, I am not worthy ... Say but the word' (Luke 7.6–7); a spirit whose gentle murmur reached highest heaven with the prayer: 'Father, forgive them for they know not what they do' (Luke 23.34).

Such was the spirit of Jesus on Calvary. But 'put ye on Christ Jesus' (Romans 13.14). We, too, have heads and hearts and members, mind and will and sensibility. Whose are they? Are they our own for us to do with them just as we please? That is the way of rebellion and of ruin, a broad and easy way with a hopeless end. Are they just seemingly ours, and really a trust confided us by God? That is the way of the Cross. 'If any man will come after Me, let him deny himself, and take up his cross daily, and follow Me' (Luke 9.23). It is a straight and narrow way, but there is a joyous rainbow of resurrection at its end.

We should, we must, put on Christ Jesus, put on His sacrificial spirit of adoration, propitiation, thanksgiving, and impetration. But putting Him on is much more a matter of God's grace than of our willing; and even our willing is first of all a willing to pray for God's grace, to pray that our minds be illumined to truth, to pray that our hearts of stone be converted into hearts of flesh, to pray that our reluctant members be steadfast in the way of God. Great and sudden changes wrought by grace would set grace in conflict with the slow and gradual processes of nature. But pray first to pray constantly; pray constantly to know as Jesus knows, to love as He loves, to do as He did. That is a prayer that draws out of us the old Adam, to mold us, mostly unaware, day by day, ever more in the loveliness of Christ our Lord.

3 [From the Latin hymn of St Thomas Aquinas, *Adoro Te Devote*. Lonergan is quoting from Gerard Manley Hopkins's English rendition of the hymn.]

The Mass

Not only are we to put on the sacrificial spirit of Our Lord, but also we are to take part in His offering of His Sacrifice. The Body that was given for us on Calvary, the Blood that was shed for us there, are present on our daily altars. The same High Priest that offered His Body and His Blood on Calvary still offers them, a clean oblation, at the continuous break of sunrise, as spinning earth ever greets new day. The Sacrifice of the Cross was bloody; the Sacrifice of the Mass unbloody; the Sacrifice of the Cross we did not witness; but in the Sacrifice of the Mass we partake. One may come as the faithful and beloved St John with Our Lady by his side. One may come as the reluctant thief in honest acknowledgement of one's sins. One may come as the repentant Magdalene who knelt weeping at the foot of the Cross. But what matters is not how one comes, but whether one puts on, prays to put on, the sacrificial spirit of Our Lord, to offer with Him His Sacrifice for the redemption of mankind and the mystery of the glory of God.

Can then 'from the Holy Sacrifice of the Mass be drawn the power to save human society?' One must make no mistake. One is not to think that human society is going to have its endless cultural, social, political, economic problems solved by some astonishing series of miracles. If problems are to be solved, they will be solved by men who have taken the time and the trouble to discover their nature, who possess the talent to think out solutions, who are gifted with the judgment necessary to proceed from abstract theory to concrete policy. As a workman does not ask an employer, so no man should ask God, to do for man what man is to do for himself. But it remains that man without the grace of God cannot begin to do for himself what he ought to do. Distrust, envy, hatred divide different sections of labor; they divide labor, management, ownership; they divide opposed political factions, distinct cultural or racial groups, separate nations. Families perish in the quicksand of lust; children grow up without homes; schools breed materialists, and universities train revolutionaries; newspapers, magazines, books exploit the disorientation of minds and the weakness of characters for the lofty aim of increasing their sales. In this Babel objectives have to be pared down to minima if they are to be even proposed; they have to be further reduced if they are to be accepted; and the performance of what is accepted is a good deal less than the promise.

So we muddle from crisis to crisis, to be tumbled from catastrophe to cataclysm. Why? Because our glorious Western civilization is on the verge of intellectual and moral bankruptcy. Once more we must learn to love, one the other. Once more we must learn that life on earth is endurable only if first we seek the kingdom of God. Once more we must learn to believe God as little children, to be able to think as objective and honest men. It is on this prior and deeper level that the Sacrifice of the Mass is the source of the power to save human society. Those who believe and hope and love do so in virtue of the Sacrifice of Calvary applied to the needs of the hour by the Sacrifice of the Mass. If their faith and hope and charity are to be intensified to the point where they become effective in human affairs, if their numbers are to be increased to the point where such effectiveness is operative on a sufficiently broad scale, that will be because, in greater numbers and more intensely, men put on the sacrificial spirit of Our Lord and with Him offer in the Mass the world-redeeming sacrifice of the Cross.

15

A New Dogma[1]

The topic assigned me read: The Assumption of Our Lady, A New Dogma. Since that title is not quite free of ambiguity, it was explained to me that very good people were perplexed over the definition of a doctrine which apparently is not contained either in scripture or in tradition. My purpose, then, is not to pronounce a panegyric celebrating the recent definition, but to deal with a problem – in fact, to deal with the same problem that I happened to treat in the theological congress held in the University of Montreal two years ago.[2]

As I pointed out on that occasion, it is important to distinguish between the doctrine that is defined by the church and, on the other hand, the reasons why it is defined. It is a matter of faith that all shall rise from the dead on the Last Day. It is a matter of faith that our Lord rose from the dead on the third day after his crucifixion. Similarly, it is a matter of faith that the body of our Lady, the Mother of our Lord and God, never knew corruption but, as did that of her Son, enjoyed an anticipation of the resurrection. By the dogma of the Assumption is meant precisely that incorruption and anticipated resurrection from the dead. Unmistakably, it is a dogma of

---

1 [An article published in *The Canadian Messenger of the Sacred Heart* 61 (January 1951) 11–15. Since 1947, Lonergan had moved from Montreal to Toronto, and was now teaching theology at the Jesuit Seminary on Wellington St West.]
2 [Bernard Lonergan, 'The Assumption and Theology,' in *Vers le dogme de L'Assomption, Journée d'études mariales* (Montreal: Fides, 1948) 411–24; now chapter 4 in *Collection*.

faith, for it has been defined by His Holiness, Pope Pius XII;[3] and, as it was taught by the universal church prior to the definition, so now it stands beyond the possibility of doubt.

Still, it is one thing to be a Catholic, and something more to be an enlightened Catholic. It is one thing to believe, as God requires us to believe, and it is another to know the reasons and explanations that are to be given for our belief. To believe is a matter of salvation; to explain belief is a matter of Catholic culture. It is this secondary but not unimportant aspect of the Assumption that I have to treat. One can manage to live without having a radio set, but it is better to have one. Similarly, one can believe what the pope has defined without knowing the reasons for it, but it is better to know something about the reasons.

First of all, then, a dogma of faith must be contained in scripture or in an apostolic tradition. For what is believed by faith is believed on the authority of God; and what is believed on the authority of God must have been revealed by God. Moreover, not any divine revelation is to the point; it must be the public revelation given to the Apostles. The church cannot base a dogma upon a private revelation made to a particular saint – for example, to a St Margaret Mary or to a St Bernadette Soubirous – for the church was founded to keep and to proclaim the deposit of faith entrusted to her through the apostles. For this reason any dogma of faith must be contained either in scripture or in an apostolic tradition. For the same reason, it is not to the point to account for the dogma of the Assumption in any other manner. When someone points out to the Most Reverend Archbishop of Canterbury that his own cathedral contains a monument to the Assumption, he may embarrass the archbishop, but he does not give the pope a sufficient reason. When it is urged that the feast of the Assumption has been preceded by a fast day for over eleven hundred years, one adduces an imposing historical fact, but not an entirely sufficient reason.

In the second place, however, one has to be clear about the meaning of the affirmation, 'Dogmas of faith must be contained in scripture or in tradition.' There is an important distinction between the explicit and the implicit, and to grasp it is fundamental in the present instance. What, then, is the distinction? It is explicitly stated in the Gospel of St Matthew that 'thou art Peter, and it is upon this rock that I will build my church; and the gates of hell will not prevail against it; and I will give to thee the keys of the kingdom of heaven; and whatever thou shalt bind on earth shall be bound

3 [By an Apostolic Constitution, *Munificentissimus Deus, Acta Apostolicae Sedis* XLII (1950) 753–73.]

in heaven; and whatever thou shalt loose on earth shall be loosed in heaven' [Matthew 16.18–19]. That is explicit. Again, it is explicitly stated in the same Gospel that a wise man builds his house on a rock that resists rain and flood and wind, and that a fool builds his house on sand [Matthew 7.24–27]. While both these statements are explicit, still here it is only implicit that Christ our Lord was a wise man and so built his church on the rock, Peter. While it is explicit that Peter is the rock, still it is only implicit that Peter is to have successors; that after Peter's death the church is not to be moved from its rock foundation and foolishly be rebuilt upon sand. To know that Peter is the rock, one has only to read; to know that the church is never to be rebuilt upon a foundation of sand, one must not merely read but also understand. What is read is explicit; what is understood is implicit.

Let me give another illustration of this difference. In the twenty-fourth chapter of St Luke there is the account of the two disciples who had their faith shaken by the passion and the death of our Lord, did not credit the report of his resurrection, and on the first Easter Sunday set out for a town named Emmaus, some sixty furlongs from Jerusalem. On their way, as you know, a stranger joined them, upbraided them for being foolish and slow of heart, and explained to them the Messianic prophecies of the Old Testament. As he spoke, their faith was enkindled afresh, their hearts burned within them, the eyes of their understanding were opened. They began to see in divine revelation what had been there all along, though previously they had not seen it. What had been said by Moses and the prophets they knew quite well; but what they knew was more a matter of reading or hearing than of understanding. They had grasped what was on the surface; they were familiar with the words; but what they had been unable to do was to begin from Moses and go through all the prophets, picking out and explaining each of the passages that referred to the redemptive death of the Messiah.

Now in the long history of the church this distinction between the explicit and the implicit constantly recurs. For Catholics accept the word of God, but they accept not only the word but also its meaning. They receive divine revelation not only with their ears but also with their understanding. On the other hand, the history of heresy is largely a matter of attending to words and neglecting meaning, of being familiar with the words, as were the disciples of Emmaus, but of being unwilling to listen to explanations such as our Lord's appeal to Moses and all the prophets. The Council of Nicea in the year 325 defined that God the Son is one in substance with God the Father; the Arians, despite their many differences among themselves, were agreed on one thing – that the consubstantiality of the Son was not in scripture, and of course it is not explicitly in scripture.

When the Council of Ephesus in the year 431 defined that our Lady was the Mother of God, the Nestorians objected that that was not in scripture, and explicitly it is not. When the Council of Chalcedon in the year 451 defined that our Lord was one person with two natures, the Monophysites objected that scripture does not talk about persons or natures, and explicitly scripture does not. When the Orthodox East broke with the West over the procession of the Holy Spirit from the Son, it was on the ground that scripture said nothing about that procession, and explicitly it does not. When in the sixteenth century Luther and Calvin left the church, it was to return, they claimed, to the purity of the gospel, to the revelation made by God Himself. What that revelation was they did not agree. But on one thing they did agree, namely, that the Catholic Church had proposed a number of dogmas not explicitly in scripture. Now the Assumption of our Lady has been defined, and people are perplexed over this new dogma which is not explicitly in scripture. But, if it is a new dogma, also it is just another new dogma. The Pope has done again what the Catholic Church has been doing all along.

But it will be asked: Is not this business of understanding the meaning of revelation rather risky? What one good and holy man or woman understands one way is understood in another way by someone just as good and just as holy. Would it not be far safer to be content with the words and pay no attention to the meaning? While this is an obvious difficulty, still that is not the solution. If one paid no attention to the meaning of revelation, one would pay no attention to revelation at all; one would take the precious talent, wrap it in a napkin, bury it in the ground, and live one's life as though God had never revealed anything at all. One has to attend to the meaning. Still one does not have to attend to the meaning discovered by private inspiration or upheld by private judgment. Catholics believe in divine revelation. They believe not merely with their ears, but also with their minds. But they reject today, as they rejected in the sixteenth century, the strange notion that a public revelation is to be interpreted by private judgment. Our Lord founded his church for all mankind, for Jew and Gentile, Greek and barbarian, slaves and freemen, rich and poor, learned and ignorant, intelligent and dull. One does not have to be a scholar to get to heaven; and even if one is a very intelligent and very learned scholar, still one has to believe just as any one else. God confided his revelation not to the experts, but to the church. It was not to the scholars, but to a backward group of Galileans, that our Lord said: 'He that listens to you listens to me; and he that despises you despises me' (Luke 10.16).

I think I have been laboring upon a point that you all know very well.

Revelation is not merely a matter of words, but also of meaning; not merely of superficial meaning, but also of profound meaning. God expects us to accept his whole message, and he has given us an infallible church to teach us as our Lord taught his apostles and disciples.

But, before applying these principles to the dogma of the Assumption, it will be well to meet a difficulty. Probably you have heard it said that Catholic thought upon the Assumption of our Lady has no basis but a mass of legendary writings, named apocrypha, that made their appearance in the course of the fifth and the sixth centuries. Now, what are the facts? I offer two. The first Roman pronouncement upon the Assumption occurs in a document that probably belongs to the pontificate of Pope Gelasius I, from the year 492 to the year 496. What was this pronouncement? It condemned as untrustworthy and unacceptable an account of our Lady's Assumption. My first fact is a document of the fifth century. My second fact is the announcement of the Feast of the Assumption as read in Roman Martyrology for a number of centuries. It runs as follows:

> The Falling Asleep of Mary, the Holy Mother of God. Though her most sacred body is not to be found on earth, still Holy Mother Church celebrates her venerable memory with no doubt that she has left this life. But as to where that venerable temple of the Holy Ghost has been hidden by divine Providence, the sobriety of the Church prefers pious ignorance to any frivolous or apocryphal doctrine.[4]

Such was the extremely cautious announcement read annually in the Basilica of St Peter's in Rome until the reform of the martyrology by Baronius in 1584, about eleven centuries after the decree of Pope Gelasius. I think you can see for yourselves that critics of Catholic doctrine, in this matter as in others, seem to have little care to be accurate even in mere matters of fact.

What, then, are the grounds for the definition of the Assumption? As you will expect, it is contained in scripture but not explicitly; it is contained there implicitly; and the way to grasp that implication is the way our Lord showed that the doctrine of his redemptive death was contained in the Old Testament. I can only sketch the argument. Divine revelation gives us a general scheme of things. Death is a natural process awaiting us all; still it is not merely natural but also a curse upon the descendants of Adam. Death

---

4 [The quotation is from a martyrology compiled c. 850–859, and is the same translation as can be found in Paul E. Duggan, *The Assumption Dogma: Some Reactions and Ecumenical Implications in the Thought of English-Speaking Theologians* (Cleveland: Merson Press, 1989) 18.]

is because of sin. For it was after Adam's sin that God said: 'Dust thou art and unto dust thou shalt return' (Genesis 3.19). Next, as death is the wages of sin, so resurrection is the fruit of the grace of our Lord and Savior Jesus Christ. To the risen Christ St Peter in the Acts of the Apostles (2.31) applied the words of the fifteenth psalm, 'that he was not left in the place of death, and that his body did not see corruption.' Such is the general scheme that is revealed explicitly.

Let us now turn to our Lady. It is plain that in this general scheme she holds a place of privilege. From Adam all men contracted original sin, and for that reason infants are baptized. But our Lady was to be the Mother of God, and so she had the privilege of the immaculate conception. Again, the curse of Eve was not upon her, for she was blessed among women, a mother yet a virgin before parturition and in it and after it. But if our Lady was free from original sin, which is the ground of death and corruption; if throughout her life she was in the grace of God, and grace is the ground of resurrection; if she was freed from the curse of Eve and the pangs of motherhood and so blessed among women that the fruits of grace were revealed not only in her soul, but also in her body; then how could she be subject to the curse: 'Dust thou art and unto dust thou shalt return'? It would not make sense. If our Lady is full of grace, as the angel said at the Incarnation and we say in the 'Hail Mary,' then hers is not the lesser grace of resurrection on the last day with the rest of us sinners, but the fuller grace of an anticipated resurrection with her divine Son. Scripture bids us: 'Honor thy father and thy mother.' Our Lord had no human father, but he did have a mother; as he died, so she died. Yet, while he has the church honor the tombs and venerate the relics of his saints, still he permits the church to know nothing of the tomb or the relics of our Lady.

Now you see how such argument admits endless development. But the important point, to which I must turn immediately, is its value. Does it establish only the incorruption of our Lady's body, or does it prove as well her anticipated resurrection? Does it yield only probability, or does it yield certainty? Is the conclusion merely something connected with the deposit of faith, or does it form part of the deposit itself? As you see, these are the basic questions; each has to be answered; and, when such answers are combined, there is a rather notable variety of possible results. Upon these issues the church has been meditating for some fourteen hundred years. Very slowly, century by century, has one point been cleared up and then another. This development can be traced in the liturgies of the East and of the West, in the sermons that have been preached and recorded, and in the works of theologians.

Let us confine ourselves to the theologians of the West. From the seventh to the ninth centuries there are two schools of thought. On the one hand, there are those opposed to the doctrine because of the suspicions engendered by apocryphal writings; they form the larger group. But there is also a smaller group that argue the matter on its own merits and favor the Assumption. From the ninth century to the middle of the thirteenth there are the same two schools of opinion, but there also is a third group, containing such illustrious names as St Anselm of Canterbury and St Bernard of Clairvaux, and they write magnificent panegyrics for the feast of the Assumption without committing themselves upon its precise significance. In the course of the thirteenth century, when theology had worked out its method with some assurance, the situation changes. There still are those afraid of apocryphal origins; on the other hand, those that favor the Assumption fall into three groups: some consider it a pious belief, others consider it certain doctrine, others argue that it is of faith or almost of faith. From the thirteenth century to the sixteenth the fully affirmative answer steadily gains ground. With the literary criticism of the Renaissance it was settled that a letter purporting to be of St Jerome was in fact a forgery. This letter had been the principal objection against the theologians favoring the Assumption; with its removal from theological consideration, the way was made straight and plane. What opponents had not dared to deny at any time then was removed from the suspicion of doubt.[5]

But the church does not hurry. During the past four hundred years there have been disputes upon the issue, but minimum positions have approximated ever more closely to the maximum. Within the past eighty years it has become apparent that the ordinary teaching power of the church, exercised by the archbishops and bishops throughout the world, was committed to the affirmation of the Assumption as a matter of faith. This, of course, is far more significant than the thought of theologians, for the church cannot err in such matters. To be quite certain of the fact, His Holiness Pope Pius XII wrote to all the archbishops and bishops. In accord with their replies he decided to define the doctrine, lest what pertains to the deposit of faith should not be preached clearly and unequivocally to all men.

May the Immaculate Heart of Mary, alive in her living body in heaven, take compassion on all her children in this world, and obtain for them the grace of inward peace with God and outward peace with their neighbor.

5   [See Martin Jugie, *La Mort et L'Assomption de la Sainte Vierge* (Rome: Biblioteca Apostolica Vaticana, 1944) 277.]

16

The Mystical Body of Christ[1]

The doctrine of the mystical body of Christ refers to a concrete union of the divine persons with one another and with man and, again, of men's union with one another and with the divine persons. Because it is a doctrine that envisages things as they concretely are, it has all the complexity, all the stout articulation and delicate ramification of concrete reality. Because it is a single doctrine, its many elements, its manifold differentiations, its comprehensive network of relations, have to be apprehended all at once in a single view. Finally, because it is a supernatural doctrine, the relevant viewpoint for that single view is the viewpoint of God himself, so that, while from books and lectures one can learn many things about the mystical body, still it is only in prayer and contemplation that one comes really to know it and to appreciate it.

In search, then, of such knowledge and appreciation, let us leave to classes and hours of study the exploration of the mystical body in its fullness and let us take as a simple clue, as a guiding thread through the labyrinth of wealth, the single but basic and familiar theme of love. Upon that theme there are many variations, but we shall consider only five. Since unfortunately a man can think or speak of only one thing at a time, each of the five variations will be considered separately. But at once I would ask you

1 [A domestic exhortation given at the Jesuit Seminary, Toronto, in November 1951. The domestic exhortation was a talk on some spiritual subject delivered to the seminary community once a month during the academic year. As a professor of theology at this time and a member of the community, Lonergan would have been invited by the Rector to give this exhortation.]

to be on the watch for the relations, and connections, and dependences that blend and fuse all five into a single doctrine with its center in Christ Jesus our Lord, at once true God and true man.

First, then, there is the love of the eternal Father for his eternal Son. As the Father is God, so also the Son is God. This love, then, is the love of God for God. Moreover, it too is God, God the Holy Ghost, who is the infinite love proceeding from the infinite lovableness of God.

Secondly, there is the love of the eternal Father for his Son as man. For the second person of the Blessed Trinity possesses two natures; he is both God and man. A moment ago we considered the love of the Father for the Son as God. Now we ask about the love of the Father for the Son as man. Because the Son has two natures, we might conclude that the Father has two loves, an infinite love that is the Holy Ghost for the Son as God, and a lesser love for the Son as man. On the other hand, because the Son is the same person in both his divine and human natures, one might argue that the Father has but a single love, the Holy Ghost, for the Son whether as God or as man.

To resolve this doubt, the gospels present us with a tableau. At the beginning of his public life, Jesus was baptized by John at the Jordan and as he came out from the water, the Holy Spirit descended upon him in the form of a dove, and a voice from heaven was heard testifying to the Father's love, 'This is my beloved Son, in whom I am well pleased' [Matthew 3.17]. The Son of Man is still the Father's beloved Son, and the love is still the Holy Ghost. Such is the stupendous corollary of the Incarnation. Because God became man, the love of God for God became the love of God for man. Because love is for a person, when God became man, when the Word was made flesh, divine love broke the confines of divinity to love a created humanity in the manner that God the Father loves God the Son.

This is the truth that theologians express by saying that the sanctifying grace of Christ was infinite. For as you know, God's love is for the loveliness that he himself produces, and sanctifying grace is the loveliness conferred upon a creature beloved by God. Since then the love of the eternal Father for Christ as man is the love of God for God, the sanctifying grace of Christ, though finite as an entity, is infinite as a grace.

Thirdly, there is the love of Christ as man for men. It is the love of the Sacred Heart of Jesus, the love of a human will, motivated by a human mind, operating through human senses, resonating through human emotions and feelings and sentiments, implemented by a human body with its structure of bones and muscles, flesh, its mobile features, its terrible capacities for pleasure and pain, for joy and sorrow, for rapture and agony. It is the love of the Good Shepherd, knowing his own, known by his own, and ready to lose his life for them [John 10.14–15]: 'Greater love than this no man hath, than to lay down his life for his friends' [John 15.13]. It is the love of a man with a mission in the world, the high mission of teaching truth: 'For this was I born and for this came I into the world that I might bear witness to the truth' [John 18.37]. It is the love of a man with an incomprehensible, an incommunicable secret. How can a man announce that he is God. Yet Christ was God. To shout that secret from the housetops was to make himself a fool. To confide it to his friends was to mystify them. To affirm it before the court of the Sanhedrin was to earn himself the penalty of an atrocious death for blasphemy. It was a frustrated love: *Quae utilitas in sanguine meo?* What is the use of living and dying for men who will not believe, or if they believe, do not love, or if they love, love only half-heartedly? Can love be love and not give all? Can Christ's love give all and be happy about it, when not met by the same total self-surrender in the beloved? But do men? Do we?

Fourthly, there is the love of the eternal Father for us. At the Last Supper our Lord prayed to his heavenly Father for all who were to believe in him. He prayed 'that all be one, as my Father in me and I in Thee, that all be one in us. I in them, and Thou in me, that they may be completely made one, that the world may believe that Thou hast sent me and that Thou hast loved them as Thou hast loved me' [John 17.20–23].

'Thou hast loved them as Thou hast loved me.' The words are startling. For we know the love of the Father for the Son. We know that that love is God the Holy Ghost. We know that that love of the Father for the Son as God was extended to the Son as man. Is it true, then, that the Father loves us as he loves his own Son? Is it true that the sanctifying grace that belongs to Christ is communicated to us? Is it true that the divine loveliness making the humanity of Christ beloved of the Father also is bestowed upon us? The answer is given by the gospel: 'Thou hast loved them, as Thou hast loved me' [John 17.23]. For Christ was baptized in the waters of the Jordan, not to obtain grace for himself but to provide an outward manifestation of the inward effect upon us of baptism in the name of the Father and of the Son and of the Holy Ghost.

As the Eternal Father loves the Son as God with the love that is the Holy Ghost, so he loves the Son as man with the same love and highest gift, the Holy Ghost. 'In the fullness of time God sent his Son to redeem those under the law and to give us an adoptive sonship. Because then we are sons, he sent the Spirit of his Son into our hearts crying out within us, "Abba, Father"' [Galatians 4.4–6].

By that adoptive sonship, by the uncreated gift of the Holy Spirit, by the infusion of sanctifying grace into our souls, we are born again. Our sins are forgiven, we are made just in the sight of God, we become his friends, his children, and heirs of the kingdom of heaven. There is implanted within us a new principle of a higher life, and from it there flow the infused virtues and gifts of the Holy Ghost.

That new and higher life is not lived in isolation. For it is the life of the member of Christ, and it flourishes in us in the measure that we are united with Christ. He is the vine and we are the branches. As branches wither and die when separated from the vine, so are we without the life of grace, when separated from Christ. As branches flower and fructify when united fully with the vine, so too do we when united fully with Christ. 'As the living Father hast sent me, and I live by the Father, so he that eateth me, the same shall live by me. He that eateth my body and drinketh my blood ... He that abideth in me and I in him ...' [John 6.57, 56].

As you know, there is not a perfect analogy between an organic body and the mystical body of Christ. The members or parts of an organism have no distinct existence of their own; what your hand does, you do, for your hand is not something for itself. But the members of the mystical body have a distinct existence of their own, so that your deeds are your own and on the day of Judgment not Christ but you shall render an account of them. Again, the member of an organic body is not for the hands or the stomach, but both hands and stomach are for the body. But in the mystical body, the members are not for the body, but the body is for the members, the members are for Christ, and Christ is for God. All things are yours; but you are Christ's; and Christ is God's [see 1 Corinthians 3.22–23].

But if in the body of Christ we remain ourselves, we do not remain our own. As the Spirit of Christ is given to us, so we are given to Christ. 'For whether we live, we live to the Lord; whether we die, we die to the Lord; so that whether we live or die, we belong to the Lord' [Romans 14.8]. 'You are not your own, for you have been bought for a high price' [1 Corinthians 6.19–20].

Since we are not our own, we have to renounce ourselves and die to ourselves. 'If any man will come after me, let him deny himself, and take up his cross daily and follow me' [Luke 9.23]. 'Amen, amen, I say to you, unless the seed falling to the ground die, itself remaineth alone. If it die, it brings forth much fruit' [John 12.24]. 'Who loves his life in this world will lose it; and who hates his life in this world will keep it unto eternal life' [John 12.25]. As St Paul told the Colossians: 'You are dead, and your life is hidden with Christ in God' [Colossians 3.3].

As he wrote to the Romans: 'You are buried with Christ by baptism; you are engrafted upon the image of his death; you have died with Christ' [see Romans 6.3–4]. As he wrote to the Galatians: 'Those who are Christ's have crucified their flesh with its vices and concupiscence' [Galatians 5.24]. As he wrote to the Corinthians: 'The charity of Christ drives us on. For we reckon that if one has died for all, then all are dead; and Christ has died for all, so that those that live, live no longer for themselves but for him who has died and risen again' [2 Corinthians 5.14–15]. As he testified of himself: 'By the law I have died to the law, that I might live to God. With Christ I am nailed to the cross. I live, not I, but Christ liveth in me' [Galatians 2.19–20].

But what does it mean that Christ lives in us? It means more than I know or can say. But at least it means that the life of grace within us does not come to us by nature, that it is the free gift of God, that properly it belongs to Christ, the natural Son of God, the immediate beloved of the Father. Again, it means that though we live that life, still we live it by renouncing ourselves and by dying to ourselves to live to Christ and with Him and in Him and by Him. It means that the perfection of that life is being perfect as the heavenly Father is perfect, that it surpasses our comprehension and our wisdom, that we cannot live it on our own in the light of our own good common sense but only in the light and through the direction and inspiration of the Holy Spirit who is sent, is given to us by the Father and by the Son and who dwells within us. It means that the goal and final end of that life is the beatific vision, a vision that was Christ's by right from the first moment of his conception, a vision that will be ours inasmuch as suffering with Christ we shall be glorified with Him.

Besides the love of the Father for the Son, of the Son for us, of the Father for us, there is another love. It is the charity of God diffused in our hearts by the Holy Ghost, who is given to us [Romans 5.5].

As St Paul wrote to the Romans: 'Who will separate us from the love of Christ? Will affliction, or persecution, or hunger, or nakedness, or peril, or sword? In all this we are conquerors through him who has granted us his love. Of this I am fully persuaded: neither life nor death, no angels or principalities or powers, neither what is present nor what is to come, no force whatever, neither the height above us nor the depth beneath us, nor any created thing, will be able to separate us from the love of God, which comes to us in Christ Jesus our Lord' [Romans 8.35, 37–39].

The same charity, reverend Fathers and dear brothers, of which St Paul wrote has been given to you by the same Holy Spirit. It is the supernatural virtues infused into the will by the omnipotent power of God, both on the reception of baptism and in the forgiveness of mortal sin in confession. It is a virtue that is increased with every increase of sanctifying grace in your souls. It is a virtue that has been given you in an abundant measure, for it led you to follow the counsels of Christ in the Society of Jesus, and it has enabled you to persevere in that calling. But also it is an exception among the virtues, for other virtues stand on the golden mean; one can be excessive in prudence or justice, in fortitude or temperance; but charity cannot be excessive, for it regards not the means but the final end. Hence the great commandment is to love God with all one's heart and all one's soul, with all one's mind and all one's strength. And the second is like unto the first, to love one's neighbor as oneself, to love one another as Christ has loved us, toward the fulfillment of Christ's prayer at the Last Supper: 'I in them, and Thou in me, that they may be completely made one in us, that the world may believe that Thou has sent me and that Thou hast loved them as Thou hast loved me' [John 17.22–23].

Let us all join our Lord in that prayer. He ever lives, interceding for us; and his prayer now is as it was at the Last Supper.

Let us join with Him, for 'wherever two or more are gathered together in my name,' he said, 'there I am, in the midst of them' [Matthew 18.20]. We are gathered together in his name.

Let us ask each for himself and each for all that his grace and his love grow ever greater within us, to an ever more complete renunciation of ourselves, to an ever fuller acknowledgement that we are not our own but his, to an ever profounder joy that the infinite love that was extended from the Son as God to the Son as man has been extended through his passion and death, through his church and his sacraments, to us.

Let us ask, not only for ourselves but for all his mystical body, that all its members be alive with the life of grace, that in our age, so blotted with anxiety and suffering, the number of saints totally given to God be multiplied, that the mystical body grow enormously to include all men in accord with the universal salvific will of the divine Father.

17

Devotion to the Sacred Heart of Jesus and the Immaculate Heart of Mary[1]

To live in a fool's paradise is a temptation denied us. Not that we are wiser than our fathers, but so obviously the world is no paradise now. Through the twenties we headed gaily to the great depression. Through the thirties we headed gaily to a second great war. Through the forties grimly we headed to victory and peace, only to discover that to secure the peace the powerful nations must stockpile A-bombs.

Hitler is credited with the invention of the 'great lie,' the lie so vast, astounding, and outrageous that denial seems feeble, disregard a confession, and refutation a long-winded, bookish, meticulous affair that no one would heed.[2] But the 'great lie' was neither Hitler's invention nor his monopoly. Satan is the father of lies, of big ones as well as little ones, of deceptions of others and of lies to ourselves. Every unrepented, rationalized sin is also a lie. The sin occurs now and then. But the lie remains with us permanently, clouding our minds, misdirecting our efforts, blocking from our apprehension the truths we need, casting a night light of glamor over the folly of the senses, the folly of the mind, the folly of the heart.

---

1 [An article published in *The Canadian Messenger of the Sacred Heart* 61 (June 1951) 345–48. See above, p. 92, n. 1.]
2 [Lonergan has in mind Hitler's remarks from *Mein Kampf*, vol. 1, chapter 10: 'The great masses of the people will more easily fall victims to a great lie than to a small one.']

Gods for Everything

Lies are as many as are sins. Like sins, they come in all sizes and offer to meet every need – domestic, economic, social, political, cultural, religious. Some last a few days, some a few years, some a few decades, some a few centuries. Only the fittest survive, but the unfit seem always to be replaced. Once dead and long forgotten, they are incredible. But they were plausible enough in their day. Take polytheism. Did he not love God who first gave Him a local habitation and a name? Did he not think, perhaps, that God would be worshiped more effectively by becoming the god of hearth and home? But there were many hearths and many homes. If there were to be gods of the hearth, why not of the fields? If of the fields, why not of the crafts? If of the crafts, then surely of the cities where the crafts flourished. If of the cities, then of the states into which cities were engulfed. If there were political gods of the nations, why not gods of commerce? Why not gods of war? Why not gods of art, of literature, of health, of eating and drinking, of love, of passion, of ecstasy – in fact, gods for everything? There were.

A Vital Process

There is a marvelous logic to falsity. It is the very same as the logic of truth. As true conclusions follow necessarily from true premises, so with equal demonstrative force do false conclusions follow from false premises. Inversely, as you need more truths to hold to a truth, so, if you would be constant in a lie, you need more lies. Lying is a vital process; it has offspring; it increases and multiplies. The further it goes, the stronger and more resourceful it becomes. Taken singly, lies are twigs to be broken with ease. But they do not come singly, or in pairs, or in sevens. They are a plague, endemic in every human culture, and, as Christopher Hollis put it, you know you are dealing with a distinct culture when you come across a really new lie.[3]

A traveler from the Orient who would understand the West has to go back to our Dark Ages to witness, in the eventual emergence of states from that chaos, the origin of the problem of church and state on which he reads such conflicting views. He has to go back to the Reformation to see how the emancipation of states from the pope, and incidentally from the Law of God, was facilitated by new religions that made each prince or each

3 [The editors were unable to trace this reference.]

reformer or each pious soul his own pope. He has to go back to the Enlightenment to watch the mountainous disagreements of the multitudinous popes relegate Christianity to Sundays and to establish Pure Reason as arbiter in things that matter. Because the representatives of Pure Reason were as little capable of agreement as the representatives of the many religions, it is a short step to Tolerance. He finds Tolerance usually described as a new and deeper understanding of Christian charity, with, however, the implication that the more basic a truth is, the less it really matters. But basic truths do matter. The radical mental vacuity of the secular university and of the state system of education is oppressive. People do grow weary of muddling from lesser disasters to greater, and, if statesmen cannot be bothered about basic truths, at least they must be concerned with what people believe. Only a common belief will enable a people to face facts, to work and to make sacrifices, to surmount obstacles, to reach solutions. So the Oriental comes to understand our age of overt myth and scientific propaganda, of terrible 'know how' and trembling 'know whether,' of starry-eyed enthusiasms and numb despair, of neurotic guilt and abolished principles, of diplomatic ineptitude and total war. To live in a fool's paradise is a temptation denied us.

'Testimony to the Truth'

'For this was I born, and for this came I into the world; that I should give testimony to the truth. Every one that is of the truth heareth my voice' (John 18.37). Such was our Lord's own description of his mission on earth. He knew what men need. He knew that by themselves they could not meet that need. 'I pray not for the world' (John 17.9), he said, for what is the world but the net of lies in which men live enmeshed, in which they struggle fruitlessly, from which there is no human escape? Indeed, what were the forces that condemned and crucified Christ himself but the lies of Pharisaic pride, the lies of an established order of vested interests, the lies of Pilate's justice, and the strange, vehement consent of the people. 'His blood be upon us!' the people shouted [Matthew 27.25].

'Every one that is of the truth heareth My voice.' But who is simply of the truth! There are those that do not hear. There are those that hear, but do not harken. There are those that harken, but do not persevere. The seed falls by the wayside. It falls on stony ground. It falls among thorns. It falls, too, on good earth, yet how varying is the yield and how rare the hundredfold of sanctity!

Grace and Prayer

Still the arm of the Lord is not shortened, nor the power of prayer diminished. Persecuting Saul fell to the ground, and there arose Paul the Apostle of the Gentiles. Western Christendom was based on the conversion of invading barbarians. The Turks were halted at Lepanto. The grace of God is needed to hear the voice of Christ, and that grace God can give us as abundantly today as ever before. The grace of God is needed to live the teaching of Christ, and that grace God can give as freely today as ever before.

If the fundamental problem of our time is the permanent human problem of reaching truth and being steadfast in it, the practical problem is prayer. Unlike the priests of Baal we do not have to shout. God is everywhere, all-knowing, all-powerful. In him we live and move and have our being. Without him we can do nothing. But faith is needed, trust is needed, charity is needed, perseverance is needed. One does not add a cubit to one's stature by taking thought. Neither does one so lightly become a man of prayer or a woman of prayer, a prayerful youth or maiden, a prayerful boy or girl, a prayerful child. Yet by the communion of saints, by the prayers of those God calls to prayer because of the prayers of others, there are in our time as in other times people that live to pray, and people that struggle to pray, and people driven by an inner grace to link by unwearied intercession the foundering hulk of humanity with the inaccessible light of God.

Such, then, in the midst of present evils and predicted woes, is the significance of devotion to the Sacred Heart of Jesus and the Immaculate Heart of Mary. As the Apostles once discovered, there are devils to be cast out, not by a mere command but only by prayer and fasting. No one of us has seen God, so the Church directs our imagination to the symbol of Christ's love – to the Sacred Heart that represents love greater than which no man hath. No one of us but has appealed to our Lady,[4] so the Church directs our imaginations to her Immaculate Heart that in faith and trust, in charity and perseverance, in sacrifice and in penance we pray for the blessings of truth and the glory of God in this world and hereafter.

4 [That is, 'There is no one of us that has not appealed to our Lady ...']

18

Humble Acknowledgment of the Church's Teaching Authority[1]

To the average Canadian, 'church' means a large stone building used on Sunday morning; 'authority' recalls Hitler and the Middle Ages; and 'acknowledgment' is a five-dollar word meaning an answer to a letter. Just what 'teaching' refers to is more obscure; in the old days it was a matter of reading, writing, and arithmetic; now it has to do, it seems, with such progressive subjects as English conversation and sandpit.[2] Finally even intensive research in the comic strips and in advertising copy might reveal no occurrence of the rare word 'humble.'

Initial Simple Fact

Instead of struggling with so strange a vocabulary, then, let us go back to the initial, simple fact. God the Son became Man, lived on earth for a few decades, then died. But that was not the end of it. I do not mean merely that he rose from the dead, ascended into heaven, sitteth at the right hand of God the Father, whence he will come to judge the living and the dead. I mean that he has remained in our midst. I mean that his few decades in ancient Palestine were but a prelude, a short and startling overture, an

---

1 [An article published in *The Canadian Messenger of the Sacred Heart* 62 (January 1952) 5–9. The subject was the General Intention for the month of January recommended by Pope Pius XII (see above, p. 93, n. 2). Lonergan is here using the Knox translation for his biblical references.]

2 [British for 'sandbox.' The reference is presumably to hands-on, practical learning.]

effective sounding of a rich and daring motif. For, when he died, he was to live again, not only in heaven, but also on earth in the lives, the hearts, the minds, the souls of countless men.

Christ in His Members

'Saul, Saul, why dost thou persecute Me?' [Acts 9.4]. These are the words heard by Saul of Tarsus on his way to Damascus. But Saul was intent, not on persecuting Christ, whom he believed already dead, but on arresting and carting off to Jerusalem the Christians of Damascus, who were still alive. What Saul did not know then was the mystery he himself was later to proclaim: 'I live, not I, but Christ liveth in me' [Galatians 2.20]. The brief earthly life of God-made-Man was but the frontispiece to the fullness of his living in the members of his mystical Body.

On the Last Day the just will hear him say: 'For I was hungry, and you gave me food; thirsty, and you gave me drink; I was a stranger, and you brought me home; naked, and you clothed me; sick, and you cared for me; a prisoner, and you came to me.' Whereupon the just will answer: 'Lord, when was it that we saw thee hungry, and fed thee; or thirsty, and gave thee to drink? When was it that we saw thee a stranger, and brought thee home; or naked, and clothed thee? When was it that we saw thee sick or in prison, and came to thee?' And the king will answer them: 'Believe me, when you did it to one of the least of my brethren here, you did it to me' (Matthew 25 [35–40]).

That They May Be One

In promising the Blessed Eucharist our Lord had said: 'My flesh is real food, my blood is real drink. He who eats my flesh and drinks my blood lives continually in me and I in him. As I live because of the Father, the living Father who has sent me, so he who eats me will live, in his turn, because of me' (John 6.55–57). The infant in the womb has its own life, yet somehow lives by the life of its mother. But God the Son is absolutely one with God the Father – one in being and essence and substance, one in knowledge and wisdom and goodness. Yet it was our Lord himself who prayed at the Last Supper, 'that they may all be one; that they too may be one in us, as thou Father art in me, and I in Thee; so that the world may come to believe that it is thou who hast sent Me. And I have given them the privilege which thou gavest to me, that they should all be one, as we are one; that, while thou art in me, I may be in them, and so they may be perfectly made one. So let the world know that it is thou who hast sent me, and that thou hast bestowed thy love upon them, as thou hast bestowed it upon me' (John 17.21–23).

Not Metaphor, but Mystery

This is not metaphor, but mystery. It is really true, the reality and the truth of our calling in Christ Jesus. But, because it is mystery, it is more by prayer than by study that we come to appreciate it and to realize it. So St Paul prayed for the Ephesians: 'I fall on my knees to the Father of our Lord, Jesus Christ, that Father from whom all fatherhood takes its title. May he, out of the rich treasury of his glory, strengthen you through his Spirit with a power that reaches your innermost being. May Christ find a dwelling place, through faith, in your hearts; may your lives be rooted in love, founded on love. May you and all the saints be enabled to measure, in all its breadth and length and height and depth, the love of Christ, to know what passes knowledge' (Ephesians 3.14–19).

We Know by Faith

How is one to say what passes knowledge! One must appeal to faith. By faith we know that our Lord is one person with two natures; he is the second person of the Blessed Trinity; he possesses a divine nature and he assumed a human nature. What perfection was bestowed upon that human nature, when even the dim sight of unbelievers sees in Christ the most winning of men! How much greater than we can fathom must have really been the perfection of a human nature assumed by a divine person! But God the Son became man, not merely to perfect the single human nature he assumed, but to perfect all men, to make them all one with himself in the Father. That is the mystery that passes knowledge. 'Thou hast bestowed thy love upon them, as thou has bestowed it upon me' [John 17.23].

Our Calling

'Put ye on Christ Jesus' [Romans 13.14]. It is our calling to forget ourselves, to forget our desires and our fears, to cast off our errors and our wilfulness, and to put on Christ. It is to desire his desires, to fear his fears, to think his thoughts, and to will his will. 'In our baptism we have been buried with him, died like him, that so, just as Christ was raised up by his Father's power from the dead, we too might live and move in a new kind of existence' (Romans 6.4).

The Church and the Mystical Body of Christ

The church, then, is not this or that stone building used on Sundays. It is the mystical body of Christ. 'Apostles and prophets are the foundation on which you were built, and the chief cornerstone of it is Jesus Christ Himself. In him the whole fabric is bound together, as it grows into a temple dedicated to the Lord; in him you too are being built with the rest, so that God may find in you a dwelling place for his Spirit' (Ephesians 2.20–22).

Just before his Ascension our Lord said: 'All authority in heaven and on earth has been given to me; you therefore must go out, making disciples of all nations, and baptizing them in the name of the Father and of the Son and of the Holy Ghost, teaching them to observe all the commandments which I have given you' [Matthew 28.18–20]. The authority of which I write is the full authority of Christ. It is an authority beyond challenge, for it is the complete authority of God the Father given to God the Son. It is the authority to make disciples of all nations, to teach them to observe all his commandments. Just as he is one with the victims of persecution, just as he is one with the hungry and the thirsty, just as he is one with the naked and the sick, just as he is one with those that eat his Body, so too he is one with the teaching authority of his church. 'He who listens to you listens to me; he who despises you despises me; and he who despises me despises him that sent me' (Luke 10.16).

Christ in His Church

On the Last Day the wicked will protest: 'Lord, when was it that we saw thee hungry, or thirsty, or naked, or a stranger, or sick, or in prison, and did not minister to thee? And he will answer them: Believe me, when you refused it to one of the least of my brethren here, you refused it to me' (Matthew 25.44–45). The trouble was that they did not recognize and so did not acknowledge Christ in the hungry and the thirsty, in strangers and prisoners, in the sick and the destitute. But, just as there is an acknowledgement of Christ in the needy, so too there is an acknowledgement of Him in the teaching authority of his church. If one acknowledges that authority to be the authority of Christ, the Son of God, there is no difficulty in being humble about it. The proud cannot stoop to listening and learning; they themselves must do the teaching. But if one sees and recognizes and acknowledges Christ in his members and in his representatives, then already one has an essential humility that can grow only as one learns of him to be meek and humble of heart.

'To Whom Shall We Go?'

'Believe Me, unless you become like little children, you shall not enter into the kingdom of heaven' (Matthew 18.3). That must be a difficult thing to do if, in our age so full of deep foreboding, men are ready to try anything except the fullness of living as members of Christ. Yet, again, how can it be difficult? As Simon Peter said: 'Lord, to whom shall we go?' [John 6.68]. There is only one church that unmistakably is his mystical body, that is spread over the face of the earth, that speaks with his authority, that demands allegiance in his intransigent way. There is only one Good Shepherd, and his voice is heard by young and old, by rich and poor, by ignorant and learned, in many tongues, over many lands.

Prayer for Grace

The difficulty is that to acknowledge Christ in his church, to hear his voice in her teaching, presupposes the gift of supernatural grace. 'Nobody can come to me without being attracted toward me by the Father who sent me' (John 6.44). The difficulty is that God gives his grace more abundantly when we pray more earnestly and more perseveringly. That is why, during the month of January, we, as members of the Apostleship of Prayer, shall pray for *Humble Acknowledgement of the Church's Teaching Authority*. We shall pray that the light of faith and the strength of good will may be given to those outside the church, that they may believe and be saved. We shall pray that those in whom the light of faith has grown dim may break away from the seduction of human opinions to acknowledge humbly the voice of Christ in the voice of his church.

19

Respect for Human Dignity[1]

'And it came to pass, when Samuel was old, that he appointed his sons to be judges over Israel ... And his sons walked not in his ways, but they turned aside after lucre, and took bribes, and perverted judgment. Then all the ancients of Israel, being assembled, came to Samuel at Ramah. And they said to him, "Behold thou art old, and thy sons walk not in thy ways. Make us a king to judge us, as all nations have." And the word was displeasing in the eyes of Samuel, that they should say, "Give us a king to judge us." And Samuel prayed to the Lord. And the Lord said to Samuel, "Harken to the voice of the people in all that they say to thee. For they have not rejected thee, but Me, that I should not reign over them"' (1 Samuel 8.1–7).

Flight from God

Contemporary psychology has made people suspicious of their motives. The ostensible purpose that lies on the surface is apt to be a piece of self-deception. The real purpose is hidden in the depths and can be brought to light only by a prolonged and expensive analysis. But what the real purpose may be is a matter of dispute among different schools of opinion. Some claim it is sexual. Others, that it is some will to power. Others, that, in the last analysis, the trouble commonly is of a religious nature. Like

---

1 [An article published in *The Canadian Messenger of the Sacred Heart* 63 (July 1953) 413–18. Again, the subject is the General Intention for the month of July recommended by Pope Pius XII (see above, p. 93, n. 2).]

the Israelites asking to be ruled by a king instead of a prophet, men today appear to want to rid themselves of Samuel's worthless sons, but in fact they want to rid themselves of God. Nor is this view surprising. For, if the ultimate end of everything is God, then man's flight from God is a violation of the order of nature.

Appeal to Science

The new king of the modern world is Science. In an earlier generation, which some of us remember, the ultimate appeal was to God, to Truth, to Virtue, to Justice, to Charity, to Christianity. But quietly and effectively that has been changed. What is undisputed now is that living must be brought into line with scientific economics, scientific sociology, scientific psychology, scientific education, scientific genetics, scientific hygiene, etc., etc. And, as few of us know any science worth mentioning, and no one knows all science, there is a great need of experts, of popularizers, of organizers, to tell us just what Science says and just how to carry out its bidding.

However, there are two very different scientific orientations. There are the old scientists who took it for granted that the real is what is out there, and that knowing it objectively is a matter of taking a good look. Of course, one must not be uncritical about the issue, for the real consists of an extraordinarily large number of extremely small knobs; one cannot actually look at them; but it is quite certain that they are out there and, while one cannot see them, still one can imagine them. There also are the new scientists, and they are committed to a quite different view of reality, knowledge, and objectivity. One can neither see nor imagine four-dimensional curved space. One can neither see nor imagine the entities of the processes of quantum mechanics. All one can do is observe, understand, and verify. Moreover, scientific knowledge is not a matter of observing unintelligently; the understanding is necessary; nor will any understanding do, for verification is necessary. So it comes about that scientific knowledge is a matter of knowing what is true; and, strangely, what is true is not what one can see or imagine, but only what one can conceive intelligently and affirm reasonably.

A New View

This difference between the old and the new scientists is of considerable importance. After all, if the real is simply a matter of extremely small knobs, and my soul is not a small knob, then my soul is not real; similarly, if my free will is not a small knob, it is not real; finally, if God is not a small knob, he is not real. But the new science has tossed overboard the old view that only very small knobs are real. The new science has introduced a new view – that what is real is what is true. To be real, it is no longer necessary to be a small knob. It is not even necessary to be imaginable. It is enough to be true. Hence, just as four-dimensional space-time can be real because it is verified, just as nonimaginable processes can be real because they are verified, so also it can be argued that, if it is true that I have a soul, then my soul is real; if it is true that I have a free will, then my free will is real; and, if it is true that God is, then God is real.

A Regrettable Lag

However, while the new view has come to dominate the field of physical research, its implications have made no great impression elsewhere. As yet it does not seem to have brought about a startling revolution in economics, or sociology, or political theory, or psychology, or psychiatry, or educational theory, or pedagogy, or genetics. Nor is this lag surprising, for what is new about the new view is not scientific but philosophic, and scientists commonly are not interested in philosophy.

But if the lag is not surprising, at least it is regrettable. For the whole orientation of the human sciences would be changed if men were conceived not as aggregates of extremely small knobs, but as persons with intelligence, initiative, freedom, and responsibility. Nor would this change of orientation be merely theoretical, for today Science is the king that has replaced the old judge; it is the last court of appeal; it rules men's lives through its ministers – the experts, the popularizers, the consultants, the planners, and the organizers. Obviously, if men are just aggregates of small knobs, then experts are needed to do their thinking for them, popularizers are needed to tell them what has been thought for them, social engineers are needed to condition them to like it, planners are needed to tell them what to do, and organizers are needed to get them to do it in the right way. Such has to be the rule of science on the old view. But, were the new view to gain the ascendant in the human sciences, then the rule of science would change. For, if men are not aggregates of small knobs, if they are persons, intelligent and reasonable, free and responsible, then the science of man will be concerned principally with his intelligence and his freedom, and it will be applied through his intelligence and freedom.

Democracy versus Autocracy

The enormous significance of that difference may be illustrated without too much difficulty. The nineteenth century was the age of increasing democracy. One country after another witnessed the reduction of monarchic power, the establishment of parliaments, the extension of the franchise, the curtailment of privileges. Hand in hand with this process went the doctrine of political economists who relied on human intelligence and ingenuity, who addressed their precepts and advice to individuals, who did what they could to discredit the alleged wisdom and beneficence of paternalistic governments. In contrast, the twentieth century is the age of increasing autocracy. The views of the old economists have been found inadequate, and the remedies of the new economists are beyond the comprehension not merely of the man in the street, but even of the average member of parliament. Even where parliaments have retained their former prestige, they have to be complemented with enormous retinues of experts and civil servants to do the thinking and the planning, to carry out the paper work, and to take care of the endless files. But why are the remedies so complex and intricate? In dealing with material things the intelligent procedure is to count and to measure, to chart tendencies and frequencies, to formulate correlations and functions, to design machines and methods, to coordinate and to check and to keep books. But it does not follow that that is the way to deal with persons, unless, of course, one takes it for granted that men are not persons, but just aggregates of old-style imaginable atoms.

Planned Society

This tendency of contemporary human science has combined with the spectacle of the gigantic enterprises of modern industry to give plausibility to the notion that the panacea for all human ills lies in a minutely designed organization both of human energy and of natural resources to secure a maximum productivity. Man as intelligent and reasonable, as free and responsible, is ruled out of consideration. In place of the free unfolding of human vitality there comes the blueprint and the quota. Instead of the continuously adaptive interplay in which the voluntary cooperation and the personal responsibility of each contribute to the personal life and development of all, there is to be a regimentation of human living, a mechanization of human activity, a leveling down of human aspirations. The worker is to have his every movement planned for him by some more intelligent expert on methods. Opportunities of employment fall under the rule of vast trade unions that have become impersonal monopolies. The administration of social security turns out to be a tool to control the birthrate. Statisticians are employed to calculate and to chart the number of people to be allowed to emigrate or to immigrate. Information is restricted to patterns that press magnates have learned to find profitable. Education ceases to transmit a culture that passes judgment on society and becomes an ever more efficiently organized department of bureaucratic government. One is assured that in due time the world will be a paradise of prosperity, security, and peace. But, while men wait for the utopia promised by universal organization, there are wars, transplanted populations, refugees, displaced persons, unemployment, outrageous inequalities in living standards, the legalized robbery of devaluated currencies, and the vast but somewhat hidden numbers of the destitute.

The Personal Factor

Such in brief outline is the picture drawn by His Holiness Pope Pius XII in his Christmas Eve Address, 1952.[2] In a key position for information on human misery, he called for 'a more intense and multiplied love for the poor ... a flood of help, headlong in its impetuosity, which may penetrate wherever there is an old person abandoned, a poor person sick, a child who suffers, a mother desolate because she can do nothing to help it.' He pointed out that, while charitable organizations are needed to meet the enormous evils of our day, still no organization can possess the personal touch nor pass on the words of kindness and comfort that the sufferer needs no less than material aid. Moreover, in this insistence on the personal factor, one can grasp in perhaps the simplest way the larger aspect of the Holy Father's discourse. On the one hand, he disclaimed any intention to pronounce on the necessity, the utility, or the disadvantages of modern industrial organization. On the other hand, he insisted that, as mere spontaneity or sentimentality leads to chaos, the planned society heads for sterility.

2   [*Acta Apostolicae Sedis* XLV (January 1953) 33–46.]

'Depersonalization'

'Wherever the demon of organization invades and tyrannizes his spirit, there are at once revealed the signs of a false and abnormal orientation of society. In some countries the modern state is becoming a gigantic administrative machine. It extends its influence over almost every phase of life. It would bring under its administration the entire gamut of political, economic, social, and intellectual life from birth to death. No wonder then, if, in this impersonal atmosphere, which tends to penetrate and pervade all human life, respect for the common good becomes dormant in the conscience of individuals, and the state loses more and more its primary character of a community of morally responsible citizens. Here may be recognized the origin and the source of that phenomenon which is submerging modern man under its tide of anguish – his "depersonalization." In large measure his identity and name have been taken from him; in many of the more important activities of life he has been reduced to a mere material object of society, while society itself has been transformed into an impersonal system and into a cold organization of force.

'If any one still doubts about this state of affairs, let him turn his gaze upon the teeming world of misery, and let him ask different classes of indigents what answer society is wont to give them, now that the individual person is being lost sight of. Let him ask the ordinary poor man, destitute of every resource, certainly not rare to find in cities, as in towns and rural areas. Let him ask the father of a needy family, a constant visitor of a bureau of public charity, whose children cannot wait for the distant and vague realization of the golden age which is always in the future. Let him put the question to a whole nation whose standard of living is inferior or very low, and which, associated in the family of nations with other peoples who enjoy a sufficient or even abundant way of life, waits in vain from one international congress to another for a stable improvement of its lot.'[3]

Return to God

The General Intention, then, for the Apostleship of Prayer in the month of July is one very close to the heart of the Holy Father and one of great moment for the temporal well-being and the eternal salvation of men. Moreover, it is supremely an object for prayer. I have said that the new view

---

3 [Translated from ibid. 37–38.]

of reality and objectivity, implicit in contemporary physics, has been disregarded by and large by human scientists because the issue is philosophic. But it also is true that the issue is theological. It also is true that the mistaken orientation of the old physicists ran parallel to a flight from God. It also is true that a correction of that orientation in the human sciences would run parallel to a return to God. Men do not return to God without the gift of his grace. 'No man can come to me, unless the Father draw him' [John 6.44]. And God, in his wisdom and goodness, wills us to cooperate by prayer in the dispensation of his grace.

The Sacred Heart of Jesus is the symbol of the personal love of God for man. To that Person and that Love let us turn in the month of July. Let us turn genuinely, honestly, sincerely, as we are, with all our sins and sufferings, our sorrows and regrets, our weaknesses and fears. Let us thereby come to know ourselves better as persons. Let us pray that the Light and the Love of his Holy Spirit may come abundantly to us and to all men, that the face of the earth may be recreated; that organized society may cease to be a source of almost inevitable sinning; that men may know men as the free and responsible persons that they really are; that man's aspirations for doing good widely and effectively may no longer be corrupted by an antiquated notion of objectivity.

PART THREE

Early Reviews

20A

Review of L.W. Keeler, s.j.,
The Problem of Error, from Plato to Kant:
A Historical and Critical Study[1]

Quod sibi auctor in hoc opere scribendo consilium proposuit, ut quae clarissimus quisque philosophus de errore senserit, quaeque deinceps hac de re in singulis fere scholis sententiae obtinuerint, accurate inquireret et diiudicaret, hoc eum felicissime assecutum esse nemo erit, ut censeo, qui infitietur. Quaestio enim subtilior atque exquisitior eademque bene definita tractatur, cui tantum abest ut philosophi vel antiqui vel recentiores satis fecerint, ut nobis contra posterisve nostris magnam huius problematis expediendi laudem reliquisse videantur. Quoniam ergo hoc libro in rem perobscuram neque satis antea ab aliis tractatam plurimum lucis allatum est, ad studiorum philosophicorum profectum eum maxime pertinere iudicamus.

Qua de causa, praetermissis multis rebus quas auctor ampla eruditione ex historia collectas de ortu et progressione huius quaestionis exposuit, cum non tam opus sit ut haec iterum declarentur, totam huius operis recognoscendi rationem in eo ponimus ut primum quod et quale hoc problema sit, deinde quemadmodum usque adhuc sit tractatum, demum quid nostrae aetatis philosophis ad tractandum relinquatur, breviter persequamur. Auctor enim ipse quamvis nominatim et proprie nisi de altera quaestione non disseruerit, tamen quae de prima et tertia sentiat, ex dictis atque criteriis suis nullo fere negotio eruitur.

---

1 Rome: Analecta Gregoriana, vol. 6, apud aedes Pontificiae Universitatis Gregorianae, 1934, xiii + 281 pp. [*Gregorianum* 16 (1935) 156–60. Lonergan wrote the review in elegant Ciceronian Latin. An English translation by Michael G. Shields follows.]

Ac primum quidem erroris problema nihil aliud est nisi mutato nomine et aspectu illud ipsum problema veritatis. Nam si cognitionis causam formalem quaerimus, manifestum est non res ipsas easque solas cognitionis nostrae contentum semper specificare et determinare posse. Hoc enim si verum esset, non alio pacto falsa cognitio gigni posset, nisi forte res ipsae essent falsae. Alia igitur est humanae cognitionis ratio ac mera terminorum et nexuum apprehensio, quoniam alia quaedam causa quae in processu cognitionis intervenire aut possit aut soleat concedatur necesse est. Quae et qualis illa sit, quando et quomodo intercedat, problema erroris proprie vocatur. Eius vero summam difficultatem hoc dilemmate indicari licet. Videtur enim esse necesse ut potentia aliqua aut cognitiva aut appetitiva interveniat: quae si cognitiva est, periculum est ne realismus et certitudo eant perditum; si vero appetitiva esse dicitur, nullo modo explicatur (excludimus enim psychoanalyticam quandam inconsciam boni in verum transmutationem) quare qui erret sententiam suam ipsa obiectiva evidentia fulciri semper vehementer testetur.

Non alias atque in ipsis rebus cognoscendis oriri posse errorem, cum ratione tum maxime usu constat, siquidem eorum naufragium respicimus qui realismo adversati sunt. Etenim ut paucissimis longam accuratamque P. Keeler explicationem complectamur, ex hac sola causa videtur Spinozae theoria esse reicienda, utpote qui mundum tam bene ordinatum cogitarit ut errorem boni indebiti privationem dicere cogeretur. Deinde purus ille phaenomenalismus, qui Hume placebat, nisi sibi ipsa phaenomena quasi contradicant, cum errore constare minime potest. Ad extremum veritas Kantiana seu mera cohaerentia esse supponitur seu cum obiecto mentis adaequatio quaedam, sequitur ut illae mentis immutabiles leges nihil nisi eundem semper fructum, numquam vero contradictiones humanas proferre possint.

Eiusmodi igitur speculationibus omissis, ad eas doctrinas veniamus quas temporibus anteactis exortas haud scio an huius problematis (non dico eius solutionis) thesim et antithesim et synthesim recte vocemus: logicam Graecorum, Stoicorum ethicam, mediaevalem de fide doctrinam. Nam cum hae tres huius problematis tractandi rationes absolutae et perfectae essent, Cartesius erroris problema omni ex parte sensit scientiamque criteriologicam invexit. Is vero ad solutionem quod attinet, cum maxime sibi constaret, in absurdam illam et nefandam vocem erupit: iudicium esse voluntatem. Quibus autem ambagibus tota haec quaestio usque eo pervenerit, paucis declaramus.

Sophistae Graeci, in eristicis suis controversiis occupati, cum alia sexcenta gravia et levia pariter commiscebant, tum de ipso erroris problemate pro sua calliditate disceptarunt. In quos Plato praeter alios illum maxime dialogum, qui Sophista inscribitur, composuit, in quo quidem doctrinam Aristotelicam de terminis et propositionibus atque etiam de loco quem error in iudicuim habeat iam adumbratam discernere videmur. Qua doctrina plene elucubrata syllogismoque invento, omnia ad diligentem erroris considerationem comparata diceres; hunc tamen laborem detrectasse Aristoteles videtur, qui modo *noûn* erroris causam, modo eum infallibilem diceret, qui in logicis errorem non esse nisi syllogismum informem affirmaret, in ethicis vero blandienti voluptati eum culpae tribueret.

Post Aristotelem conveniebat inter philosophos iudicium quodammodo esse liberum et voluntarium; quemadmodum autem hoc fieri posset, silebant. Ita Pyrrhonici, qui omnem assensum cohibendum esse docuerunt. Ita Stoci et Epicurus, qui tali ratione errorem explicare conati sunt. Ita ipse S. Augustinus, qui hanc aetatis suae sententiam tacite assumpsit neque umquam suspicari visus est quantae nobis admirationi haec sua negligentia futura esset.

Quamquam erroris problema Scholasticis in mentem non venit, eos tamen maxime natura actus fidei cruciabat. S. Thomas breviter hanc quaestionem tractavit, sed vertente saeculo quarto decimo magnum cominus praelium initum est. Nam omnes satis immodici in sua quisque sententia proponenda erant; Thomistis Scotistisque nimis intellectualistica, Nominalistis nimis voluntaristica sententia placebat; postea eremitae Augustiniani mediam quandam opinionem invexerunt, finem tamen belli non fecerunt. Illud enim, quod iam a Scoto propositum erat, denuo post renata in Hispania studia philosophica agitabatur, utrum enuntiatio mentalis dividenda sit in apprehensivam et iudicativam. Cui quaestioni cum aliis respondens Suarez iudicium esse ipsam nexus apprehensionem affirmavit; at ita efficitur ut in falso iudicio nexus qui non existat apprehendatur, id quod ne voluntas quidem imperare potest; praeterea, dum de fide tractat, suae de iudicio sententiae Eximius Doctor oblitus esse videtur et assensionem quandam a nexus apprehensione distinctam supponere non dubitavit. Neque praetereundum est eiusmodi contradictionem adhuc e scholastica doctrina non esse sublatam: aliud dici solet iudicium cum de primis principiis, aliud cum de fide vel de errore sermo est factus.

Quibus omnibus perspectis, magis interpres quam criticus ad mentem S. Thomae indagandam P. Keeler aggressus est, tamquam in hoc clarissimo philosopho non perfectam rei praetermissae solutionem sed utilissimas ad solutionem indicationes inventurum se crediderit. Illud praecipue ostendere contendit, aliam S. Thomae nexus apprehensionem fuisse, alium assensus actum; illam quasi in ordine pure intelligibili versari, hunc obiectivam intellectualis contenti existentiam affirmare. Qua ex distinctione deduci licet non ideo nos errare quod falsa apprehenderimus sed quod praecipites in assentiendo fuimus; dato quidem proprio intellectus obiecto ita non assentiri in nostra potestate non est ut assensus a nexus cognitione distinctus remaneat; contra, cum propositio sine plena evidentia menti se sistit, locus indebito voluntatis influxui praebetur. Quod solutionis fundamentum non ipsam solutionem auctor denominat; mirum sane ait futurum fuisse, si S. Thomas, quamvis tantum tamque difficile problema numquam opera data investigasset, per occasionem illud leviter in transitu attingens plane solvisset.

Quod si auctor in exponenda S. Thomae doctrina his fere finibus se continuit, non certe vana quaedam modestia eum deterrebat, perinde ac si iam cuiusvis esset totam rem dirimere. Quin immo, illud et nos in contrariam partem afferre velimus quod quilibet ad haec de Suarezi schola responderit: aut apprehendi aut non apprehendi illam obiectivam intellectualis contenti existentiam; nam ea si apprehenditur, non est cur ulterius vel iterum assensu quodam ponatur, sed ipsa apprehensione iamiam sufficienter affirmari videtur; si vero non apprehenditur, non est cur umquam rationabiliter fiat assensus; sola illa conspicitur ratio cur assentiendi vel facultas vel functio existat ut, dato insufficienti affirmandi motivo, homo perversus et improbus perperam iudicare possit! At esto hoc fieri posse, tamen error nondum explicatur. Dicis enim voluntatem indebite influere. An eo usque influit voluntas ut qui falsa opinatur et illud credat, non propter voluntatis influxum sed propter obiectivam rerum evidentiam se ita opinatum esse? Quo concesso, de infallibilitate conscientiae actum esse nemo est quin videat. Haec argumenta, licet non satis explicata, tamen, si penitus considerentur ac iuste perpendantur, ad hanc quaestionem solvendam omnino pertinere putamus, nec quemquam iis prius satis facturum suspicamur quam luminis intellectualis naturam quamque rationem hoc lumen cum errore habere possit indagarit et perspexerit.

Iam vero silentium auctoris, qui hanc rem integram reliquit, libenter imitamur. Neque enim ei hoc silentium vitio vertendum est, qui opus historicum et criticum conscripturus alia, quae magis speculativa sunt, optimo iure omittere decreverit. Libet tamen etiam atque etiam rogare ut, postquam haec solida fundamenta iecerit, aliis quoque libris conscriptis exspectationi nostrae et cupiditate satis faciat.

Hoc unum querimur quod fato aliquo inviso factum est ut tot tamque praeposteris mendis typographicis totus liber aspersus sit. Alteram eamque emendatam editionem ut quam primum auctor curet expetimus et obsecramus.

20B

Review of L.W. Keeler, s.j.,
The Problem of Error, from Plato to Kant:
A Historical and Critical Study[1]

No one, I think, would disagree that the author of this work has succeeded admirably in achieving his purpose, namely, to examine carefully and assess the opinions of all the major philosophers regarding the problem of error and the opinions on this topic that have prevailed in successive schools of thought. For his treatment of the question is quite subtle and detailed and at the same time clearly outlined, yet the treatment of it by both ancient and more recent philosophers has been so inadequate that one would think they had left to us or our successors the glory of settling it. Since this book, therefore, throws a great deal of light upon a very abstruse matter and one that has not been satisfactorily treated by others, it is, in our judgment, a most valuable contribution to philosophical studies.

We shall leave aside, then, the many historical details about the emergence and development of this question which the author with great erudition has gathered and narrated, since there is no need to repeat them here. Our sole purpose in this review is to consider briefly (1) the nature of the problem of error, (2) how it has been dealt with up to now, and (3) what remains for contemporary philosophers to deal with in addressing it. In fact, although the author himself has expressly and properly discussed only this second point, nevertheless from the statements he makes and the criteria he uses one may easily gather what his opinions are regarding the first and third.

1   [An English translation by Michael G. Shields of the preceding Latin text.]

To begin with, the problem of error is simply the problem of truth under a different name and considered under a different aspect. For if we inquire about the formal cause of knowledge, it is clear that things by themselves alone cannot always specify and determine the content of our knowledge. If this were true, false knowledge could not be generated in any other way – unless perhaps the things themselves were false. Human knowledge, therefore, is not a mere matter of apprehending terms and nexuses, since it must be acknowledged that there is some other cause that either can or often does intervene in the cognitional process. What this is, what its nature is, and when and how it intervenes – this is properly what is meant by the problem of error. The extreme difficulty of this problem may be indicated by the following dilemma: it is apparent that some faculty, either cognitive or appetitive, must intervene in the process; if it is a cognitive faculty, there is the danger of destroying realism and certitude; but if it is an appetitive faculty, there is no way to explain (apart from some unconscious psychoanalytic transmutation of good into truth) why someone who is in error always vehemently maintains that his opinion rests solidly upon objective evidence.

Both reason and, above all, experience make it clear that error can arise from no other source than the very objects to be known, since in fact we regard the position of those who reject realism to be bankrupt. And so, to summarize Father Keeler's lengthy and accurate explanation, for this reason alone it seems necessary to reject the theory of Spinoza, inasmuch as he thought the world to be so well ordered that he was compelled to say that error is the privation of an undue good. Next, Hume's pure phenomenalism is incompatible with error, unless the phenomena were somehow to contradict themselves. Finally, whether Kant's notion of truth is considered as mere coherence or as a certain correspondence between the mind and an object, it follows that those unchangeable laws of the mind could always produce only the same results, but never give rise to human contradictions.

Setting aside such speculations, then, let us go back to those doctrines of past ages which, we would suggest, could rightly be called the thesis, antithesis, and synthesis of the problem (I do not say, of its solution): Greek logic, Stoic ethics, and the medieval doctrine about faith. For while these three ways of dealing with the problem were finished and complete in themselves, Descartes saw the problem of error everywhere and introduced the study of criteriology. But as to its solution, since he was quite consistent with himself, he uttered that absurd and outrageous dictum,

'Judgment is will.'[2] We shall briefly explain by what turnings and twistings this whole question of error arrived at this point.

In the course of their eristic controversies, the Greek Sophists, besides the 600–odd[3] topics, serious and frivolous, which they treated indiscriminately, debated the problem of error with their typical cleverness. Plato wrote against them in several dialogues but especially in *The Sophist*, in which we may see foreshadowed Aristotle's doctrine on terms and propositions and also on the place of error in coming to a judgment. With the complete working out of this doctrine and the discovery of the syllogism, one might say that the stage was set for a serious study of the problem of error; but Aristotle seems to have shied away from this task, at one time saying that the mind (*nous*) is the cause of error and at another time that it is infallible, in matters of logic declaring error to be simply a defective syllogism, and in matters of ethics blaming it on the allurement of pleasure.

After Aristotle there was general agreement among philosophers that judgment was somehow free and voluntary, though they did not say how this could be. So, for example, the Pyrrhonists, who taught that all assent should be withheld; so also the Stoics and Epicurus, who tried to explain error on such a basis. St Augustine himself tacitly accepted this current opinion of the age without ever suspecting, it seems, how amazed we would be at this negligence on his part.

Although it did not occur to the Scholastics to consider the problem of error, the nature of the act of faith was a vexed question for them. St Thomas treated this question only briefly, but in the fourteenth century a great battle was joined. All sides went to extremes in propounding their views. The opinions of the Thomists and Scotists were overly intellectualistic, those of the Nominalists too voluntaristic. Later, the Hermits of St Augustine proposed an intermediate opinion, but that did not end the war. Following the revival of philosophical studies in Spain there was considerable discussion of a question previously proposed by Scotus, namely, whether mental propositions are of two distinct kinds, apprehensions and judgments. To this question Suárez, among others, answered that a judgment is simply the apprehension of a nexus; but the consequence of this is that in a false

2 [See Keeler's discussion of Descartes on pp. 162–77 of *The Problem of Error.*]

3 [Obviously an expression for an indefinite large number. Lonergan uses it again in *Divinarum Personarum Conceptio Analogica*, p. 18: 'And there are 600-odd further points that call for a new kind of understanding.' (Lonergan, *The Triune God: Systematics*, vol. 12 in Collected Works of Bernard Lonergan, trans. Michael G. Shields, ed. Robert M. Doran and H. Daniel Monsour (Toronto: University of Toronto Press, 2007) 753.]

judgment a nonexistent nexus is apprehended – something that not even the will can command. Moreover, in his treatment of faith Suárez seems to have forgotten what he had said about judgment and had no hesitation in supposing some assent to be different from an apprehension of a nexus. And we should not overlook the fact that this sort of contradiction has not yet been eliminated from Scholastic philosophy, holding judgment to be one thing when speaking of first principles, and another thing when speaking of faith or error.

Accordingly, Keeler has undertaken his investigation of the mind of St Thomas more as an interpreter than as a critic, as if he felt that in this illustrious philosopher he would find, not the complete solution to a neglected problem, but rather helpful pointers towards a solution. His main objective is to show that for St Thomas the apprehension of a nexus is one thing and the act of assent is another, and that the former exists in the purely intelligible order while the latter affirms the objective existence of an intellectual content. From this distinction we may conclude that we err, not because we have apprehended what is false, but because we have been precipitate in assenting. When presented with the proper object of the intellect, we are powerless to withhold assent, such that assent remains distinct from knowledge of a nexus; on the other hand, when a proposition is present in the mind without complete evidence for it, there is an opening for the will to exercise undue influence. The author calls this a basis for a solution, not the solution itself; and it would surely have been quite remarkable, he says, if St Thomas, who had never deliberately addressed this very difficult problem, had nevertheless completely solved it when occasionally touching upon it in passing.

If in his exposition of St Thomas's thought the author has confined himself within these limits, it is certainly not out of false modesty, as if anyone could now settle the entire question. However, we ourselves, taking the opposite course, wish to state the objections that anyone might make to these arguments of the Suarezian school: the objective existence of an intellectual content is either apprehended or it is not; for if it is apprehended, there is no reason why it should be further affirmed or affirmed again in some act of assent, but seems rather to be already sufficiently affirmed in that apprehension itself. But if it is not apprehended, there is no reason why assent is ever reasonably given. The sole reason why a faculty or a function of assenting exists appears to be that, when the motive for affirming is insufficient, a perverse and bad person may be able to make a bad judgment! But supposing this could be so, error is still not yet explained. For you say that the will has undue influence. Or is the will influential to this extent, that one who has erroneous opinions also believes that he holds those opinions, not because of the influence of the will, but because of objective evidence of things? If this is granted, then obviously that means the end of the infallibility of consciousness. We believe that these arguments, even though not fully developed, nevertheless if considered carefully and weighed fairly are certainly part of the solution to this question, and we suspect that no one will do them justice who has not investigated and clearly understood the nature of intellectual light and the relation this light can have with error.

But now we shall be happy to imitate the silence of the author, who left this matter aside. Nor is this silence to be held against him, since his intention was to write a work of critical history, and he rightly chose to omit more speculative matters. We would earnestly beg him, however, now that he has laid these solid foundations, to satisfy our eager expectations in further writings.

Our sole complaint is that by some cruel fate the book abounds with so many egregious typographical errors. We implore the author to get out a corrected edition as soon as possible.

21

Review of E.I. Watkin, *The Catholic Centre*[1]

The Catholic Centre is conceived both as a criterion of truth and as a norm of action. Because Catholicism is central, it is true. Because this centrality is an ideal never perfectly achieved, Catholics must ever strive to achieve it.

The work is not a treatise. Disregarding the genres of the specialists, Mr Watkin meditates in public on the liturgy as the perfect expression of the Catholic Centre and on adoration as its inner spirit. A philosopher, he relates it to the antitheses of idealism and realism, rationalism and irrationalism, fluidity and fixity, divine immanence and divine transcendence. His atmosphere is less rarefied when Buchmanism[2] leads him to write on guidance in prayer, modern sensitiveness calls for an essay on the problem of suffering, and the dangers of institutional religion inspire a homily on unconsciously materialistic deformations of the Catholic attitude. Traditionally central is his splendid analysis of the concept of law and his contention that centrality cannot be too central: the Catholic Centre is not a compromise; one must 'come in' or 'go out'; one must tend to the perfection of the saints or sink towards infidelity.

Perhaps the fundamental value of the work is apologetic. A convert has peculiar advantages in this field, and Mr Watkin writes persuasively for the highly cultivated mind that in England frequently finds its way to Rome.

1 New York: Sheed & Ward, 1939, 247 pp. [*The Montreal Beacon* 6 (28 June 1940) 5. Editorial heading: 'Catholics Must Ever Strive ...']
2 [An evangelical religious movement founded at Oxford in 1921 by American-born Frank Buchman (1878–1961) to promote individual and national moral regeneration (Moral Re-Armament).]

Appreciative of religious values, fond of balanced discussion, unconsciously convinced of the futility of pure theory – a conviction that is part of the national culture – such a mind will find its sensibilities delicately honored, its objections forestalled, its manifold tendencies towards the Catholic Centre encouraged by this genial flow of positive affirmation and earnest criticism, of keen analysis and winning explanation.

However, the author's intention is not merely apologetic. The centrality of Catholicism is an ideal, and this not only supplies an answer to those who would argue from the poor fish in Peter's net to the inadequacy of his bark, but also is a premise to a number of fresh conclusions, advocated developments, desirable reforms. Here, while the fundamental principles are indisputable and the fact that the issues are raised is extremely wholesome, it remains, I think, regrettable that the treatment of them is so summary as to be open to an equally summary charge of amateurishness. It is not to be fancied that the author attempts to settle all manner of questions with a phrase, after the fashion of the pontifical novelist or columnist. When I used the term 'amateurish,' I had in mind the highest standards of Catholic thought, that centrality of form and method which by an untiring effort for explicit articulation achieves the universalism characteristic of Scholasticism.

As is plain, Watkin could not have sought such universalism, such centrality of expression and argument, without sacrificing his appeal to the eccentric milieu for which, perhaps, he primarily writes. But there is a deeper antinomy than that of explaining the centre to those on the periphery. The author is a profound and original thinker with a contribution to make, both to Catholic philosophy and to the orientation of theology; but, because he does not dominate these fields as a master, he is impotent to effect the developments he would see realized. The only way to improve a trade is to practice it better than its professionals.

This difficulty, a greater man though not so keen a philosopher, Cardinal Newman, could not overcome. His success and the unquestioned value of his work may well encourage Watkin not to be unduly depressed if 'old Catholics' venture to criticize. As he himself maintains, things may not be infallibly right and yet be infallibly profitable.

22

Review of Moses Coady, *Masters of Their Own Destiny*[1]

Moses M. Coady's *Masters of Their Own Destiny* is now in its second French edition; the original English is published by Harper's. It must be read by everyone interested in modern problems. Through its pages breathes the authentic spirit of Canada, a Canada facing the new age, facing its fundamental economic problem, and attaining a solid solution that is the admiration of the hemisphere.

Universal Application

It is sometimes thought that the method employed by the Antigonish Movement[2] cannot be applied universally, that it can work only under such special circumstances as are found in northeastern Nova Scotia. Nothing could be further from the truth. The essence of the cooperative movement

1 New York: Harper's Publishing, 1939, xi + 170 pp. [*The Montreal Beacon* 50 (2 May 1941) 3. Editorial introduction:
'*Quebec's Opportunity*
The social function of the popular school is to train and equip the masses for economic independence. Unless the masses achieve economic independence, we are doomed to the quiet death of uninspired regimentation under an intellectually insignificant bureaucracy.']
2 [The Antigonish Movement is described as follows at http://www.stfx.ca/institutescoady/text/about_antigonishmovement: 'The Antigonish Movement is a people's movement for economic and social justice that began in Nova Scotia, Canada during the 1920s. This local community initiative originated as a response to the poverty afflicting farmers, fishers, miners and other disadvantaged groups in Eastern Canada. Two prominent founders of the

is to teach free enterprise to those who in a regime of free enterprise have not had the initiative to look out for themselves.

Why does the proletariat today include almost everyone? Why is the control of industry in the hands of fewer and fewer? Radically it is our own fault. We leave our affairs to others, because we are too indolent and too stupid to get to work and run them ourselves. The results are palpably ruinous: our system of free enterprise cannot survive if only a few practise free enterprise.

Practical Education

Masters of Their Own Destiny is a singularly pertinent book to present discussion. It shows in the concrete what practical education is. It reveals how ignorant, how unimaginative, how narrow-minded, how shortsighted, how stupidly selfish is the human material with which the economic reformer has to deal. It provides the educator with very concrete and very definite objectives.

In particular, it explodes a specious fallacy. It will do us not the slightest good if we establish the world's finest technical schools and, at the same time, fail to teach the technique of economic independence as it is taught by the St Francis Xavier [University] Extension Department. If our schools produce more competent technicians, then the companies will be able to have a greater product with less labor; unemployment will increase and wages will decrease; the companies will be unable to sell their greater product, and this will increase unemployment and decrease mass purchasing power still more; the government will have to undertake vast relief schemes, and the taxes will ruin the companies. There is no way out along such lines.

The technical training needed at the present time is in the technique of cooperation. That first of all and most of all. That can change the face of the province as it has changed eastern Nova Scotia, Sweden, Finland. Nothing else can or will.

---

movement, Rev. Jimmy Tompkins and his cousin, Rev. Dr Moses Coady, were teaching at St Francis Xavier University and saw the need to reach out to the rural areas. They used a practical and effective strategy of adult education and group action, which began with the immediate needs of the local people. The Antigonish Movement enabled people to change their lives and their futures. Over the next two decades, this pioneering effort in university education became known worldwide as the Antigonish Movement.']

Once the technique of cooperation is grasped, then all else follows easily. People will see before them the vision of economic independence; they will understand the necessity of study; they will cooperate with teachers in making their children do their lessons faithfully and well; they will welcome every opportunity to learn, for they will realize that that is the one condition of their survival and, at the same time, of the survival of free institutions.

Quebec's Opportunity

The province of Quebec is in an extremely fortunate position. Walter Lippmann, the profound American commentator, recently accused American educationalists of having successively thrown overboard every part of the cultural heritage of western civilization.[3] That accusation cannot be made against Quebec. Our universities stand in the oldest and finest European tradition; see the splendid article by Professor E.R. Adair on the 'Teaching of History at McGill' in the recent number of *Culture*, the Franciscan quarterly.[4] Our classical colleges are stamped with the sixteenth-century humanistic movement that lies at the root of all modern developments. If it is true that our popular schools appear ill adapted[5] to popular needs, it is also true that this lack of adaptation lies in the absence of positive social inspiration in the nineteenth-century movement that created state popular schools. For that reason this defect is not peculiar to Quebec but recognized to be universal: obviously if there is not a social idea, there cannot be a practical end for popular education.

But what the nineteenth century failed to conceive, the twentieth makes manifest: the social function of the popular school is to train and equip the masses for economic independence. It is a vast task, but a necessary task

---

3 [Walter Lippmann, 'Education versus Western Civilization,' *The American Scholar* 10:2 (Spring 1941) 184–93. Originally an address delivered under the auspices of Phi Beta Kappa at the annual meeting of the American Association for the Advancement of Science, Irvine Auditorium, University of Pennsylvania, 29 December 1940. See also the content of Quotation 1605 in *Respectfully Quoted: A Dictionary of Quotations*, ed. Suzy Platt (Washington, DC: Library of Congress, 1989), from a speech that Lippmann gave to the Harvard Class of 1910 at their thirtieth reunion, 18 June 1940.]

4 [Lonergan is probably referring to 'The Study of History at McGill University,' in *Culture: Sciences Religieuses et Sciences Profanes au Canada* 2 (1941) 51–62.]

5 [The editors have changed the printed 'inadapted' to 'ill adapted.']

and the clear goal of the historical forces at present in ferment. Unless the masses achieve economic independence, then we are doomed to the quiet death of uninspired regimentation under an intellectually insignificant bureaucracy. Democracy will be a noble experiment that failed.

To meet this challenge of the age, Quebec, I say, is in an extremely fortunate position. It has in abundance the leaders that can define and diffuse the inevitable social ideal of our time. The Antigonish Movement attributes its success basically to the broad culture its originators received in Quebec, Montreal, and Rome. The technical inspiration of the movement lies in England. The success of the execution was derived from training received in Canadian schools of agriculture and economics. We have the same roots, the same heritage. We have few of the blunders of educational experiment to correct. If we want to, we can set to achieving the real task of popular education on its practical side.

But remember, legislators can pass wise laws in vain. All depends on the initiative and the devotion of those who carry them out.

23

Book Notice of Jacques Maritain, *The Living Thoughts of St. Paul*[1]

M. Maritain grasps St Paul as the first and greatest of the stream of converts who have illumined the church: he was a Hebrew of the Hebrews, who nevertheless broke the cords of cultural limitation to perceive and announce the universality of the Gospel, the primacy of the spiritual, and the liberty of the sons of God; he was a thinker whom the categories of abstract thought may chart but cannot represent. His doctrine is presented in seven well chosen extracts from the Epistles, which are preceded by an Introduction and a sketch of St Paul's life, and are linked together by Maritain's brief explanatory reflections. The Westminster Version of the text is used, with occasional alterations. Professional exegetes may enter some reserves with regard to points of interpretation, but at any rate it is to be hoped that the book, in Mr Binsse's adequate translation, will render a service to the vast numbers who are more worthy of rebuke than were Chrysostom's audiences.

---

1 Trans. Harry Lorin Binsse, New York and Toronto: Longmans, Green and Company, 1941, 161 pp. [*Theological Studies* 3 (1942) 310–11.]

24

Review of Caryll Houselander,
This War Is the Passion[1]

The 'Grail' is a movement of deep spiritual culture that slipped over to English girls from Holland when the J.O.C. moved majestically from Belgium to France.[2] It is part and parcel of the general 'secession of the proletariat' of our time: a movement of souls, alienated by the vacuous hopes and strident stupidity of our civilization, and gathering round various centers to grow inwardly and then burst outwardly in the creation of a new order. Such centers are manifold. For if our Western culture is everywhere the same dry rot, if the human spirit is always the same, it remains that the splendid vision of truth is not grasped equally by all. Accordingly, one may discern a mystical faith, an ardent devotion, a heroic enterprise no less in communists or racialists than in *jocistes* or followers of the Grail; for faith

1 New York: Sheed & Ward, 1941, x + 185 pp. [*The Canadian Register* 7 (11 April 1942) 5. Editorial caption: 'A Book for Our Days. Spirituality and War.']
2 [The Grail was founded as a movement of Catholic laywomen in Holland in 1921 by Jacques van Ginneken, s.j., a professor at the University of Nijmegen, and a group of his students. The movement unites married and single women of all races, backgrounds, and professions in a common effort to bring spiritual values to all areas of modern society.

The Jeunesse Ouvrière Chrétienne (JOC) is a movement of young workers founded by Joseph (later Cardinal) Cardijn (1882–1967) as a curate in Belgium. The movement spread first in Belgium and France, and then throughout the world in a variety of spiritual movements. Its characteristic organization of small groups for the apostolate of 'like to like' and its method of formation (see-judge-act) were widely adopted and praised by Pius xi and succeeding popes.]

and devotion and enterprise are the very fiber of any human effort to create anew what has decayed. Still, the measure of the works of man is not the effort but what that effort serves. If the goal is a foul and narrow material- ism, there result the hideous perversions of communism and industrialism. If the goal is a proud and exclusive racialism, there results the terrible thun- der of the Nazi beast and machine. If the goal is the imitation of Christ, then no matter what the storm of troubles nor the virulence of persecution, Christ must arise in the new Easter of a renascent Christendom. It was so when Rome had its Indian summer under the Antonines,[3] then crumbled and vanished in the wandering of barbarian war-bands; for the answer to that abomination of desolation was the creative work of Augustine and Benedict, Gregory and Hildebrand, the work that made European culture the finest of all time. It is so again today when Europe stands in ruins and a new challenge goes forth to the wide world to create once more.

The mystical faith of the Grail is also the faith of St Paul and the Catholic Church, faith in the Mystical Body of Christ in whom we all are one, from whom we draw the bread and bloodstream of life, to whom we return in the consummation of charity that thinks no evil and refuses no good. This faith is dynamite. Even though the many carry it about carefully encased against the spark of generosity, still every now and then it does explode in a Curé d'Ars, a Don Bosco, a Thérèse, a Bernadette of Lourdes. Nor is our day any exception. On the contrary, the sterile encasement of dull use and wont is wearing thin. Explosions are easier to provoke than to prevent. Among them is the Grail that has drunk deep of the traditions of Catholic spirituality and has found in the peculiar conditions of the war in England a chance to prove its mettle.

This War Is the Passion is not a study in speculative history, though it might be. It is a series of essays originally written for the *Grail Magazine*, some before the war was thought of, others less polished but more tense and vital, minted by the war itself. In them the deep spiritual culture of the Grail leaps to flame – a flame as practical as an acetylene torch, as realistic as the soul of a young woman who meets the challenge of her life and day

---

3 ['Antonines, a collective name of certain Roman emperors of the second century, namely Antoninus Pius (86–161); his adopted sons, Marcus Aurelius (121–180) and Lucius Verus; and Commodus (161–192).' The 'Indian sum- mer' of the Pax Romana ended with Commodus. *The Columbia Encyclopedia*, 6th ed. (New York: Columbia University Press, 2001–2005).]

without blinkers. Among a people uprooted, reassorted, organized in a total war, taught fear and pain, fatigue and privation, and the great sorrow we too witness in the homes of our war-bereaved, the question is not whether one chooses to suffer. Too obviously Donoso Cortés, that profound and neglected philosopher of nineteenth-century Spain,[4] was right in summing up the vast long scroll of mankind in a single phrase: 'Blood must flow; the only question is whether it flows in hatred or in love.'[5] Where the natural man hates and, like Jan Valtin,[6] draws strength from his hatred, where the communist disseminates lies to hate the more, the Christian has to love. Calm-eyed, deft, exact, Caryll Houselander analyzes hatred, the hatred that springs from fear which all feel, the hatred that springs more nobly all about her from indignation at a planned and wanton slaughter of the innocents. She cannot ride rough-shod to a facile victory; yet she does do much to enable those who share her spirit to fulfil in some poor way the commandment of loving one's enemies when sirens have shrieked and the ack-acks roar and bombs tumble down for hours. Our oneness in Christ is the intuition she knows must be lived. To see Christ in the wounded, to see him in the surging mass of destitute without food or clothing or homes, to live Christ in the aching fatigue and crushing monotony of a nurse's nights in a first-aid hut or a worker's shift at the machines, to relax in Christ lest nervous prostration overtake one, how to pray with a mindless body, with the senses, with a throbbing head in the relentless routine of total war, why and how to learn to suffer, what to hope – these are her practical themes.

They are practical. Lesser souls can be betrayed. They may feel that a war begun pretentiously in the high name of Christian civilization is being prostituted by press magnates and political agitators to intrigue and calumny and hatred and the miasmic materialism exhaled by the world about us. Caryll Houselander cannot be betrayed. The glorious Easter of her

4   [Donoso Cortés (1809–1853) was a Spanish statesman and writer on philosophy, politics, history, and theology. His early writings and speeches espoused a bourgeois liberalism but he later moved towards a quasi-theological traditionalism and conservatism.]
5   [The editors were unsuccessful in locating the source of this remark in Cortes's writings.]
6   [Richard Julius Herman Krebs, alias Jan Valtin, was an active member of the Communist Party in the 1920s and 1930s. As a professional revolutionary, agitator, spy, and would-be assassin, Krebs traveled the globe from Germany to China, India to Sierra Leon, Moscow to the United States, where an attempted assault landed him a stint in San Quentin.]

journey's end is not an organization, nor a political movement, nor even the flush of successful propaganda. It is the good deed crying to be done here and now, with no red tape. It is growing in Christ, being him more and ever more in his adoration of the eternal Father, in his vicarious satisfaction for our day's heaped-up mountain of sin, in his compassion that not only tries to alleviate suffering but also seeks to share the sufferings of others. Strip off all things – possessions, homes, friends, careers, leisure, privacy, even our prized opportunities for Mass, the sacraments, the nourishing and the spreading of the faith by schools and press and wireless – still we have our bodies and our souls to give to God, and that was all Christ had, that was all the Apostles had, nor were they unsuccessful dying without issue. Who stakes life and soul on that achievement cannot be betrayed. Such a one is the salt of the earth, the light of the world, mothering the Christian civilization that will arise on the ruins of this war. For this war is the Passion, and its Easter a renascent Christendom.

'Lo, the Kingdom of God is within you!' [Luke 17.21]. Passiontide and Easter are not separate events, nor is the Christian a utopian or millenniarist. The Risen Christ rises again as secretly as on the midnight that followed his thirty hours in the tomb. He rises in hearts of which he takes charge, in which he imperiously rules, on which he has made a mark that doubt and weariness, confusion and relapse can cover over but rarely can efface. For such, *This War Is the Passion* may be a precious book, for its repeated flashes of spiritual insight transcend the movement from which it sprang and the circumstances under which it was written. Like all intense spirituality, it can be misinterpreted by the wrongheaded. But that is a danger no honest son or daughter of the church need fear, provided that they will be guided. St Bernard wrote to a pupil that had become Pope: he who has himself for a master has a fool for disciple.[7] The call to sanctity can be

---

7 [St Bernard (1090–1153) wrote an ascetical treatise, *De Consideratione*, to a fellow Cistercian and former pupil, Eugenius III (1145–53). For one English translation, see *Five Books on Consideration: Advice to a Pope*, Cistercian Fathers Series, The Works of Bernard of Clairvaux, vol. 13, trans. John D. Anderson and Elizabeth T. Kennan (Kalamazoo, MI: Cistercian Publications, 1976; 2nd printing, 1982). The piece of advice Lonergan cites here seems not to be a direct quote but a paraphrase of the substance of book 2, paragraph 11, pp. 59–60. An earlier and more exact wording of the advice can be found in Letter XXIV to Oger, Regular Canon of St Nicholas des Prés monastery, who had resigned his abbacy against the advice of Bernard: 'For he who makes himself his own master, subjects himself to a fool as his master.' Bernard goes on to cite his own experience that 'it is far more easy and safe to govern many others than my own single self.']

transmuted into temptations that lie outside ordinary experience, that might deceive even the elect. Against them stands the rock of Peter, which, in the double rhythm of its secular expansion is organizational as well as mystical, authoritative as well as inspired by individuals without authority, in a word, organic. 'But in all these things, one and the same Spirit worketh, dividing to everyone according as he will' [1 Corinthians 12.11].

25

Review of Dietrich von Hildebrand,
Marriage[1]

In the Nietzschean 'revaluation of all values' that has been and remains the main preoccupation of our time, marriage was among the latest to undergo the sea-change. As late as the nineteenth century, full three hundred years after the German reformer repudiated reason and the Tudor got himself another wife and church, the sacrosanctity of marriage remained an inviolate principle. Ruskin, inveighing against the industrial revolution, attacked the since rarer pharisaism of believing that to be the complacent and righteous father of a dozen children was to observe the whole Law and the Prophets. Huxley blithely tossed God and Christianity aside yet insisted on the supreme value of Christian morality. Marx, with his communism of wives, got himself no more in his own age than the reputation of a lunatic. It was reserved for our contemporaries to be more coherent and thorough in their ardor of destruction. Thus artists like D.H. Lawrence wished sex purified of all intellectualism that man might be engulfed in the simpler rhythms of lower life-forms. Psychologists in the wake of Freud became obsessed with repressions and aimed at procuring their victims a balanced mind by encouraging a moderate and systematic indulgence in vice. Eugenists now

1 New York and Toronto: Longmans, Green and Co., 1942, vi + 64 pp. [*The Canadian Register* 13 (23 May 1942) 5. Editorial caption: 'Christian Marriage. Values Sound – Doctrine Vague.' Von Hildebrand's book was written in German. No translator is mentioned on the English title page, but at the end of the preface we read, 'I want to express my deep gratitude to Dr. Emmanuel Chapman and Mr. Daniel Sullivan for all their help in the translation of this little book.']

are captivated with the ideal of scientific breeding and, no doubt, look forward to the utopia when the whole citizen body will be guinea pigs for their laboratory. More modest social workers set their hearts on the immediate goal of more divorces and fewer children for the proletariat. Governments dare not venture, even in the present rubber shortage, to interfere with the big business – over $250,000,000 a year in the U.S. alone – of supplying inefficacious contraceptive devices. Publishing houses, magazine editors, film magnates appear convinced that the sale of their products on the grand scale is a matter of striking the right note in salaciousness. For all to see, the revaluation of the value of married life is pretty much a fact, and to so ingenuous a child of our day as J.W. Krutch[2] nothing perhaps is more amusing than the way in which the Victorians sublimated an elemental biological urge with the high-sounding phrase, 'The world well lost for love.'[3]

Against this biological materialism, which considers love no more than a matter of endocrine glands and hormones,[4] Dietrich von Hildebrand reacts by setting forth in a first chapter the natural significance of conjugal love and, in a second, its supernatural significance as a sacrament. As an antidote to the poisonous dogmas current in magazines, novels and pseudo-scientific books, this work is excellent. God created man and woman, he created them one for the other; he saw that his work was good. Christ is the bridegroom and the church is his spouse; St Paul bids husbands to love their wives as Christ has loved his Church; and towards the attainment of this ideal love the sacrament of marriage incorporates husband and wife in a special way in the Mystical Body of Christ.

2 [Joseph Wood Krutch (1893–1970), an American scholar, academic, and naturalist. He taught at Columbia University 1937–52, giving courses on English Drama from Dryden to Sheridan and on Modern Drama from Ibsen to the present. He published critical studies of Samuel Johnson, Edgar Allen Poe, and Henry David Thoreau, and was the drama critic for *The Nation* 1924–52. He later turned to lyrical writing about the life of the desert, after his move to Tucson, Arizona, in 1952. Lonergan likely has in mind his book *The Modern Temper: A Study and a Confession* (New York: Harcourt, Brace and Co., 1925; 6th printing, 1933) and in particular his chapter on 'Love – or the Life and Death of a Value' (84–114) and his chapter on 'The Tragic Fallacy' (115–43).]

3 [The phrase derives, it seems, from the title of John Dryden's 1678 play *All for Love; or, The World Well Lost*, which is a reworking of Shakespeare's play *Antony and Cleopatra*.]

4 [For representative passages, see Krutch, *The Modern Temper* 101–102 and 136–37.]

However, the work aims at being something more than an antidote to contemporary aberrations as well as something more than a correction of the uninstructed or unbalanced view that sex is not so much sacred as nasty. From the preface and from repeated remarks in the course of the exposition, one can gather that the author considers these pages to be an original contribution to the philosophy and the theology of marriage. In this claim there is this much truth, that the movement originating with von Hildebrand not only has not been condemned but, in the opinion of perhaps all writers in theological reviews, contains elements that are destined to enrich Catholic thought. On the other hand, the most downright member of this school, Dr Herbert Doms, whose *Von Sinn und Zweck der Ehe* was published incompletely in English as *The Meaning of Marriage* (Sheed & Ward),[5] received a very deliberate though unofficial rebuke from the Master of the Holy Office; and while von Hildebrand carefully avoids not only the more venturesome formulae but even the very name of Doms, it remains that he shares in the latter's fundamental outlook.

Von Hildebrand's affirmation is this: while the primary end of marriage is the procreation and education of children, the primary meaning of marriage is love, the natural love intended by God when he made Adam a helpmate like unto himself, the supernatural love intended by Christ when he raised marriage into the sacrament that showed forth his own love for his spouse, the church. The difficulty is the studied vagueness of the position. A book has been written on *The Meaning of Meaning*,[6] and it concluded that 'meaning' has over eight hundred meanings. Which of these is meant by von Hildebrand, what is a primary meaning, what would be a secondary meaning, are so many questions conveniently left without an answer. So far is such lack of precision from Catholic philosophy and theology that it reminds one rather of Anglican comprehensiveness. It would indeed be

---

5 [Herbert Doms, *Von Sinn und Zweck der Ehe* (Brelsau: Ostdeutsche Verlagsanstalt, 1935); *The Meaning of Marriage* (New York: Sheed & Ward, 1939). For further information on Dr Doms and the subject of marriage, see *Collection*, 17–18 & nn. 2, 3; 41 nn. 65, 66; 46 n. 73.]

6 [The reference is likely to C.K. Ogden and I.A. Richards, *The Meaning of Meaning: A Study of the Influence of Language upon Thought and of the Science of Symbolism* (London: Kegan and Paul, 1936); see *Philosophical and Theological Papers 1958–1964*, vol. 6 in Collected Works of Bernard Lonergan, ed. Robert C. Croken, Frederick E. Crowe, and Robert M. Doran (Toronto: University of Toronto Press, 1996) 206 & n. 51. Note that here Lonergan says that the pair of authors 'arrived at 900 meanings for the English word "meaning."']

unjust to say that the author is combating biological materialism by reaffirming Victorian romanticism, for his roots are in the second chapter of Genesis and in the fifth of the Epistle to the Ephesians. On the other hand, it cannot be denied that he shares the romanticist vagueness and thinks in a misty middle distance where ideal love and plain fact merge.[7]

7 [For a series of letters touched off by Lonergan's review of von Hildebrand's book *Marriage*, see below, Appendix.]

26

Review of George Boyle,
Democracy's Second Chance[1]

George Boyle is a Wise Man from the East. Like his prototypes, he has seen a star and follows it. Besides the labor of editing the *Maritime Cooperator*, he has produced a book that bears fresh witness to the vitality, the realism, and the profundity of the social movement emanating from a Catholic and Canadian University, St Francis Xavier, Antigonish.[2]

To George Boyle there exists no question that democracy missed its first chance. Our modern world is very new as well as very bad. But Mr Boyle is not at all concerned to show the newness of our cities, our industries, our economic structures and techniques. What appalls him is their badness. The organic cap of the earth – the accumulated savings of the millennia that make the difference between a garden and a gravel pit – are being destroyed at a fantastic rate. The countryside is emptying into the cities. The cities have birthrates below the net reproduction rate, and among the offspring there is a disquieting tendency to neurasthenia. Again, the too closely knit urban society makes men mere cogs in worldwide depressions and wars; and men without a saving contact with the organic life of nature and its rhythms lose their mental ballast to plunge recklessly along the courses advocated by demonic genius.

To this vast challenge the only response is a Toynbeean 'Withdrawal and Return.' Obviously socialism is no solution, for that 'nationalization of capitalist errors' only puts more wealth into the hands of fewer, to redirect

---

1 New York: Sheed & Ward, 177 pp. [*The Canadian Register* 17 (20 June 1942) 5. Editorial caption: 'Path to the Future. Withdrawal and Return.']
2 [See above, p. 143, n. 2.]

careerists from business to palace intrigue and turn citizens into guinea pigs for the experiments of social theorists. A democratic solution has to be a program of education both intellectual and moral. But where are the sciences to be taught, and who are the teachers, and what is the hope that the mass of men would understand the lessons and carry them out? Such education on such a scale exceeds the limits of any schooling. It can be carried on only by the school of life itself. It has to be a withdrawal from the modern world and the creation of a new environment and culture under the inspiration of new values and new ideals.

A blueprint for at least part of such a withdrawal is the first section of Boyle's book. His exposition of 'Ideas and Attitudes that Underlie Rural Life' is an attempt to work out the ideals and values that must inspire a successful rural movement. Since at present it is ideas that make the farmer's brightest son gladly descend to the level of a clerk, since it is ideas that make farming appear a narrow and dreary life in comparison with an office or factory existence compensated by the conspicuous consumption of nationally advertised products, then, as in first aid, one must begin by removing the cause. Ideas are merely ideas: they can be changed. Silly ideas might be thought to be changed easily, but this change will require a thorough refashioning of rural educational programs and rural teachers and rural attitudes towards life. There must be created what has not yet existed, a distinctive rural culture. Country life must become self-sufficient emotionally and intellectually before it can attempt the economic self-sufficiency of withdrawing from the network of aberrations driving our world mad.

Despite an appearance of fragmentariness, the second section of the book really is integral with the first. There is needed a buffer state between the present world and the pioneers of the new. The cooperative movement supplies such a buffer. At once it provides the springboard towards a rural movement, the protection of such a movement in its early stages, and finally the nucleus of techniques that will make possible the return. For there is withdrawal only that there may be return, a return in which the achievements of the West may be integrated in a decentralist order through cooperatives and on the basis of the organic rhythms of rural life.

Naturally such a program raises a number of questions. One might be inclined to ask whether our economic and social structure is not rather a sick man needing treatment than a dying man awaiting burial. But really such an issue only affects the amplitude of the program envisaged. Undoubtedly there has to be a rebirth of rural living. Undoubtedly such a rebirth would be a most potent agent in the vast educational work that must accompany any democratic solution of social problems. Undoubtedly the organic and integral mentality fostered by a life in touch with nature has to spread through the whole fabric of society and completely oust the mechanist and fractional thinking that has landed us where we are. And if the last point is Mr Boyle's soundest claim to entitle his work 'Democracy's Second Chance,' it cannot fairly be objected that he aims merely at converting men from Descartes to Aristotle. For the mass of men know nothing of either philosopher, and, most likely, never will.

27

Review of Andrew J. Krzesinski, *Is Modern Culture Doomed?*[1]

The question is of manifest interest. It is not merely, 'What is to be done after the war?' It is, 'Are things already so bad that there is no hope for the future?'

The author's answer involves a distinction between the two poles in modern culture. There is the materialistic, anti-traditional tendency. Its obvious representative is in the field of economics: eighteenth-century capitalism, nineteenth-century communism and twentieth-century nazism. Such is the great materialist trinity: communism is a collectivist reaction against capitalist individualism; nazism is a nationalist reaction against the international character of finance and world revolution. Despite their differences and oppositions, all three agree in their dedication of man, soul and body, to the goods of this world. None of them acknowledges and submits to a higher end or a higher law for man. Their consequences are not a matter of abstract deduction. The experiment has been performed and still is being performed on the quivering body of humanity. The results are not pleasant.

But materialism is only one pole in modern culture. True, it rules most practical politics and newspapers, most popular books and universities. Still, it is not the whole show. There remains the traditional and Christian element in modern culture and its ever renewed vitality, its profound respect for the deeper and more real aspirations of man, its capacity to survive the

---

1 New York: Devin-Adair, 1942, 150 pp. [*The Canadian Register* 30 (19 September 1942) 8. Editorial caption: 'Significant Book. An Optimistic Answer.']

aberrations of noisy factions and seemingly powerful groups, give solid grounds for optimism. This is a viewpoint which propaganda agencies for the boosting of morale would do well to investigate.

The author was formerly a professor in the University of Cracow, the home of Copernicus, the pride of Poland. He writes with the peculiar distinction of the European scholar familiar with the thought of many lands and, if he does not mention Toynbee or Sorokin, it must be remembered not only that their works are recent but also that no one would expect to find such serious efforts in English. His approach to his problem is classical: he works out very excellent definitions of culture and of civilization and has sixty pages of fine analysis on the characteristics and implications of materialistic living. It has been impossible to convey to the reader any impression of the high quality of this analysis, for nearly all the author's sixty pages would be needed to do so. But the work is to be recommended wholeheartedly. With the degree of accuracy and refinement possible in its brief compass, it squarely meets the ultimate problem of our day.

28

Review of André Maurois,
I Remember, I Remember[1]

In the role of a French Anglophile, Maurois is best known to English letters. Indeed, his studies of Disraeli, of Shelley, of Byron, had been taken somewhat as a matter of course after his meteoric rise to fame in 1917. Then, at a time when the fortunes of war were low and nerve ends frayed, his *Silence of Colonel Bramble*[2] attained by art what diagnosis and explanation could never do. It gave the French an insight into the character of their allies; and it delighted the English to find a Frenchman who understood them so well. Still the book was by an unknown author. Not only was it his first; not only did his military superiors oblige him to use a pseudonym,[3] but he was not a man expected to write. For the liaison officer who became a noted writer in 1917 had been, before the war, a Jewish millowner and executive in a small provincial town near Rouen.

I Remember, I Remember recounts his exceptional life. His father, Ernest Herzog, had been, after 1870, a chief actor in transferring the family mill from annexed Alsace to French territory, managing the liquidation of the old property and organizing the migration of some four hundred Alsatian laborers to the new enterprise at Elbeuf. So it happened that into haunting

1 Trans. Denver Lindley and Jane Lindley. New York & London: Harper, 1942, vi + 310 pp. [*The Canadian Register* 52 (20 February 1943) 8. Editorial caption: 'An Autobiography. Exceptional Life Story of André Maurois.']
2 [André Maurois, *The Silence of Colonel Bramble*, trans. Thurfrida Wake; verses trans. Wilfred Jackson (New York and London: J. Lane Co., 1920). The original was published in 1918: *Les silences du colonel Bramble* (Paris: B. Grasset).]
3 [André Maurois is a pseudonym of Émile Salomon Wilhelm Herzog, his birth name.]

memories of lost Alsace as well as a closed Jewish family Émile was born in 1885. Till eight years of age the boy was taught privately, with English and German, music and horsemanship thrown in as extras; attractively enough, the riding master was the most successful. Next, he went to the local junior Lycée and, when twelve, began to commute daily by train to the Lycée Corneille in Rouen. Throughout the course he regularly took first place, in classics and literature, in mathematics and philosophy; his subsequent career is a tribute not only to the soundness of the curriculum but also to the excellence of the teachers. As Maurois remarks: 'Today, having traveled in many countries and observed many colleges, I can better realize the extraordinary good fortune we French students enjoyed in having as masters, when we were ten years old, men qualified to teach in any university in the world.'[4]

Though formal education ended at seventeen or eighteen (the chronological framework of the book is skimpy), its imprint was soul-deep and still remains. The year of military service, shared with Étienne Gilson, was flavored with literary nostalgia. Then, returning to Elbeuf and the woollen mill, he began to learn the trade from the ground up and in less than a decade, despite half-submerged longings for letters, he occupied a commanding position in the firm, having met and mastered a crisis that demanded a fairly complete transformation of the enterprise. Janine Marie Wanda de Szymkiewicz he met in Paris, wooed in Geneva, educated at Oxford,[5] and presented to his parents at Haguenau, where the Alsatian setting, fragrant with reminiscence, conquered them and other plans. The war followed the birth of a daughter, yet, kind in its cruel way, it brought forth the *Colonel Bramble* that opened to Maurois the doors of French literature, English society, and American universities. From then his life became public, and membership in the French Academy brought its triumphant crown in 1938.

I need not say that this autobiography is full of interest and entertainment; alone to the point is a word of assurance that Denver and Jane Lindley know translation as a fine art.[6] While a Catholic weekly cannot but

---

4 [*I Remember, I Remember* 21.]
5 [Maurois took Janine to England and arranged for her education at a school in Brighton and, later, supported her when she took courses at Oxford. See his own account, ibid. 93–95.]
6 [Both are explicitly indicated as the translators of this edition, which is the first part of Maurois's *Mémoires* (New York: La Maison française, 1942), translated later by Denver Lindley as *Memoirs, 1885–1967* (New York: Harper & Row, 1970).]

regret the decadence of the humanism in which Maurois was nurtured, it must, because Catholic, pay a tribute to any humanism in our inhuman day. The count of those who know letters and so can understand men dwindles perpetually. Foreign affairs are bungled by pressure groups without a shadow of insight into the culture and history and minds of other nations. Domestic affairs gain momentum as they approach the technician's utopia when a succession of 'security' plans will have made citizens into guinea pigs for the grand-scale experiments of commissars under the laboratory conditions guaranteed by a secret police. As Maurois found in France, the humanist with his love of reconciliation, of order, of spreading understanding, has little leverage in such a world. He does not command the vast monopolies of the printed word. He wastes his time addressing the vested interests of the right or the militant hatred of the left, for the modern breakup of humanism has followed the old breakup of religion, and only the cold steel arms of mechanized peace and war give distracted humanity a common factor. Still, on this dismal background, it is all the more a duty to bow low to a Jew, a French patriot, an academician, who was taught German in his boyhood by ex-Chancellor Bruning's aunt,[7] who was delighted as a young man with the lilting imperialism of Kipling's verse, who married the daughter of a Russian, and having toyed with socialism and played the industrialist, having met all the celebrities and left them, having made and lost a fortune, finds delight as well as refuge in the lecture halls of America. To his eternal credit be his refusal to jump on the press wagon of the calumniators of France.

7 [*I Remember, I Remember* 18–19.]

29

Review of Francis Stuart Campbell, *The Menace of the Herd*[1]

There is an increasing consciousness of the fact that men of good will have to join against the forces of destruction in the modern world. One of the most obvious struggles will be the next peace settlement, and in this regard the men of good will will have little more than their benevolence. Because, then, 'pep without purpose is piffle' and purpose without knowledge is impossible, there is a great debt of gratitude due to the author of this book. He has exceptionally intimate knowledge of Europe. He has great critical ability. He writes vividly, vigorously, entertainingly.

Perhaps his basic purpose may best be judged from a recent article he contributed to the distinguished Catholic quarterly, *Thought*,[2] in which he brings his own modes of expression into line with those of the noted Italian exile, Guglielmo Ferrero.[3] I think it was Disraeli who said that men

1 Milwaukee: The Bruce Publishing Co., 1943, xiv + 398 pp. [*The Canadian Register* 9 (24 April 1943) 5. The book carries a subtitle, *Procrustes at Large*. The author's name given here is a pseudonym for Erik von Kuehnelt-Leddihn, a learned Austrian Catholic philosopher. Editorial caption: 'Critical Commentary on Mass Democracy.']

2 [Francis Stuart Campbell, 'A Conservative's Reflections on the Future of Europe,' *Thought* 17 (September 1942) 499–512.]

3 [Guglielmo Ferrero (1871–1942), Italian journalist, novelist, and historian, who devoted his life and his writings to the cause of liberalism. When liberal intellectuals were forced to leave Italy in 1925, Ferrero refused and was placed under house arrest. In 1929, after officials of the League of Nations intervened, he was allowed to accept a professorship at Geneva.]

are governed either by force or by tradition.[4] In any case this disjunction squares very well with Ferrero's basic distinction between legitimate and illegitimate government, where 'legitimate' means simply that the government is accepted spontaneously, unquestioningly, loyally by the mass of the governed. With such an acceptance, force is superfluous; without it, force is a necessity, while the use of force only increases discontent and resistance to make still more force inevitable; the long-run consequence is a naked tyranny and, when opportunity arises, revolution.

In the light of this correlation, it follows that an essential requisite for a satisfactory treaty will not be the establishment of European governments on the model of the United States or of England or, for that matter, of any theoretic ideal; the essential requisite will be the establishment of governments capable of meeting acceptance by the governed and so capable of ruling without force, without persecuting minorities, without turning into tyrannies that effect a general instability and will result in another general collapse after another twenty years. To avert such a tragedy ensuing upon the second war for the rights of small nations – in the present case the now widely disregarded Poland – it is obviously necessary to prepare the public mind, to provide knowledge of Central Europe, to combat the widespread views that will make the next peace no better and no more successful than the last.

But if this was the author's aim, he does not make it sufficiently clear. For sufficient clarity is, as Cicero put it, not the possibility of being understood but the impossibility of being misunderstood. One reviewer took him to mean that in *The Menace of the Herd*, the herd is the people and the menace is democracy. But while such a view finds a great deal of confirmation in his pages, but no less in the popular support of Nazism in Germany, still it cannot be reconciled with his patent admiration of England or his unquestioning acceptance of the American Republic. After all, England and the United States have a better title to the name 'democracy' than Nazi Germany or Soviet Russia.

Perhaps the author has attempted too much in a single volume, but two criticisms, I think, go more deeply. In the first place, the author is not immune from archaism: I use the word in Toynbee's sense, who divided political thinkers, in times of crisis and disintegration, into futurists who wish to tear up everything by the roots to remodel the world on the pattern

4 [The editors have found some independent supporting evidence that words to this effect are attributed to Disraeli, but have been unsuccessful in locating the precise place where he wrote this, or the occasion on which he said it.]

of some theoretic ideal and, on the other hand, archaists who find the cause of all evils in the desertion of the retrospectively good old ways of a past that, unfortunately, is gone forever. No doubt the futurism of de la Bedoyère's Dawnists[5] is at present the great danger, but what is needed is not reaction but a definition of the mean. A second criticism is that the author has attempted to fit profound thoughts into striking images. The fit is Procrustean. The root of his 'herdism' is not any instinct but the lack of a supernatural orientation in life. Without the egalitarian justice of the Last Day, men inspired by memories of Christian ideals will insist on egalitarian justice in this world only to lose themselves, as today, in the cumulative, interlocking, and crushing evils of mass production, mass living, mass education, mass amusement, mass emotions, mass hatreds, and mass wars. That is the menace. What the author is dealing with in his earlier chapters is not any new contribution to political psychology but only another application of Aristotle's brilliant antithesis of true and false self-love (*Nicomachean Ethics*, IX, 8) and Augustine's theory of history in terms of two loves, love of the City of God and love of the City of the World. Even at the expense of reducing popular appeal, I think the author should have related his ideas to the traditional perspective.

Finally, to justify my initial paragraph, there are roughly 210 million Catholics and 65 million Protestants on the continent of Europe. Unless Christians in the United Nations (even in Canada despite our somewhat colonial status in foreign affairs) take an interest in their fate, then the peace settlement will be the exclusive work of Russia, powerfully backed by its international affiliations, and of our own Dawnist monopolists of the daily press and semi-educated parliamentarians. Under such auspices the peace risks being bungled. We have much to do, and Mr. Campbell offers more than stimulus to do it.

5   [On 'Dawnism,' see Michael de la Bedoyère, *Christian Crisis* (London: The Catholic Book Club, 1940) 36–58.]

30

Review of Harry M. Cassidy, Ph.D., *Social Security and Reconstruction in Canada*[1]

Over a century ago the classical economists divided social activities into two classes: the profitable and the unprofitable. The profitable were entrusted to the undoubted beneficence of intelligent self-interest. The unprofitable residue was handed over to the state. The inadequacy of this conception – social evils result from sloppy thinking – has presented us in the year 1943 with an economic system that runs only by fits and starts and with a political system overloaded with the ever mounting residue of unprofitable business.

Dr Cassidy's book – he calls it a *Tract for the Times* and avows its propagandistic intention – is concerned with the now enormous unprofitable residue. What is to be done about social insurance against old age, invalidity, sickness, industrial accident, unemployment? about family allowances? educational and recreational facilities? widows, orphans, and incompetent parents, housing, sanitation, preventive medicine, clinics, hospitals, asylums? juvenile and adult penal institutions? systems of probation and parole?

Dr Cassidy studies what Canada has done in a number of these fields, compares the results with those in three other countries, takes at face value the social-security platforms of our three political parties, and asks what have we to do. Though his discussions and answers, if compared with the

---

1 Toronto: The Ryerson Press, 1943, x + 197 pp. [*The Canadian Register* 7 (10 April 1943) 5. Editorial caption: 'Another Tract for Our Time.']

Beveridge Report,[2] merely scratch the surface, it remains that they are too nuanced and detailed to be reproduced satisfactorily in a review; fortunately there is no need to reproduce them, for the book itself is required reading. Outstanding, however, are his sense of political possibilities (or at least his universally conciliatory attitude), his stress on the essential importance of trained personnel and continuous field research, his insistence that Canada remedy, through sound organizational and administrative procedure on the federal, provincial, and municipal levels, the haphazard accumulation of more or less makeshift solutions that are our modest possession at present. Incidentally, are we not a modest people?

Comments, if in order, are slightly complex. The aims of 'social security and reconstruction' are the highest in quality: '"Come, you that are blessed by my Father, possess you the kingdom prepared for you from the foundation of the world. For I was hungry, and you gave me to eat; I was thirsty, and you gave me to drink; I was a stranger, and you took me in; naked and you covered me; sick, and you visited me; I was in prison, and you came to me." Then shall the just answer him, saying, "Lord, when did we see thee hungry and fed thee; thirsty and gave thee drink? And when did we see thee a stranger and took thee in? Or naked and covered thee? Or when did we see thee sick or in prison and came to thee?" And the king answering shall say to them: "Amen I say to you, as long as you did it to one of these my least brethren, you did it to me"' (Matthew 25.34–40).

It might be inferred that with social security Canadians will get to heaven by paying their taxes. However, there is a serious condition to the success of the program. No attempt whatever is made to discuss the economics of the $1,000,000,000 a year state expenditure. The author is a specialist. He discusses one technical issue: if you wish a plan for security, then this, very tentatively and approximately, is the way to go about it; and please remember that, should unemployment rise above, say, 8 percent, the plan can hardly be expected to work.

Though first-rate propaganda, it will not clarify popular thinking to give the name 'social security' to a method that breaks down when security is most needed. In particular, Catholics must not fancy that the reconstruction envisaged is the reconstruction of the social order in the sense of Pius XI; it is simply a reorganization of the residual (and mostly misplaced) governmental functions that have been multiplying and accumulating for

2   [*Social Insurance and Allied Services*, a Report by Sir William Beveridge, presented to Parliament, November 1942, 300 pp.]

a century under the evil influence of a mistaken economic system. Such reorganization does not go to the root of the matter; it merely works out an elaborate palliative for a monstrous disease.

Unless I am mistaken, Canadians want a cure and not a wheelchair. They want to be shown how to do things for themselves. They do not want to be the raw materials for social or economic engineers who attain their noble ends through propaganda, government fiat, vigorous taxation, and trained personnel. They do want to live a social life based upon the person's informed, intelligent, and organized freedom. That is the goal, distant, arduous, yet not desperate. To that in all things we must work, or our democracy is a fake. But meanwhile we must be content with interim policies; and in the long run we shall have to face deficiencies though not to the tune of a billion a year. From both of these viewpoints all that Dr Cassidy proposes merits full consideration.

31

Review of K.F. Reinhardt, *A Realistic Philosophy*[1]

It has been urged that too frequently the *philosophia perennis* passes from one book to another without passing through any mind. In the light of that complaint the present work must be judged an exception[al] outline of Scholastic philosophy. Dr Reinhardt, now engaged as professor of Germanic languages at Stanford University, has put into a book materials collected and developed during the past twelve years while he was conducting an extension course under the auspices of the University of California. Of German birth and education, the recipient of doctorates from the University of Freiburg, he was a publisher, an editor, and an author before turning professor in a foreign land. His experience makes Dr Reinhardt's main concern the orientation of mind necessary for the solution of current problems of reconstruction. With this concrete end in view, he discourses with a remarkable wealth of general erudition upon such staple topics as being, the existence of God, human freedom, ethical and political laws, the state, justice, the dignity of labor, ownership.

The backbone of the work is standard doctrine and argument. The author's personal contribution lies in his practical aim, in his selection of topics, in a sense of breadth conferred by citations from many sources. Discussion of epistemological questions is sidetracked neatly by a brief but competent survey of the field of philosophic systems and an option for realism. The presentation of Scholastic thought is better than average,

---

1 Milwaukee: The Bruce Publishing Co., 1944, 268 pp. [*The Canadian Register* 52 (17 February 1945) 8. Editorial caption: 'Philosophia Perennis.']

certainly adequate for a general audience not discouraged by a polysyllabic style, but too brief to satisfy the philosophically trained still in search of something more exact and convincing than what already they have been told. There is an index, a glossary of terms, and a suggestive bibliography of a general nature.

It is to be hoped that the book will have a wide diffusion among the minority capable of reading nonfiction and desirous of grasping a perspective of current events on a profound level. Though it does not answer all questions, it does much to supply a background and basis upon which questions can be discussed fruitfully.

32

Review of *Mediaeval Studies,* VIII[1]

Mediaeval Studies continues its patient and solid work of reducing our *libertas errandi* in interpreting mediaeval documents. I. Th. Eschmann, O.P., brings to book those who would foist on St Thomas an acceptance of the moral validity of the notion of collective guilt; the investigation is thorough but incomplete; a further article is promised. Professor Gilson works out the puzzle of St Augustine's references to Egypt in his account of the works of the Platonists. Dr Landgraf gives valuable notes on mediaeval usage of the terms 'editio' and 'facultas,' and on the mediaeval manner of citing authors. Armand Maurer, C.S.B., publishes a corrected text of a question by Siger of Brabant on *esse* and *essentia* and conducts an admirable analysis to the conclusion that Siger did not understand the real distinction. George Klubertanz, S.J., deals with the same question in St Bonaventure, to find that *esse* and *essentia* do not differ, while *existere*, in its technical sense, meant for St Bonaventure *esse hic et nunc*; it would seem that there is a patron saint for the naive epistemologists who are concerned exclusively with the real as a 'something out there.'

Alexander J. Denomy, C.S.B., gives a detailed study of the *De Amore* of Andreas Capellanus and raises the question of a doctrine of two truths being advanced in the twelfth century. V.L. Kennedy, C.S.B., argues that the date of the Parisian decree on the elevation of the Host at Mass should be set a few years later than 1208. John Hennig investigates Cataldus

---

1 Toronto: Pontifical Institute of Mediaeval Studies, 1946, 318 pp. [*Theological Studies* 8 (December 1947) 706–707.]

Rachav in a study of the early history of diocesan supremacy in Ireland. Professor Gilson's notes on the history of *ens* are useful not only to philosophers but also to theologians concerned with the Latin equivalents to *hypostasis*. Dr Anton Pegis argues for caution in interpreting *De potentia*, q. 3, a. 5, as though Aquinas attributed a doctrine of creation to Aristotle.

J.R. O'Donnell, C.S.B., gives us the text of the treatise of William of Auvergne, *De bono et malo*. Sister Mary Jeremy, O.P., studies the sources of Caxton's *Golden Legend*. B.J. Whiting draws attention to the poetical works of Froissart. The volume closes with a series of brief notes by A.J. Denomy, Johannes Quasten, Francis Lee Utley, Raphael Levy, L.K. Shook, C.S.B.

33

Review of Donald Williams, *The Ground of Induction*[1]

The author conceives the problem of induction as the problem of the transition from particular to general propositions. His purpose is to solve the problem, and the whole interest and value of his work lies in the solution he proposes. His approach is purely logical. He does not consider it part of his business to give any account of the manner in which we arrive at particular propositions; accordingly, he ignores the possibility that the ground of induction is prior to the transition from particular to general propositions and in the formation of the particular propositions themselves. Assuming particular propositions, he also assumes logic, in the sense of that term made familiar by symbolic logicians, and also mathematics, at least to the extent that mathematics are required for an elementary theory of probability.

The substance of his argument is as follows: The problem of induction is solved if it can be shown to be a valid procedure to affirm of a class what one knows from a sample of the class. But that procedure can be shown to be valid. Therefore, the problem of induction is solved. The major premise is assumed. The minor is established by showing that under the least favorable conditions it is antecedently most probable that the composition of a sufficiently large sample will nearly match the composition of the total class.

---

1 Cambridge: Harvard University Press, 1947, 213 pp. [*Thought* 22 (December 1947) 740–41.]

With regard to the proof of the minor, I believe the author to be correct. What he has to say on this aspect of the issue is a solid contribution that is worth knowing, namely, that logic and mathematics ground a probable inference from a number of instances to the general case. Granting so much, I must also grant that the author has solved the problem of statistical induction in cases in which the investigator wishes to know approximately what the chances are that the next M he meets will have the property P, provided that he knows nothing about M or P except what he has learnt from his sampling in this particular investigation. Granting so much, I must further grant that if the author can work out a satisfactory theory for the cumulation of probabilities, he will be able to extend his theory to solve the problem of statistical induction in cases in which the investigator possesses more knowledge about M and P than is involved in the work of sampling, provided that this further knowledge is of the type that sampling is.

The author acknowledges the limitations of his work on p. 162. On p. 161 there is an admission that shows that the title ought to have read not *The Ground* but *A Ground of Induction*. But in general he writes, not merely without the perspective of such limitations, but as though any limitations were unreal or, if real, then only temporary. He brushes aside as a fancy of natural scientists, Hegelians, and schoolmen the notion that a single instance is sufficient to warrant general conclusions and that resort is had to plural observations only to diminish the danger of error in the observation of the single instance (p. 122). But is it just a fancy, or is it a plain matter of fact? Scientific induction, in point of fact, is not a matter of taking a sufficiently large sample and generalizing through the premise that the composition of the sample matches the composition of the population. Scientific induction is constructed on the assumption the single instance is a sufficient warrant and that plural observations are a necessary safeguard.[2] Does Williams wish scientific procedure to cut off its excellent legs and use his excellent crutches? I do not think so. It just happened that Williams saw a vague resemblance between the problem of the transition from particular to general propositions and the problem of scientific induction, and another vague resemblance between the probability of statistical inference and the probability of scientific generalization. Since he had done some solid thinking with regard to statistical inference, he rewarded himself with a logical holiday and proceeded to write rather brashly not only of statistical inference but of science and even philosophy.

2 [For details on Lonergan's approach to induction, see *Insight* 312–14, 326.]

34

Review of William R. O'Connor, *The Eternal Quest*[1]

This investigation of the teaching of St Thomas Aquinas on the natural desire for God, after a preliminary chapter in which apparently conflicting texts are presented, takes over and elaborates the fourfold classification of opinions worked out by P. Brisbois in *Nouvelle revue théologique*, 1936.[2] Then, returning to the text of St Thomas, it develops an interpretation that coincides with none of the four. The author's basic contention turns upon a distinction between desire in the intellect for knowledge and desire in the will for happiness. There is in the intellect a natural desire for the vision of God, for intellectual curiosity is natural to man; accordingly, knowledge of God's existence is followed naturally by a desire to know God's essence or quiddity. But this does not imply in the will any natural desire for the beatific vision; man's will tends naturally not to any specific beatitude but only to beatitude in general. Objectively, it is true that knowing *quid sit Deus* and possessing perfect beatitude are identical; but that objective truth is evident *immediately* only to those already in possession of the beatific vision, and in them desire is replaced by fruition. Hence, while there is a natural desire for the vision of God, there is no natural desire for the vision of God as beatific.

1 New York, Toronto, London: Longmans, Green and Co., 1947, 290 pp. [*Theological Studies* 9 (1948) 125–27. O'Connor's book is cited in the first footnote in Lonergan's 1949 lecture 'The Natural Desire to See God,' in *Collection*. See the editorial notes there by Frederick E. Crowe, esp. p. 268.]

2 [E. Brisbois, s.j., 'Le désir de voir Dieu et la métaphysique du vouloir selon Saint Thomas,' *Nouvelle revue théologique* 63 (November 1936) 978–89; (December 1936) 1089–1113.]

This account of what St Thomas said has the splendor of simplicity, accuracy, and objectivity, as well as the merit of not having been said (to my knowledge) before. The author may be congratulated sincerely and warmly. It remains, I think, that exception should be taken to two aspects of the general perspective in which he has placed the foregoing account.

He insists very strongly that for both Aristotle and Aquinas natural appetite is always 'a real and positive movement proceeding from the natural form in the direction of the natural good or end of the object' (p. 106). This real and positive movement is a *motus* in the strict sense of imperfect act (p. 113). The natural *velle* of the will towards its end is a *motus*, not in the broad sense of operation, but in the strict sense of imperfect act (p. 121). Such statements are more than puzzling. Matter has a natural appetite for form. From what form does this movement, natural appetite, proceed? What is moving? To what category does the movement reduce? Again, there is a natural inclination to fall that pertains to a stone at rest in an elevated position. Is this natural inclination a movement? Does it reduce to the category, *ubi*? Can the same thing be at movement and at rest simultaneously with respect to the same category? No doubt the natural inclination to fall is really distinct from the substantial form of the stone. But it is not interpreting St Thomas to adduce later speculations on the nature of final causality to prove that the natural inclination of the stone to fall is more than a natural relation of finality in the accidental *forma gravitatis*. Finally, with regard to imperfect act, one cannot eat one's cake and keep it. If *motus* and imperfect act are so taken that only God and the blessed have operation without movement (as in *In II Sent.*, d. 11, q. 2, a. 1), then in this life willing the means is just as much an imperfect act as naturally willing the end. If *motus* and imperfect act are taken as movement from one contrary to another, as determined in the *Physics* (*In III De anima.*, lect. 12 §766), as incompatible with sensation (ibid.), as presupposing an extended and divisible subject (*In VI Phys.*, lect. 12), then no act of will can be an imperfect act.

Though the author does not explicitly discuss the possibility of introducing into Thomist thought the later hypothesis of *natura pura*, still he cannot avoid this issue entirely, and two of his appendices hover about it. He affirms that man's natural beatitude would be a perpetual process of advance in knowledge of God; vision is not to be attained naturally, and so natural desire remains unsatisfied; this is only to be expected, since perfect beatitude is natural only to God, while the beatitude natural to a creature is imperfect; over this imperfection, unbaptized infants do not appear to be distressed. To the objection, *nihil in natura frustra*, he answers that, though this statement is simple, still its meaning is complex: it means that the desires of nature are satisfied, provided there are no impediments; when there are impediments, it means only that the desires of nature would be satisfied if the impediments were removed; the impediment to the satisfaction of natural desire for the vision of God is the 'inferiority of nature,' and it is removed by the grace of the light of glory. But might not the objection be pressed? Impediments are *per accidens* and, in an ordered universe, they occur only *in minori parte*. Is then grace *per se*? Is it required by the order of the universe? Against this, one might appeal to the view that there are extinct biological species despite their natural desire for conservation (*Summa contra Gentiles*, 2, 55, ¶13).[3] But again one can object: did Aquinas adjust Aristotle to make provision either for *natura pura* or for extinct biological species? Or, to come back to Cajetan, is it not unhistorical to attribute to Aquinas's arguments from reason a rigor that at least sometimes they do not possess? In a word, I do not think that the author has evaluated adequately the significance of Aquinas's views on natural desire.

In conclusion, the work handles admirably its main issue; it is a valuable fund of information on subsidiary issues, and this fund is made available by an index; there is also a large bibliography. Unfortunately, the footnotes are consigned in a lump to the end of the book.

3   [See below, p. 203, n. 2.]

35

Review of Dom Illtyd Trethowan,
Certainty: Philosophical and Theological[1]

This is an instructive work written by a vigorous and inquiring mind. While the discussion ranges from logical positivism to mystical experience, the central concern is the reconciliation of the properties of the act of faith, which at once is certain yet free, rational yet due to divine grace. Though the author has more material than he can fit smoothly into the space at his disposal, the somewhat choppy presentation of exact information does not interfere with the strong logical structure and its strictly speculative intention. Indeed, I find the basic viewpoint most attractive:

> Theology is the queen of the sciences. But a philosopher may say, 'I am a philosopher and not a theologian,' and, although this is not a satisfactory state of affairs, it does make good sense; whereas the theologian who says, 'I'm a theologian and not a philosopher,' is talking nonsense. (p. 65)

Slightly less than the first third of the book is merely philosophic. The position adopted is a dogmatic intuitionism that recalls Fr Sebastian Day's significant work on *Intuitive Cognition*.[2] Certainty is to be taken rigorously

1 Westminster: Dacre Press, 1948, viii + 170 pp. [*The Modern Schoolman* 27 (1950) 153–55.]
2 [Sebastian J. Day, *Intuitive Cognition: A Key to the Significance of the Later Scholastics* (St Bonaventure, New York: Franciscan Institute, 1947). There is a hint of irony in Lonergan's description of Day's book as 'significant.' For it is evident from his remarks in the last *Verbum* article, which appeared originally in 1949, that he did not regard the book as significant because he agreed with its position. On the contrary, for Lonergan the book's significance lies, first, in the

(p. 11), and it has to provide its own guarantee (p. 9). By ruling that doubtful knowledge is not knowledge, it seems that incomplete knowledge is not knowledge. There follows an identification of knowledge with certainty. There also follows a disregard of elements or factors within knowledge, so that our apprehensions are said to be affirmations in the form of judgments (p. 40). This knowledge-apprehension-affirmation-certainty is intuitive: while Aquinas contrasted (*Summa contra Gentiles*, 2, c. 98, ad fin.), the author identifies the Platonist confrontation of knower with known and the Aristotelian identity of knower in act and known in act (p. 22). A sharp distinction between sense and intellect is deprecated, and so an intellectual intuition of bodies is affirmed (p. 36). The doctrine of species is under a cloud, for it risks changing the object (p. 30), and for the same reason the construction by intellect of its object is set aside (p. 37). Indeed, the author is so opposed to distinction, analysis, explanation that, while admitting a difference between immediate and inferred knowledge, he proceeds to contend that the demonstration of God's existence is not syllogistic but an immediate inference (p. 42).

After the reader is introduced to theology and to the supernatural order, various theories of the acts of faith, current among Catholic theologians, are passed in review. All are found unsatisfactory. With this pronouncement it would be difficult to disagree. But probably it will be contended that the author's proposal, while headed in the right direction, fails to reach the goal. He would ground faith on a supernatural intuition of God as revealing. This assures the intervention of grace, the sufficiency of evidence, and the certainty of faith. But it leaves faith free not immediately but only *in causa*. The real difficulty, however, is whether the alleged intuition exists. The author appeals to the normality of mystical experience and argues that mysticism involves an intuition of God, and that faith is the beginning of the mystical life; what can be overwhelming in mystical experience should be rudimentary in faith, where it would provide the element of intellectual evidence that is needed. It remains that the author seems to wish he did not have to account for the faith of those in the state of mortal sin. More boldly, in the name of intellectualism, he attacks the theologians who advance that mystical experience radically is affective rather than intuitive.

----

fact that it 'put[s] down in black and white' the logical consequences of conceptualists' inadvertence to their own acts of understanding, and, second, in the possibility that, having read and studied the book, conceptualist interpreters of Aristotle and Aquinas 'will be roused to something better than his [Day's] and their suppositions.' See *Verbum* 195.]

The weak point of the work seems to me to be the notion of intuition. Faith cannot be a conclusion, for it is a new and supernatural beginning. But on the author's philosophy, certainty must be either a conclusion or an intuition. Really it is this premise that forces the affirmation of an intuition of God in faith, that leads to an a priori interpretation of mystical experience, that brings up the embarrassing faith of sinners, that excludes from faith immediate freedom, that would give rise to further difficulties if the term 'intuition' were given an exact meaning in an adequately systematic presentation.

But it is not in such consequences that the real weakness lies; rather it is in the very notion of intuition. The definition of truth is correspondence between judgment and reality. The criterion of truth is evidence. Now, to postulate intuitions is unquestionably simple and simplifying. At once the definition and the criterion of truth are made to coincide. At a stroke the critical problem is eliminated, for if evidence is evident intuition of reality, there is neither need nor possibility of proceeding rationally from the criterion to the definition of truth. Unfortunately, the postulated intuitions do not seem to exist. In its first moment on each level, knowledge seems to be act, perfection, identity; such identity of itself is not a confrontation; confrontation does arise, but only in a second moment and by a distinct act, of perception as distinct from sensation, of conception as distinct from insight, of judgment as distinct from reflective understanding. On this showing confrontation is not primitive, but derived; and it is derived from what is not confrontation, not intuition, not formal and explicit duality. Admittedly, it is difficult to justify such derivation. Overtly to accept such difficulty is a basic and momentous philosophic option. Still it seems to me to be the way of honesty and truth, and I should like very much to see so acute and so transparently honest a thinker as Dom Trethowan explore it.

36

Review of Étienne Gilson,
Being and Some Philosophers[1]

The work presents to a wider public the lectures given at the Mediaeval Institute in 1946. If to settle recondite points scholars will also want the somewhat similar *L'être et l'essence*,[2] everyone more at home in English will be grateful for the opportunity to assimilate the massive argument along the line of least resistance.

What is meant by 'being'? The very question is misleading. A geometer has to be able to define 'circle,' but he need not care whether our powers of observation and our instruments of measurement are capable of determining whether or not there is a single circle. But can the meaning of 'being' be of that type? Can 'being' be meant without 'existing' being meant? Further, to move to a profounder level, can questions about the meaning of 'being' be settled by straightforward argument? For it would seem that any principles invoked in argument would presuppose some determinate meaning of 'being' and so only beg the question.

Professor Gilson's critical reflection on the issue is through history. The implications of supposing the meaning of 'being' to be like the meaning of 'circle' or of 'man' are displayed in three cycles. First come the affinities of

1 Toronto: Pontifical Institute of Mediaeval Studies, 1949, xi + 219 pp. [*The Ensign* (28 May 1949) 10. Editorial caption: 'Gilson Approaches Notion of "Being" through History.' *The Ensign* was a Catholic weekly published in Montreal by Robert W. Keyserlingk for the Canadian Bishops, October 1948 to December 1956. A carbon of the autograph of this review can be found in the library of the Lonergan Research Institute, and this was followed here. One change is noted below, n. 3.]
2 [Étienne Gilson, *L'être et l'essence* (Paris: J. Vrin, 1948).]

Parmenides, Plato, Plotinus, Marius Victorinus, pseudo-Dionysius, Eriugena, and Eckhart; in a second chapter are Aristotle, Averroes, and Siger of Brabant; in a third Avicenna, Scotus, and Suarez. The complete breakdown of this position appears in the violent oscillations of the series: Wolff, Hume, Kant, Hegel, and Kierkegaard. In a fifth chapter the position of St Thomas Aquinas is presented as the solution to the problems raised. The work closes with a discussion of cognitional questions from a logical and grammatical rather than a psychological viewpoint.

Extremely valuable for the brilliant series of historical insights it offers, the book has a much deeper significance. Against the apparent fact that metaphysics has been tried and found wanting, M. Gilson sets the historical fact that, while a large number of philosophers have tried to think 'being' and bungled, one has seen that 'being' has to be not conceived but affirmed, and he[3] has been rather neglected.

Along with this special relevance to the thought of our day, the work makes a serious contribution to the method of philosophy. Aristotle had employed the dialectic of opinions. Aquinas had affirmed that while conclusions depend upon principles, and principles upon grasp of the relations of their terms, still judgment on the validity of the initial terms is a matter of wisdom. At least for those who can learn a lesson from the experiments conducted by history, M. Gilson has provided a technique for developing that ultimate wisdom. In this respect the present work complements his *Unity of Philosophical Experience*.[4] But since once may be chance, and twice may be coincidence, let us ask for a third performance. Modern wisdom has room for development and, though Gilson likes neither the name nor the thing, so also has critical realism.[5]

3   [The word 'he' is what appears in the autograph. The text published in *The Ensign* has 'this.' It is clear that 'he' refers to Aquinas.]

4   [Étienne Gilson, *The Unity of Philosophical Experience*, The William James Lectures, Harvard University (New York: Charles Scribner's Sons, 1937).]

5   [The last sentence is omitted from the *Ensign* edition, and is perhaps the most important sentence in the entire review. On Gilson and Lonergan's critical realism, see 'Metaphysics as Horizon,' in *Collection* 188–204. See also Lonergan's second review of Gilson's book, which, in the present volume, follows immediately.]

37

Review of Étienne Gilson, *Being and Some Philosophers*[1]

In the light of the 'unity of philosophical experience' M. Gilson endeavors to determine the content of the most basic of terms, 'being.' As indicated in the preface, the work is not history but philosophy, not narrative but argument. It remains that the argument is a massive affair, an extraordinarily erudite application of the method Aristotle named 'dialectic.' It draws upon the thought of some two dozen philosophers from Parmenides to Sartre, and it considers them not in isolation but in their originating affiliations and their consequent influence. To offer a summary of such a work is, of course, to strip it of its amazing wealth of insights and to deprive it of a great part of its effectiveness. But I can do no better than summarize, and so, having uttered a warning that M. Gilson is much more convincing out of a capsule than in one, I proceed to encapsulate him.

Being, then, is not to be taken as what can be thought and talked about. From that would follow, as for Plato, that Ideas are because of their determinacy and that sensibles are not because of their indeterminacy. Again, it would follow, as for Plotinus, that the very first principle must be the One, beyond being and beyond intelligence, in the astounding hypostatization of the principle of identity that, nonetheless, found its way into the minds of such Christian thinkers as Marius Victorinus, the pseudo-Dionysius, John the Scot, and Eckhart.

1 Toronto: Pontifical Institute of Mediaeval Studies, 1949, xi + 219 pp. [*Theological Studies* 11 (1950) 122–25.]

Next, being is not to be taken as substance, the compound of matter and form. Aristotle thought so. But Aristotle also acknowledged something more. His method begins with the question, *An sit?* And though subsequently he forgets the existence he begins by affirming, that neglect has resulted in the strangest array of followers holding among themselves violently opposing views. To remain with Aristotle in all things was the ideal of Averroes who, by positing a single intellect for all men of all times, anticipated the lines of the pure metaphysic of substance worked out by Spinoza.

Thirdly, being is not to be taken as what stands in some relation to existence. There are a variety of such positions. Avicenna identified 'existing' with 'being necessary': God is existence; other things are essences with an accidental necessity and so a somehow accidental existence derived from God. Duns Scotus broke the Greco-Arabic block of necessity by taking existence as a mode of essence. For him God is essence; but because that essence is infinite, it is individual; and because it is individual, it exists. Similarly, every other essence, as it acquires its full range of determinations and so its *haecceitas*, also acquires the mode or degree called existing. On this view, to exist is to be real, and as matter, form, accidents each have their proper degree of reality, so each has its proper degree of existence within a single existing thing. Suarez distinguished two meanings of being: there is the participial meaning, existing; there is the substantive meaning, real essence, which prescinds from existence. This Suarezian distinction was taken over by Wolff who distinguished between a basic science of ontology, which deals with being by prescinding from existence, and on the other hand the derived sciences of cosmology, psychology, and natural theology, which deal with existent beings.

It was from the dogmatic slumbers, not of metaphysics in general but of Wolffian ontology, that Hume awakened Kant. In Hume Kant found the empirical acknowledgement of existence lacking in Wolff's ontology, and in Wolff he found the basis of scientific knowledge lacking in Hume. Put them together, and there will result the unknown thing-in-itself, the a priori categories of experience, and the transcendental illusion consequent upon use of the categories outside the realm of possible experience. Unfortunately, Kant could not keep Hume and Wolff together. Hegel, the supreme essentialist, took essence as the concrete universal, the universal with the maximum of determinations. In contrast, being was the least of concepts; it was what remained when all determinations were removed from essence. Yet, little as being was for Hegel, at least it merited mention; and that was more than he could grant to the sensible and external existence sometimes mistaken for being. Still, there also is an existence internal to each of us. Kierkegaard was unimpressed by Hegel's thinking out all art, religion, and philosophy. What matters, as he averred, is not thinking Christianity but being a Christian. If for Descartes thinking proved existence, for Kierkegaard thinking resulted in not existing. Accordingly, he left being to 'objective' thought, and turned to 'subjective' existence.

Hence M. Gilson reverts to Aquinas to identify 'to be' and 'to exist' and to distinguish 'thinking' and 'knowing.' Perhaps the briefest way of putting his position is to begin from Aristotle's reconciliation of the universality of science with the individuality of the real. Knowledge or science, then, is twofold: knowledge in potency is of the indeterminate and universal; but knowledge in act is of the determinate; it is a 'this' with respect to a 'that' (*Metaphysics*, xiii, 10, 1087a 15–18). Aquinas developed Aristotle by specifying the transition from knowledge in potency (i.e., thinking) to knowledge in act. Beyond conception, beyond the singularity from reflection on phantasm, beyond the principles of abstract truth, knowing in act requires an existential judgment. Similarly, the being known by knowledge in act requires, beyond substantial form, beyond individuating matter, beyond accidents, a further ontological component named 'existence.' Hence '… every *ens* is an *esse habens*, and unless its *esse* is included in our cognition of it, it is not known as an *ens*, that is, as a *be-ing*' (p. 204). 'Existence lies beyond abstract representation' (p. 202). 'Being is not and cannot become an object of purely abstract cognition' (p. 204). 'All real knowledge includes a judgment of existence' (p. 206).

Such seems to be the substance of M. Gilson's position. To note a few of the accidents: the opinion that Aristotle was seriously involved in a problem of universals does not seem plausible. The attempt to place the Thomist existential component, *esse*, among Aristotle's four causes is mistaken, for *esse* is neither agent nor end, neither matter nor form, but a fifth type of cause that, like matter and form, is internal. Again, M. Gilson does not seem to acknowledge a concept of being; at any rate, the reader will find himself confronted with the problem of determining whether such a concept exists and in what it consists. And there will be the further problem that, if 'to be' is 'to exist,' then what is the metaphysician's *ens ut sic*? Finally, the insistence upon a 'return to sense' and the affirmation of an intuitive experience of acts of existing (pp. 206–207) are strangely reminiscent of something like Kierkegaard's aesthetic sphere of existential subjectivity.

But such matters and others on which difficulty or disagreement might arise do not seem to me to affect the validity of M. Gilson's central contentions. Being is existing, and thinking is not knowing. With unobtrusive dexterity he has lifted the old disputed question of essence and existence quite out of the context in which it was likely to remain a perpetually disputed question. By the same stroke he has indicated a method to tackle all disputed questions at their roots. If speculative theology has languished, if philosophy is regarded as a poor relation of the empirical sciences, the cause has been the scandal of the persistence of disputed questions with little reasonable hope of their solution. That is the problem that exists. Not only has M. Gilson aimed at the root of the problem that exists but also his method is a new departure. One will not find it described in Georges van Riet's 670-page study of the philosophic methods evolved by Scholastic writers in the last one hundred years.[2] Moreover, it is a particularly elegant method. For an appeal to history as experiment is not more argument or more theory. It is an appeal to fact and possesses the peculiar decisiveness of that appeal. Further, it is not an appeal to obscure fact that a succession of scholars barely can determine; it is an appeal to the critical moments in the history of philosophy, with great figures and the emergence of new schools marking their occurrence, and with very little scope left to plausible fiction in determining their significance and their relationships. Only fresh experiment on this high level can invalidate M. Gilson's identification of being and existing.

2   [Georges van Riet, *L'épistémologie thomiste: Recherches sur le problème de la connaissance dans l'école thomiste contemporaine* (Louvain: Éditions de l'Institut Supérieur de Philosophie, 1946).]

38

Review of Joseph Buckley, S.M., *Man's Last End* and André de Bovis, *La sagesse de Sénèque*[1]

With increasing insistence, historians have been advancing that the Renaissance constitutes a watershed in Catholic theological thought on nature and grace. In 1928 in *Gregorianum*, Fr Elter argued impressively that theologians prior to Sylvester Maurus took it for granted that perfect beatitude was to be had by man only in the beatific vision.[2] With no less impressiveness in 1929, though his work does not seem equally well known, Fr Doucet in *Antonianum* argued that theologians prior to Cajetan took it for granted that there existed in man a natural desire for the supernatural vision of God.[3] Recently both these positions have been overshadowed by the more radical contention of de Lubac[4] that only after Baius did it become a common view that the state of pure nature, as now understood, was a concrete possibility; and a startling confirmation of the accuracy of de Lubac's history has been given by Rondet,[5] inasmuch as the Tridentine theologian Dominicus Soto, O.P., is claimed to have affirmed that, had man been created *in puris naturalibus*, he could not know his last end, since that would have been supernatural.

1 [Buckley] St Louis: Herder, 1949, 249 pp. [de Bovis] Collection: 'Théologie,' vol. 13, Paris: Aubier, 1948, 231 pp. [*Theological Studies* 10 (1949) 578–82.]
2 [E. Elter, S.J., 'De naturali hominis beatitudine ad mentem Scholae antiquioris,' *Gregorianum* 9 (1928) 269–90.]
3 [Victorinus Doucet, O.F.M., 'De naturali seu innato supernaturalis beatitudinis desiderio,' *Antonianum* 4 (1929) 167–208.]
4 [Henri de Lubac, *Surnaturel: Études historiques* (Paris: Aubier, 1946).]
5 [Henri Rondet, 'Le problème de la nature pure et de la théologie du XVIᵉ siècle,' *Recherches de science religieuse* 35 (1948) 481–521.]

If the history of the matter is becoming clearer, the speculative issues are so complex that a generous lapse of time will have to be granted, I suspect, before all concealed suppositions have been detected and sound judgment can be passed upon the relative merits of the medieval and the Renaissance positions. Accordingly, it is as valuable, if incomplete, contributions to the contemporary process of investigation, clarification, and criticism that the books under review are recommended.

In the main Fr Buckley's work is speculative and systematic. His topic is very closely related to the Thomist statement, 'Beatitudo perfecta est soli Deo naturalis,'[6] which was developed by O'Mahony's *Desire of God* over a decade ago.[7] But, as his title indicates, he treats not of man's beatitude but of man's last end and, indeed, not of the end that might happen to be last, but of the end that intrinsically is last. Such an end is good in itself, willed because of itself (terminative), and the ground both of the goodness and of the willing of anything else (architectonic). These requirements are met by divine goodness as presented to the will in the beatific vision. Again, they are met by divine goodness considered from a metaphysical viewpoint as the final cause of all things in any order. But from the viewpoint of human psychology there appears no last end to be attained by man except through the beatific vision. For apart from the vision man knows divine goodness not directly and in itself but indirectly and *per speciem alienam*. Accordingly, he knows that divine goodness is the ground of all other goodness and desirableness, but he does not know it inasmuch as it is that ground. Hence, divine goodness as presented to his will is not architectonic and so lacks a property of an end that of itself is last. Again, in the vision right willing follows necessarily; but apart from the vision right willing has to be postulated to ensure stability; for apart from the vision one has to argue that men will be content with their lot because they ought to be. Finally, since divine goodness is the last end metaphysically, it is useless to look elsewhere for a last end psychologically; but apart from the vision, man can attain divine goodness only *per speciem alienam*; and to say that man attains his last end *per speciem alienam* is tantamount to saying that properly he does not attain a last end at all.

This vigorous thesis, which throws not a little light on Thomist usage of the term *finis ultimus*, has its repercussions. For Fr Buckley a merely natural

6   [*Summa theologiae*, 1, q. 62, a. 4 c. Actually, the text has '… soli Deo beatitudo perfecta est naturalis …']
7   [James E. O'Mahony, *The Desire of God in the Philosophy of St. Thomas Aquinas* (Cork: Cork University Press, 1929).]

order involves antinomies. The will tends to beatitude in general. In a merely natural order man can attain a reasonable perfection and satisfaction. But beatitude means more than that, so that the tendency to beatitude in general can find no good or set of goods in which it can rest simply. Again, within a merely natural order there is no concrete and determinate good which both is and is attainable as the principle of subordination and coordination of other goods of that order. Finally, within a merely natural order man's last end is, as it were, to have no last end but to remain open.

The alert reader will recognize in such statements a variation on the traditional theme emphasized by de Lubac in the section of *Surnaturel* entitled 'Esprit et Liberté': a rational creature cannot be impeccable naturally.[8] But while Fr Buckley acknowledges a certain affinity between his thought and that of de Lubac (p. 180), he stoutly maintains the concrete possibility of a state of pure nature on the ground that de Lubac has not satisfactorily shown such a possibility not to be a necessary dogmatic postulate. And if one puts the obvious objection, *nihil in natura frustra*, Fr Buckley would answer that he would very much like to know for certain just what that affirmation means. For him human nature as rational is determinate only with respect to broad categories such as truth, goodness, happiness. Further determinations are a matter of divine providence and of history, so that in a sense a state of pure nature is a state of indetermination.

It might be expected that Fr Buckley is an advocate of the natural desire for the vision of God. In fact, he regards that position as a contradiction in terms. Capacity and exigence mean the same thing to him, so that if the matter of the moon had a capacity, it also would have to have the exigence to be part of an animal organism.

May we add our congratulations to Fr Buckley on the appearance of his well-informed, clear, alert, and solid work a good word for the publishers who had the kindness to print the footnotes at the foot of the page, and so spare readers the perpetual inconvenience, not to say annoyance, of turning to the back of the book?

André de Bovis offers a thorough, documented study of the basic ethical and religious doctrines of the Roman Stoic philosopher, Seneca (4 B.C.–64 A.D.). An introductory section is followed by seven chapters on such ethical first principles as the supreme good, the last end, and their relation to the

---

8 [de Lubac, *Surnaturel* 187–321, with a statement of the question in the introduction, 187–88.]

moral goodness and the happiness of man. The dominant notion is the *honestum*, defined as what accords with right reason and, again, as what accords with nature. A minor antinomy results from the twofold definition inasmuch as conflict does arise between right reason and sensitive nature. But the major difficulty of Seneca's position is brought out by forcing the transition from the abstract *honestum* to a concrete end, from the ideal norm of reason and nature to the real good to be attained by moral living. This reveals that probably the happiness of man, certainly his good and end, consists for Seneca simply in the self-realization effected by moral living. Now if the moral end is immanent in the individual, there spontaneously arises the question of justifying morally the sacrifice of the individual for the common good. To this there appears no adequate answer (p. 132).

Correctly, the author warns one against any anachronistic determination whether Seneca thought as a monotheist or as a polytheist. The divinity exists. But its unicity does not preclude the existence of subordinate powers and deities (p. 156). One, immortal, powerful, intelligent, it also is immense and makes of the universe its temple. Indeed it is an active member of the universe, everywhere present and effective, though not all-powerful nor a creator. Destiny, fate, world order, divine law, reason, nature are so many aspects of it; nonetheless, Seneca at times seems to break through the logic of Stoic orthodoxy and to desert rationalist monism for a God transcendent and personal. Fear of God is rejected on the ground that God is good; but gratitude, even love, is recommended; still, the possibility of the efficacy of prayer is more than doubtful. Suffering is understood in its moral significance, yet the problem of evil proves too grave; its existence seems to vitiate the whole perspective of the concept of God.

To the author, Seneca provides the spectacle of a purely human, a thoroughly laicized wisdom. Ethical doctrine is based on human right reason to find in the ideals of that reason its norm and in the actuation of those ideals man's end. As human reason is its own absolute, God is not properly the moral absolute nor is He given any significant function in moral living (p. 86). The good to be attained lies within the reach of merely human effort; it consists in man's conquest of self by self; it places the highest of values within the self to be realized by the self; so that if Stoicism has its harsh and repellent aspects, it also has its seduction in the glory of man (p. 147). For man and God differ accidentally but essentially are alike: both have reason; but what in God is perfect, in man is perfectible. Thus, the self-perfection of moral living is equated with self-divinization. What makes a man wise is what makes God God. God is model and authority and judge of goodness. But by that very token, the wise man is the equal of Seneca's God, in quality of being, if not in length of days!

But if André de Bovis offers us a concrete indication of the Lyon-Fourvière concept of theological laicism,[9] it is only in scanty asides that he attempts to integrate this picture with the general problem of the differences between medieval and Renaissance theology. A conscientious historian of Seneca's thought, he is content with the contrast between Stoic and Christian wisdom, between a divinity cut to human measure and God at once personal and incomprehensible, between moral perfection achieved by human effort and holiness achieved by grace in answer to prayer. Yet such objective studies have the value of giving thought a concrete turn and of providing a touchstone to test necessarily abstract theorems. That is a matter of no little importance if, as it seems, the current alternatives ultimately are: (1) conceiving the supernatural as another essence or nature and so at once parallel to and utterly distinct from nature; and (2) conceiving it as some approximation to an existentialist communion of man with God as he is in himself, and so at once the act and perfection of natural aspiration; it is man's, yet utterly beyond natural right, desert, or achievement, for it is with God as he is God.

9 [The series in which de Bovis's book appears all have the following: Théologie: Études publiées sous la direction de la faculté de théologie s.j. de Lyon-Fourvière.]

39

Review of Eduard Stakemeier,
Über Schicksal und Vorsehung[1]

In the present work Professor Stakemeier of the Faculty of Theology at Paderborn is concerned with contemporary problems in the perspective of contemporary general culture. In a brief introduction he recalls a remark of Pius XI on the advantage enjoyed by Catholic doctrine inasmuch as it can be presented in simple language, intelligible to anyone, without thereby suffering any substantial loss. Accordingly, he has made it his aim throughout his book to be non-technical even in the sections in which such graciousness is not commonly expected of a theologian. In correspondence with the manner is the theme that takes concrete form in the question: 'Wie kann Gott zulassen, was an furchtbarer Sinnlosigkeit und Ungerechtigkeit so offenkundig vor allen Augen liegt?'[2] The problem of evil is today oppressively obvious, and it is to be handled, not with the philosophic calm of a Leibniz, but with the religious vigor of a Joseph de Maistre.[3]

The work falls into three parts that deal successively with belief in fate, with faith in divine providence, and with the effects of either attitude on human character. Accounts of belief in fate are drawn from Lao-tse and Confucius, from ancient and Renaissance astrology, from the mythology of

---

1 Lucerne: Verlag Räber & Cie., 1949, 349 pp. [*Theological Studies* 12 (1951) 259–60.]
2 ['How can God permit what to everyone appears obvious absurdity and injustice?']
3 [Joseph de Maistre (1753–1821), a French ultramontane writer. At first influenced by the eighteenth-century rationalists, after the Revolution of 1789 he came to see the church as the safeguard of political stability.]

Greek epic and drama, of Germanic saga, and of Virgil, from the philosophy of Seneca, from Mohammedanism, from the anthropocentric theology of Luther and the theocentric theology of Calvin. The sources of a new and secularized fatalism are found in the picture of man drawn by modern scientists, by modern historians, and by modern philosophers. Then the problem of suffering is ushered in to provide, as it were, an experimental test of the validity of Confucian, Buddhist, Greek, and modern views of fate. The first part closes with a chapter on literature and drama as the liberal surrogate for catechetics and sermons and, after a review of fatalistic notions running from Goethe to Ibsen (to mention the most familiar names), there is a thesis on the function of poetry in expressing the deeper and unformulated movements of a period and in exploring the relations between fate and human character.

In the second part the doctrine of divine providence is set forth from the Old Testament, from the Gospels, and from St Paul. There follows a dogmatic treatment of the divine plan, divine governance, free will, predestination, and the end of man, with particular attention paid to such personal issues as reliance on providence and prayer of petition. Under the title of a theodicy of providence come discussions with a slightly more speculative turn. Are the good unlucky and the evil lucky? Is suffering inevitable or is it a punishment for sin? Is suffering mere natural necessity that has nothing to do with providence? Does the evil in the world upset the order of providence? What is the meaning of the Cross of Christ?

The third part is named an excursus and deals with the respective effects of the opposed doctrines on human character. There is a general thesis that man, created in the image of God, heads for nihilism if he has no belief in divine governance. It is then shown that love of one's neighbor is a quite different precept in the wisdom of China, India, or Greece and in the wisdom of Christ: the point becomes especially vivid in a down-to-earth account of the attitudes of pre-Christian husbands to their wives. After charity there is discussed *Seelengrösse* – it is without the overtones of our 'magnanimity' – in its bearing on conduct, humility, and charity. The work ends with a contrast between the Stoic wise man and the Christian saint.

The author operates from the basis of a broad culture and aims at the effective communication of common doctrine. Difficulties to be met are drawn from the pages of influential names or from the depths of the heart of man. If the answers are not new, they are clear and robust. If the argument is not so much thought out as quoted out, its concrete procedures and its knack of treating questions that are asked possess the significance of a model for a needed layman's theology.

40

Review of *Sciences ecclésiastiques*, III[1]

Sciences ecclésiastiques for 1950 maintains the standards we have come to expect. Two articles on theology, two on asceticism, and one on moral philosophy occupy over 180 pages. Notes on psychology and theology occupy 30 more, and there are some 40 pages of book reviews. To discuss all contributions would be impossible; therefore, I shall direct my attention particularly to the leading article of over 60 pages by R.P. Jules Paquin on John of St Thomas's account of the *lumen gloriae*.[2]

With unfailing clarity and precision, Fr Paquin follows John step by step through an extremely complex issue. The *lumen gloriae* is an accident, a quality of the first species, a disposition, a supernatural operative habit, an illumination, a *medium sub quo*. It is not the act of vision, nor divine concursus, nor purely extrinsic, nor the divine essence as object or as species. It is with respect to the divine essence a material cause and with respect to the act of vision both an efficient and a material cause. The intellect elicits the act of vision, and it does so as no mere instrument. Still the whole operative power for the act comes from the *lumen gloriae*.

Dogmatic notes are worked out with care. A single exception is, perhaps, the question whether the act of vision can be infinite. There is overlooked a relevant distinction between (1) a truth, and (2) the metaphysical conditions of a truth. To say that the humanity of Christ exists by an infinite act does not mean that the humanity of Christ does not exist. Again, to say that

1 Montreal: Les Éditions de l'Immaculée Conception, 1950, 250 pp. [*Theological Studies* 12 (1951) 292–93.]
2 ['La lumière de gloire selon Jean de Saint Thomas,' pp. 5–67.]

an immanent activity such as knowing cannot have an extrinsic metaphysical condition is false; God contingently knows finite existences, for he would not know them as existing if they did not exist and they need not exist; still, there is no contingent entity in God. Probably enough, John of Ripa's[3] views do not call for such careful treatment; but a general theological note does.

The main speculative problem in the beatific vision was, for John of St Thomas, the 'vitality' of the act of vision. This is a rather remarkable notion. It has nothing to do with the Thomist doctrine of the natural desire to see God. It is not conceived as denoting a substance 'cui convenit secundum suam substantiam[4] movere seipsam, vel agere se quocumque modo ad operationem' (*Summa theologiae*, 1, q. 18, a. 2 c.). Its most conspicuous instance is not God, as Aquinas held (ibid. a. 3 c.), nor is its meaning so elastic that one might claim 'quod se intelligit, dicitur se movere' (ibid. ad 1m). On the contrary, each vital potency of a creature has to move itself, as in the doctrine of Peter John Olivi (*In II Sent.*, q. 58, ad 14m [Quaracchi: Collegium S. Bonaventurae, 1924, vol. II, 461–515]),[5] with the important difference, however, that John of St Thomas accepts the Aristotelian axiom of 'quidquid movetur, ab alio movetur.' As one would expect, a syncretism of views from such opposed sources calls for an exceptional display of mental gymnastics. The act of vision has to be the product of the efficient causality of the possible intellect, otherwise it would not be a vital act. At the same time, the possible intellect cannot have the slightest native capacity for producing the act, otherwise the act would not be absolutely supernatural. John rejects the alternative solution to his problem, namely, the equally extraordinary 'potentia obedientialis activa,' and correctly, on his suppositions, concludes that the total operative power comes from the *lumen gloriae*, that nonetheless it is the possible intellect that does the producing.

Fr Paquin is to be congratulated on his thorough account of a really splendid specimen of dialectical ingenuity and, no less, on his care to make it plain that he is expounding John of St Thomas's thought on John of St Thomas's suppositions.

3 [John of Ripa, an Italian Franciscan theologian who flourished as a professor at the University of Paris, 1357–68. In his commentary on the *Sentences*, he tried to make clear as possible the character of the beatitude communicated by God to his creatures.]

4 [Thomas's text has 'naturam.']

5 [See Lonergan, *Verbum* 211, n. 90.]

41

Review of Eduardo Iglesias, s.j., *De Deo creationis finem exsequente*[1]

Many have been fascinated by Aquinas's affirmation that God operates in all other operations inasmuch as he creates all finite principles of action, conserves them, applies them, and uses them as instruments. On this topic Fr Iglesias published in 1946 his work, *De Deo in operatione naturae vel voluntatis operante.*[2] The thesis was that Aquinas taught mediated concursus and that he was right in doing so. The same contention remains in the present work, where it becomes the hypothesis of a theory on the nature of divine knowledge and providence, predestination and reprobation, efficacious and sufficient grace.

In substance, the proposal is that, if one accepts mediated concursus, then one moves out of the context of the controversy *de auxiliis*[3] into the

---

1 Mexico, D.F.: Buena Prensa, 1951, 310 pp. [*Theological Studies* 13 (1952) 439–41.]

2 [Mexico, D.F.: Buena Prensa, 1946. Lonergan's lengthy review of this book appeared in *Theological Studies* 7 (1946) 602–13 and is included in *Collection* 53–65. He refers to it later in this review.]

3 [A controversy on the manner in which divine grace operates, the help (*auxilium*) it affords to human beings, and the reconciliation of the efficacy of grace with human freedom. It became more acute at the end of the sixteenth century in the respective positions of the Jesuit theologian Luis de Molina (1535–1600) and the Dominican theologian Domingo Bañez (1528–1604). For a summary statement by Lonergan of the key issues involved in the controversy and Aquinas's position, see *Grace and Freedom*, vol. 1 in Collected Works of Bernard Lonergan, ed. Frederick E. Crowe and Robert M. Doran (Toronto: University of Toronto Press, 2000) 448–50.]

context of the thought of St Thomas, and, though all difficulties do not vanish at once, still one is incomparably better off. For the context of the controversy was set by Scotus, who invented immediate concursus and did so because of his theory of divine knowledge (pp. 148–49). But in the writings of Aquinas, divine omniscience and the efficacy of divine will rest on the absolute perfection of God. Hence there is no need to postulate immediate concursus to make God omniscient and to endow his will with efficacy, and so there follows a great mitigation of the problem of reconciling divine dominion with human freedom. For it is immediate concursus that conflicts with contingence and liberty, and not at all divine omniscience and efficacy. Inversely, it is not immediate concursus that makes grace efficacious, but divine omniscience and efficacy (pp. 163, 188, 194, 290).

I believe the foregoing, as a general scheme, to be valid and correct. In my opinion reservations have to be made on the author's contentions for mediated concursus; these I have expressed on a previous occasion (*Theological Studies* 7 [1946] 602–13). I find completely unacceptable, however, the effort to deduce divine knowledge of the futuribles from divine knowledge of the possibles without any recourse to divine wisdom; and as the author believes that he succeeds, where it seems clear to me that he fails, his whole position becomes, in my judgment, ambiguous.

Quite rightly, Fr Iglesias maintains that God knows the possibles, not as mere assemblages of abstract properties, nor merely as contained virtually in finite causes, but in themselves and in the setting of their circumstances, conditions, and causes. However, he argues that in each such setting there is a knowable, necessary nexus between the possible event, considered concretely, and its circumstances. Because the nexus is knowable, it follows from divine omniscience that God knows it. Because the nexus is in the field of the possibles, it follows that this divine knowledge is prior to any act of divine will. On the other hand, though the nexus is necessary, it is to be conceived on the analogy of 'Socrates, dum sedet, necessario sedet,' and so it cannot conflict with contingence or liberty. Hence the author concludes that God, prior to any act of will, knows what he could produce through the mediation of created free wills (pp. 88–89).

This conclusion, I submit, is either trivial or contradictory. It is trivial if it means that God knows that under determinate circumstances Peter, since he is free, could either sin or not sin. It is contradictory if it means that God knows that under determinate circumstances Peter would sin. For in the very circumstances in which Peter sins, (1) it is possible for him to sin, for that is what he does, and (2) it is possible for him not to sin, for he is free. Hence, the same possible circumstances must bear two nexus; on the author's showing both must be necessary; but the terms of the two nexus are contradictory, for the one is sinning and the other not sinning; and it is impossible for both of a pair of contradictories to be necessary.

42

Review of H. Paissac, O.P., *Théologie du Verbe: Saint Augustin et saint Thomas*[1]

Is the statement *ideo Filius quia Verbum* a matter of faith, or a permanently valid contribution to theology, or an intrusion of philosophic speculation into Catholic doctrine? Such approximately is the question to which Fr Paissac seeks an answer by studying ecclesiastical pronouncements (pp. 11–33), outlining the thought of St Augustine (pp. 34–60), indicating earlier sources (pp. 64–102), recalling the contributions of Aquinas's medieval predecessors (pp. 103–116), and in three main sections investigating the thought of Aquinas himself (pp. 117–231). The general conclusions that emerge from the work are (1) that, while the Church has shown marked favor to the psychological analogy, official documents do not imply more than the validity of some comparison between divine generation and human mental process; (2) that St Augustine was not engaged in philosophic speculation but in carrying forward a long-standing Catholic effort to attain an *intelligentia fidei*; (3) that St Thomas's effort was similarly theological; and (4) that the church might take advantage of theological clarifications to allude to the intellectual character of the generation of the Son.

The more concentrated part of the work is the study of St Thomas; in general it is conducted admirably. Relevant texts are taken in chronological groups. The *De natura verbi intellectus* is regarded as spurious. Later distinctions between impressed and expressed species, between transcendental and predicamental relations, are ruled out as irrelevant in an historical

---

1 Paris: Éditions du Cerf, 1951, 248 pp. [*Theological Studies* 13 (March 1952) 121–25.]

inquiry. The absence in Aristotle of any explicit theory of an inner word, Richardian influence in Aquinas's commentary on the *Sentences*, the procession of the Son from the knowledge of the Father, the procession of the Holy Spirit from the Word, all are acknowledged. Finally, though Fr Paissac can insist upon a theory of the course of St Thomas's intellectual development, he is also capable of pointing out when he goes beyond the text.

This interpretative theory finds its inspiration in the surprising Augustinian contention that the name 'Word' is relative in the same fashion as is the name 'Son.' The surprise has its ground in our Aristotelian habits of mind: we take for granted the existence of real distinctions both between the soul and its potencies and between the potencies and their acts, so that for us an inner word is not in the category of relation but in the category of quality. Fr Paissac sees the same surprise behind the fact that, when St Thomas in his *Sentences* asked whether the name 'Word' is applied to God personally, his answer was hesitant because he distinguished, as did St Albert, between relations *secundum esse* and relations *secundum dici*. The name 'Word' belongs to the latter class: it denotes something absolute to which a relation accrues, and not something relative as does the name 'Son.' Hence we are given the rule that in the transition from the creature to God only relations *secundum esse* survive: 'ce qui chez nous est relatif seulement par dénomination ne peut pas conserver son caractère relatif quand on le transpose en Dieu; au contraire, ce qui chez nous est relatif par essence peut, une fois transporté en Dieu, demeurer relatif' (p. 134). It is in the light of this criterion that the development of St Thomas's trinitarian thought is studied, that the position in the *De veritate* is assimilated to that of the *Sentences*, that the dawn is found in the *Contra Gentiles*, and the fully developed position in the *De potentia*. Clearly this is an exceedingly complex issue. I shall endeavor to indicate what seems to me to be correct by formulating precise questions and offering reasoned answers.

First, does St Thomas hold the rule enunciated above, that a relation *secundum dici*, when transferred to God, ceases to be relative? I do not consider that statement descriptive of the facts. According to *In I Sent.*, d. 27, q. 2, a. 2, sol. 1, and *De veritate*, q. 4, a. 5, the name 'Word' denotes something absolute to which a relation accrues. This is what is meant by a relation *secundum dici*. But in the *Sentences*, the name 'Word' is applied to God either essentially or personally. In the *De veritate*, the name 'Word' in its proper sense is applied only personally. In both cases, then, the rule breaks down, for the relation *secundum dici* can or does remain a relation when transferred to God.

Further, the name 'Love' is applied to God both essentially and personally. When applied essentially, it denotes something absolute; when applied personally, there accrues to it a real relation, indicated by the designation '*Amor procedens*.' Nor is this relation *secundum dici* considered a defect of trinitarian thought but merely a shortcoming of human language (*Summa theologiae*, 1, q. 37, a. 1). Indeed, the *De potentia* (q. 7, a. 10, ad 11m) explicitly, and the already cited solution in the *Sentences* implicitly, advance that the distinction between relations *secundem esse* and *secundum dici* regards the meanings of names and not the reality of relations.

Secondly, are the relations of origin of the names 'Word' and 'Proceeding Love' intrinsic to what these names denote? It is, I think, this intrinsic or essential relativity that Fr Paissac finds in the *Contra Gentiles* and the *De potentia*. An inner word, whether concept or judgment, is essentially the term of the cognitional process of objectification. Moreover, such essential relativity is not asserted in the *Sentences*, though it is present in the *De veritate*. Finally, it is not to be confused with the relation *secundum esse*. Just as one cannot abstract 'son' from 'father,' so one cannot abstract 'foot' from 'animal' (*In Librum Boethii de Trinitate*, q. 5, a. 3); but 'son' is relative *secundum esse*, and 'foot' is relative *secundum dici*.

Hence, despite essential relativity, the names 'Word' and 'Proceeding Love' denote something absolute in the *Contra Gentiles*. The Word is God's concept of God, *Deus intellectus*; and *Deus intellectus* is shown to be identical with divine being (*Contra Gentiles*, 4, c. 11, ¶11).[2] Similarly, Proceeding Love is *Deus amatus*, which is identified with divine willing and so with divine being (*Contra Gentiles*, 4, c. 19, ¶7).

Thirdly, is this position maintained? If one examines the *Contra Gentiles*, one finds that it argues, as did St Athanasius and Richard of St Victor, from God the Father to God the Son. In the *De potentia*, God the Father remains the starting point, and if relations are treated before persons, still persons are treated before processions. But in the *Summa* there is a new beginning: it is from God, the common name of Father, Son, and Spirit, as in St Augustine and the *Quicumque*. From that starting point, by means of the psychological analogy, are developed the notions of procession, relation, and person, and then in reverse order is undertaken the presentation of trinitarian doctrine with the relations reappearing as properties and the processions as notional acts. It is this *via doctrinae* that in full clarity exhibits God as a single absolute being in which there are processions and rela-

2 [The reference reflects Lonergan's habit of counting the paragraphs in the Marietti edition of *Summa contra Gentiles*.]

tions. It is within this context that there emerges the doctrine that the name 'person' denotes a relation as subsistent; as Cajetan has noted (*In I Summa theologiae*, q. 29, a. 4), and as Paul Vanier has recently reaffirmed,[3] this involves an advance upon the *De potentia*. It would seem that, as the name 'person,' so also the name of a person, will denote a relation as subsistent. Further, if the names of persons denote relations as subsistent, then they are relations *secundum esse*; and so our conclusion is the same as Fr Paissac's.

Fourthly, what precisely is the relation of the inner word to its origin? Fr Paissac has the exceptional merit of not attempting to answer this question by appealing to empty metaphysical categories. He is out to expound and defend the psychological analogy, and so he gives metaphysical categories their psychological content. The inner word is the immanently produced term of the cognitional process of objectification, and essentially it is relative to the objectifying knower. This is excellent. Still, what is the producing, the objectifying? Both Son and Spirit know, yet neither produces a word. If all knowing involves an object, not all knowing involves a process of objectification. Fr Paissac does not face this issue, yet it is the heart of the matter, the essence of the psychological analogy. In us, as I have argued previously,[4] the act of defining thought is both caused by and because of the understanding that grasps an essence; the act of judgment is both caused by and because of the reflection that grasps the sufficiency of the evidence; the act of will is both caused by and because of the judgment of value, the *verbum spirans amorem*. Now God understands, utters, and wills. He does so by a single infinite act. Since there is only one act, there is no causation. Still the uttering is because of the understanding, and the willing is because of both understanding and uttering. In us that 'because' is operative not naturally but intelligibly. But God's nature is intellectual; his *esse intelligibile* is his *esse naturale* (*Contra Gentiles*, 1, c. 47, ¶5); his intellect is his substance, and his understanding is his being; and so in him that 'because' is an eternal *emanatio intelligibilis* (*Summa theologiae*, 1, q. 27, a. 1), a communication of nature, and the ground of real relations of origin. Moreover, though the procession of Love is not a generation, the procession of the Word is a generation; and so *ideo Filius quia Verbum*.

3 [Paul Vanier, 'La relation trinitaire dans la Somme théologique de saint Thomas d'Aquin,' *Sciences ecclésiastiques* I (1948) 143–59.]
4 [Lonergan is referring to the *verbum* articles which originally appeared in *Theological Studies* between 1946 and 1949.]

Fifthly, what is the theological status of the psychological analogy? Fr Paissac admits that it is only probable, yet would contend that it is unique, so that a theologian is not altogether at liberty to fall in with contemporary sociological preoccupations and set up some new analogy that conceives the divine persons as a sort of divine family. I agree with this conclusion; its paradox is, I suggest, only apparent. Judgments are true or false, certain or probable. Acts of understanding are perfect or imperfect, fruitful or sterile. Primarily, the psychological analogy is not a judgment but a technique for understanding; since what is to be understood is a mystery, the understanding it yields cannot be more than imperfect and fruitful (DB 1796 [DS 3016, ND 132]), and the judgments resting on imperfect understanding will be only probable. On the other hand, since the psychological analogy is suggested by scripture, since its formulation was repeatedly attempted by the Fathers, since St Thomas made it so thoroughly his own, its position is unique. The need is not to invent something new but, as Fr Paissac contends, to master what has been achieved. Like an old painting protected by successive coats of dust and varnish, the brilliance of the psychological analogy has been obscured. *Théologie du Verbe* is a laudable effort at restoration.

PART FOUR

Reviews and Book Notices from the Roman Years

43

Review of Jules Chaix-Ruy,
Les Dimensions de l'être et du temps[1]

M. Jules Chaix-Ruy possesses the never common merit of a stimulating awareness of the philosophic problems that concern our time and of the main lines of their solution. If his basic attachment seems to be to Augustine, Pascal, and M. Blondel, if on the notions of space and time he balances Kant, Schopenhauer, and Heidegger with Newton, Clarke, and Einstein, still his main purpose is to orientate the bewildered existential subject of our day through a coherent and constructive criticism of Feuerbach and Nietzsche, Sartre and Jaspers, the historicism of Croce, and, it seems to him, the somewhat precipitate procedures of Louis Lavelle.[2]

'Nous ne vivons jamais, mais attendons toujours de vivre' puts to us the problem of our existence or, rather, to me the problem of mine. For the future is never more than another present, so that if I live only in the future, never shall I live at all. Again, it is beyond my powers to erase the future from the present, for my present is never more than a moving point of time. What then is needed is a qualitative change in me, a shift in the center of my existing from the concerns manifested in the *bavardage quotidien* towards the participated yet never in this life completely established eternity that is tasted in aesthetic apprehension, in the inner utterance of truth, in the partial success of moral struggle.

---

1 Collection: Problèmes et Doctrines IV, Paris-Lyon: E. Vitte, 1953, 315 pp. [*Gregorianum* 36 (1955) 137–38.]
2 [A French philosopher (1883–1951) and professor at the Sorbonne. He founded a movement known as philosophy of the spirit, which aimed at a renewal of metaphysics in reaction to positivism and classical rationalism.]

As there are qualitative levels to time, so too there are to being. Hence M. Chaix-Ruy's work bifurcates from an initial chapter on existence into two chapters on temporality and three on thought, being, and essence. In the latter triad as in the former pair, he seeks to lead his readers to the central positions that also are traditional. But, perhaps, I had best explain my use of that word in the present context. Augustine relates that it took him years to discover that the name 'real' did not have the same connotation as the name 'body.' M. Chaix-Ruy is anxious that others make the same discovery with a similar impact upon their thinking and living. It is in that real sense that his goal is traditional.

If it is incumbent upon me to express a personal opinion, perhaps I may meet with a distinction the criticism that L. Lavelle's thought suffers from a neglect of the phenomenological approach. While I agree that our basic objective must be to understand things as they are, also I am somewhat adamant on the point that, inherent in the very notion and the entire method of phenomenology, there lurks a specious and superficial epistemology that must be overcome and discarded no less than superficial living and superficial views on reality. Existential dialectic has to transform the whole man, and the attractiveness of phenomenology is just part of the maya to be dispelled.

44

Review of Paul Vanier, S.J., *Théologie trinitaire chez saint Thomas d'Aquin: Évolution du concept d'action notionelle*[1]

Notional act is attributed to God the Father inasmuch as he generates God the Son; also it is attributed to both Father and Son inasmuch as they are the principle whence proceeds the Holy Spirit. The difficulty of a theological conception of the former notional act is well known and was put succinctly by Louis Billot in the following dilemma. 'Porro relatio paternitatis secundum modum intelligendi praesupponit actum generandi, et rursus actus generandi praesupponit suppositum generans iam constitutum.'[2]

Commonly the mind of St Thomas on this issue is settled by appealing to the opinion expressed in the *De potentia*, while the few writers aware of the divergences between this work and the *Summa theologiae* endeavor to eliminate them by speculative procedures that, of course, have nothing much to do with an objective interpretation of the text. Fr Vanier's fundamental merit is that he has placed this abstruse issue in its historical perspective, and his reward has been a set of conclusions of exceptional interest.

He distinguishes between a Dionysian and an Augustinian mode in formulating the basic concepts in trinitarian theory. The former takes God the Father as starting point; it unfolds in much the same manner as the evolution of trinitarian dogma; and it reaches theological systematization

---

1 Université de Montréal: Publications de l'Institut d'Études Médiévales, XIII; Paris: Vrin, 1953, 156 pp. [*Gregorianum* 36 (1955) 703–705.]
2 ['The relation of paternity by way of understanding presupposes the act of generating, and conversely the act of generating presupposes the generator as already constituted.' Louis Billot, *De Deo uno et trino* (Rome: Gregorian University Press, 1935) 619.]

through the theorem *bonum est diffusivum sui,* to conceive God the Father as *fontana Deitas,* communicating the Infinite Good to Son and Spirit and finite good to creatures. The latter approach begins, not from God the Father, but from the divine nature or substance; it is not content to affirm that the three divine persons are objectively consubstantial, equal, and eternal; but it also insists that our concepts also should be simultaneous, and so it assigns mutually opposed relations as the constitutive ground of the persons.

At first sight it might seem that medieval theologians were divided on the relative merits of the two modes of conception. Fr Vanier argues that the facts are more complex. Instead of two opposed views, he finds two levels in the development of theological thought. Elements of the Dionysian construction are almost ubiquitous. But their dominance in Richard of St Victor does not prevent him from beginning in Augustinian fashion from the divine nature. Moreover, the Dionysian principle *bonum est diffusivum sui* changed from an asset to a liability when the development of theological method made explicit the impossibility of demonstrating mysteries. Hence, while it continues to be repeated, at the same time it is enervated by its systematic context and so, perhaps, is to be regarded as a mere survival with no more than a symbolic value.

In the writings of St Thomas it is found that 'Le *Commentaire sententiaire* de saint Thomas offre donc sur la théologie trinitaire un ensemble de positions identiques à celles de la *Somme* et du *Compendium* et divergentes de celles du *De Potentia* et du *Contra Gentiles*: la subsistance du Père expressément attribuée à la relation; la priorité du Père, comme personne distincte, sur la génération; l'évanouissement dans notre esprit de tout aspect du concept de personne par la suppression de la relation; la signification du mot *personne* reportée *in recto* sur la relation; l'omission d'une relation d'émanation, perçue comme action notionelle; la distinction très nette entre la puissance génératrice et la puissance créatrice' (p. 123). So brief a citation, of course, cannot do justice to the sweep of Fr Vanier's analysis or to his firm yet precise grasp of subtle differences. But it does set forth clearly the result of his exacting labors: the Dionysian mode [of] conception is revealed in a whole series of manners in the *De potentia;* it is systematically eliminated from the *Summa theologiae;* and if no one will be surprised that the *Contra Gentiles* stands with the *De potentia* and the *Compendium theologiae* with the *Summa,* a problem of the first order arises from the agreement of the *Scriptum super Sententias* with the latter works.

To meet this issue Fr Vanier reviews the general evidence for a later revision of the *Scriptum* by St Thomas. To this he adds his own findings. While the *Scriptum* agrees with the *Summa* and differs from the *De potentia* on a series of basic points, there is no lack of evidence that the *Scriptum* contains too much of the older Dionysian viewpoint to be a single coherent piece. Moreover, insofar as the work of Hannibald de Hannibaldis[3] is representative of St Thomas's original *Scriptum*, further confirmation is forthcoming for the assertion that the text that alone is at our disposal contains a series of corrections of the views St Thomas initially entertained.

Perhaps the minimum conclusion to be drawn is that the theologian can no longer appeal to the *De potentia* for evidence on St Thomas's definitive trinitarian thought on the ground that, since the articles there are longer, therefore they are more profound. But if this is granted, more follows for, once the superiority of the *De potentia* has been challenged, the issue has to be investigated, and so Fr Vanier's work cannot be disregarded by any serious theologian concerned with trinitarian thought.

The only criticisms I have to offer lie in a rather remote part of the field of methodology. There is an elementary stage of historical investigation that has to be content with ill-defined, descriptive concepts. So New Testament scholars work out explanations in terms of Semitic mentality, eschatology, and the like; and in somewhat similar fashion Fr Vanier speaks of Aristotelian, Dionysian, Augustinian streams of thought. I should be inclined to expect or, at least, hope that a more developed methodology will eventually eliminate such makeshifts in favor of sharply-defined concepts and of well-formulated dialectical principles of development. But if I find a weakness in this aspect of Fr Vanier's work, I also am inclined to believe that the application of a still to be developed method will recast rather than change his conclusions.

3   [A Dominican theologian and cardinal; died 1272. He studied theology under St Thomas Aquinas and wrote his own commentary on the *Sentences*.]

45

Review of B. Xiberta, O.C., *El Yo de Jesucristo: Un Conflicto entre dos Cristologias*[1]

A brief introduction (pp. 9–16) is followed by an outline of some twenty-five opinions on the consciousness of Christ (pp. 10–82), by a diagnosis of current discussion, a statement of dogmatic requirements, and the presentation of a solution (pp. 85–156).

While everyone will find useful the workmanlike review of opinions, Fr Xiberta's many admirers may find his own treatment of the matter disappointing. Perhaps the root difficulty lies in his formulation of the issue. Liberal Protestants can ask how the man Jesus became conscious of his messianic vocation. Déodat de Basly[2] can ask how the *homo assumptus* was conscious of the divinity. But Fr Xiberta puts himself a false question when he inquires how the soul of Christ is conscious of the divinity. For what is conscious is a subject and, as Fr Xiberta rightly claims, there is in Christ only one subject, the Word.

Unfortunately, it is left to the reader to divine how Fr Xiberta would have answered his proper question, namely, How is the Word conscious of the Word through his human nature, How does a human consciousness without any commingling of divine consciousness constitute the Word as

---

1 Barcelona: Editorial Herder, 1954, 172 pp. [*Gregorianum* 36 (1955) 705–706.]
2 [Déodat de Basly, O.F.M. (1862–1937). Among his published articles is 'L'Assumptus Homo. L'emmêlement de trois conflits: Pélage, Nestorius, Appollinaire,' *La France Franciscaine* 11 (1928) 285–314. For a discussion of Déodat de Basly's Christology and a list of his publications, see Herman Diepan, 'Un scotisme apocryphe: La christologie du P. Déodat de Basly, O.F.M.,' *Revue thomiste* 49 (1949) 428–92.]

conscious of the Word? At least, I think, he would have seen that the Council of Chalcedon demands not only a single person but also two natures unconfused, not only a single subject but also a divine consciousness and a human consciousness without one merging into the other. There would follow, I suggest, a more nuanced diagnosis of contemporary discussion. Instead of seeing simply a conflict between an orthodox and a heterodox Christology, he would have adverted to a twofold dogmatic requirement demanding both a single divine subject and, at the same time, the natural unity of that subject's human consciousness; in consequence, he would not have tended to regard theologians that insist on the natural unity of Christ's human consciousness as victims of a lamentable aberration when, in fact, they are safeguarding a truth of faith to which his view hardly can be said to do full justice.

There is a further aspect to the matter, and it has to do with the fundamental question of method. Fr Xiberta is concerned to bring out the dogmatic issues without any metaphysical or psychological frills. But if dogmatic truth and theological subtlety are quite distinct, there is the whole history of dogma and theology to emphasize their interdependence. In the present instance, the necessary subtlety seems to be a distinction between the unity of the subject and the unity of a human nature: the unity of the subject is the unity formulated in the principles of identity and non-contradiction or, again, the unity that adds to *ens* only a negation and consequently derives, as does *ens*, from *esse*, but the unity of nature is the intrinsically intelligibile unity, the *unum per se*, that derives from essence or nature. Christ's human consciousness is a unity in a plurality of potencies, habits, and acts; it is a unity in virtue of Christ's human nature and not exclusively in virtue of the divine subject; but also it is a unity that is easily overlooked when one scorns the labor of analyzing consciousness and when one adopts a theory of the hypostatic union that grounds the transcendental attributes of the man Jesus in the divinity.[3]

3   [For further treatment by Lonergan of Xiberta's Christology and methodology, see *The Ontological and Psychological Constitution of Christ*, vol. 7 in Collected Works of Bernard Lonergan, trans. Michael G. Shields, ed. Frederick E. Crowe and Robert M. Doran (Toronto: University of Toronto Press, 2002) 125–31, 281–83.]

46

Book Notice of F.L.B. Cunningham, O.P., *The Indwelling of the Trinity: A Historico-Doctrinal Study of the Theory of St. Thomas Aquinas*[1]

The first five chapters are devoted to a statement of the issue and to the teaching of scripture, the Greek and Latin Fathers, and the earlier Scholastic writers. The remaining four chapters set forth an account of Aquinas's view in the *Summa theologiae* and compare it with his *Scriptum super Sententias* and with the views of Alexander of Hales, of St Bonaventure, and of St Albert the Great. The last sixty or so pages are devoted (1) to transcripts of manuscripts attributed to Alexander of Hales, Eudes Rigaud, and an unidentified writer, (2) to four tables, of which the most notable indicates parallel passages in four commentaries on the *Sentences*, and (3) to a bibliography and two indices. Though it seems to me unfortunate that footnotes are printed, not where they are wanted but at the end of chapters, it remains that the Priory Press has produced a beautiful book.

The author believes that there is nothing new to be said on Aquinas's doctrine on divine inhabitation, and so, while he is conversant with the many opinions of theologians on the issue, his principal effort is directed to a clear and forceful statement that (1) divine inhabitation does not result from sanctifying grace as an effect of divine causality but (2) from a quasi-experimental knowledge constituted by the love and wisdom that are rooted in grace, where (3) this experimental knowledge presupposes God's presence by immensity and, (4) though only habitual, suffices to constitute

1 Dubuque, IA: The Priory Press, 1955, xvii + 414 pp. [*Gregorianum* 37 (1956) 664–65.]

inhabitation. While the author considers that there are different concepts of divine mission in Aquinas's *Summa* and *Sentences*, he maintains the doctrine of inhabitation to be the same in the two works and to resemble that of St Bonaventure rather than that of St Albert.

47

Review of Johannes Brinktrine, *Die Lehre von Gott.* Zweiter Band: *Von der göttlichen Trinität*[1]

This compact and well-informed manual, after an introduction dealing with the notion of mystery (11–17), offers an account of 'Scripture and Tradition' in thirty-six pages (17–52) that include a three-page excursus on the *Comma Ioanneum*[2] and four pages on imagery, liturgy, and manifestations of Christian piety. There follows a *Spekulativer Teil* in which are treated processions (52–103), missions (103–110), relations (110–124), persons (124–163) and the perfection, operation, and perichoresis of the persons (163–184). There follow an appendix on non-Christian trinities (184–209) and four indices.

I experience some difficulty in reconciling the author's theses: he denies a real distinction between the two processions, identifies the relations with the processions, and yet affirms three real and really distinct relations. Also, I find his grasp of the psychological analogy and of the structure of the treatise in Aquinas's *Summa* somewhat feeble. On the other hand, his pages abound in information on a large variety of theological and related topics.

---

1 Paderborn: F. Schöningh, 1954, 237 pp. [*Gregorianum* 37 (1956) 665.]
2 [The Johannine Comma: A clause (Greek: *komma*) inserted in 1 John 5.7–8 which makes explicit reference to the Blessed Trinity. It is omitted in most modern versions of the Bible and discounted by modern biblical scholars. For a thorough review of the controverted text, see Raymond E. Brown, s.s., *The Epistles of John*, The Anchor Bible 30 (Garden City, NY: Doubleday, 1982), appendix IV, pp. 775–87.]

48

Book Notice of S. Thomae Aquinatis, (1) *In octo libros de Physico Auditu sive Physicorum Aristotelis Commentaria,* (2) *In Aristotelis Libros Peri Hermeneias et Posteriorum Analyticorum Expositio,* (3) *In Librum de Causis Expositio*[1]

Fr Pirotta has aimed at an accurate reproduction of the Piana edition of the *Commentary on the Physics.* The Latin translation of Aristotle is accompanied with indications of Bekker's pages and columns; the text of St Thomas is divided into continuously numbered paragraphs; and there are one hundred and ten pages devoted to an *Index Alphabeticus Nominum et Terminorum.*

Fr Spiazzi has reproduced the Leonine editions of the commentaries on the *Peri Hermeneias* and on the *Posterior Analytics,* together with their prefaces and indices. He has omitted the Greek text and has not added the Bekker pagination.

Fr Pera has done an enormous amount of work. He has collated the first Venice edition, the Antwerp, and the Parma editions; he has also drawn upon the edition of the *Liber de Causis* in R. Steele's edition of Roger Bacon's commentary and made what use he could of the work of C. Vansteenkiste and H.D. Saffrey which appeared after his own was completed. Besides laboring for an intelligible text and adding illuminating references, he regularly reproduces the Greek text of Proclus from Dodds's edition and a Latin translation whenever St Thomas refers to Proclus. Fr Caramello provided an introductory essay of some twenty-five pages on the literary, historical, and doctrinal aspects of the *Liber de Causis.* There are five indices.

---

1 (1) Editio novissima, cura et studio A.M. Pirotta, o.p., Naples: M. D'Auria, 1953, 660 pp. (2) Cura et studio R.M. Spiazzi, o.p., Turin: Marietti, 1955, xviii + 440 pp. (3) Cura et studio C. Pera, o.p., Turin: Marietti, 1955, lviii + 174 pp. [*Gregorianum* 37 (1956) 691.]

49

Book Notice of Plotinus, *The Enneads*[1]

Stephen MacKenna (1872–1934), one of the great line of unprofessional
scholars that have enriched English letters, confided to his private journal
on his thirty-sixth birthday that to translate and interpret Plotinus seemed
to him 'really worth a life.' He resigned a lucrative post as European representative of the *New York World* and head of its Paris office, settled in
Dublin, and went to work not only on Greek language and philosophy but
also on the masters of English prose style. His translation, published in five
volumes by the Medici Society between 1917 and 1930, is considered by
the Regius Professor of Greek at Oxford to rank among the few great translations in our time. But for some years the work has been out of print and
hard to come by, and the publishers are to be congratulated on reissuing it
in a single, elegant volume.

To take advantage of subsequent advance in Plotinian studies – notably,
Henry and Schwyzer's critical edition of the first three enneads, Harder's
German translation (1930–1937), and Cilento's Italian (1947–1949) –
some revision was imperative. This work was entrusted to B.S. Page, who
had collaborated with MacKenna in the translation of the sixth ennead.
Several hundred modifications have been introduced, though many are
slight, and about a quarter of the total occur in the tractates *On the Kinds of
Being* (VI, 1–3), which Mr Page had translated for the original edition.

---

1 Trans. Stephen MacKenna, revised by B.S. Page, preface by E.R. Dodds, introduction by Paul Henry, s.J.; London: Faber and Faber, 1957, ii + 635 pp.
   [*Gregorianum* 40 (1959) 389–90.]

Besides the translation of the *Enneads* and of Porphyry's *Life of Plotinus*, there are reproduced from the first edition MacKenna's account of his principles of translation and of his terminology, and there are added a truly eloquent tribute to MacKenna by Professor Dodds, a learned essay on Plotinus by Paul Henry, and three appendices containing a selected contemporary bibliography, a concordance of the systematic and chronological order of the tractates, and a list of references to the sources of Plotinus's quotations.

50

Review of M.F. Sciacca, *Saint Augustin et le néoplatonisme, La possibilité d'une philosophie chrétienne* and Maurice Nédoncelle, *Existe-t-il une philosophie chrétienne?*[1]

In 1954 a leading Italian philosopher, Professor Sciacca of Genoa, was invited to occupy the *Chaire Cardinal Mercier* at Louvain. He took as his topic the philosophic element in the thought of St Augustine and, with the greatest delicacy and discernment, discussed (1) the role of Neoplatonism in St Augustine's conversion, (2) his strictly philosophic stand against the skepticism of the Academy, (3) his grasp of the ontological unity of man's composite nature, and (4) the dialectic of human nature implicit in 'Fecisti nos ad Te, Domine.' From the first, second, and fourth of these themes there naturally arises the question of a Christian philosophy. For St Augustine, in his own way, was helped by the Neoplatonists; he did not hesitate to appeal to purely philosophic arguments; yet when it came to the goal of philosophic aspiration, the attainment of happiness, he found man's mind and man's virtue in need of Christ's truth and grace. With natural and supernatural so intertwined in St Augustine, Sciacca was able in a very brief conclusion to enter his plea for the unified and integrated Christian view that distinguishes rather than separates the philosophic and religious moments in the thinking of the concrete person.

Canon Nédoncelle, professor at the University of Strasbourg, opens his essay with a rapid sketch of the relations between Christianity and philosophy. In sixty pages, he outlines (1) the philosophies that existed at the

---

1 [Sciacca] Louvain: Publications universitaires; Paris: Béatrice-Nauwelaerts, 1956, 69 pp. [Nédoncelle] Je sais – je crois, 10, Paris: Fayard, 1956, 121 pp. [*Gregorianum* 40 (1959) 182–83.]

birth of Christianity, (2) the gradual patristic development of the notion of a Christian philosophy and its later medieval decline, and (3) in modern times the violent swings of the pendulum from Renaissance exaltation of man to Reformation contempt of nature, from Descartes to Pascal, from the optimism of Leibniz to the pessimism of Kant, from Hegel to Kierkegaard. Against this backdrop there is set the debate of 1931 (Bréhier, Gilson, Blondel) with its prolongations into the present, and the work concludes with a suggestive essay along the personalist lines which Canon Nédoncelle so ably represents. The philosopher, he would contend, is to yield place to the theologian at the moment of encounter with Christ. Meanwhile, he is not to fear that the light of faith and the help of grace will make him less objective or less critical or even, indeed, deprive his work of that measure of universal relevance and significance that concretely it is given philosophers to attain.

Evidently the question of a Christian philosophy is not dead. Nor will it die, for in substance it asks how a Catholic can attempt total reflection on man's situation. But it will do no harm to recall that the twelfth century was steeped in Augustine, yet baffled by problems in method and concept formation that were solved only in the early thirteenth by the systematic and ontological distinction between the orders of grace and nature. Further, this distinction is stretched to a separation of philosophy and theology only when there intervenes a further methodological component, namely, that the one valid scientific ideal is an abstract deductivism. Thirdly, against that ideal much contemporary thought, correctly I believe, is in revolt; but to refute effectively, one must replace, and the replacement must be better than a contrary exaggeration. So I am led to suggest that the issue which goes by the name of a Christian philosophy is basically a question on the deepest level of methodology, the one that investigates the operative intellectual ideals not only of scientists and philosophers but also, since Catholic truth is involved, theologians. It is, I fear, in Vico's phrase, a *scienza nuova.*

51

Book Notice of Bernard Piault, *Le Mystère du Dieu Vivant*[1]

Fr Piault, professor at the Grand Séminaire de Sens, aims to bring the dogma of the Blessed Trinity to the people. He does so beautifully through the scriptures, outlines of patristic thought, an account of Greek and Latin trinitarian theology, and indications of the relevance of the dogma to one's spiritual life and to the human community.

1   Je sais – je crois, 17, Paris: Fayard, 1956, 126 pp. [*Gregorianum* 40 (1959) 156.]

52

Review of Bartholomaeus M. Xiberta, O. Carm., *Tractatus de Verbo Incarnato, I. Introductio et Christologia, II. Soteriologia* and *Enchiridion de Verbo Incarnato. Fontes quos ad studia theologica collegit*[1]

Fr Xiberta is professor of theology in the International Carmelite College in Rome and Member of the Pontifical Roman Academy of St Thomas. Well-known for his scholarly research, he published in 1949 an *Introductio in sacram theologiam,* and the present ample treatise may, perhaps, be regarded as a concrete application and illustration of his earlier account of theological method.

Since he believes in a division of the sciences, he leaves to historians, apologists, and exegetes practically all discussion of biblical issues. While this creates the unfortunate impression that his treatment of scriptural issues is superficial, full compensation is made by his erudition in other fields. The annotated bibliography, which includes scriptural topics, runs to seventy pages and the *Index onomasticus* to eighteen. In particular, the extensive and carefully indexed companion volume of *Fontes,* to which the treatise frequently refers, not only reproduces relevant papal and conciliar documents but also draws upon the best available editions to provide an original and abundant collection of extracts from [the] Fathers and [from] heretics.

This wealth of information must not lead one to expect a genetic account of the development of dogmatic formulae after the fashion of

---

1 [*Tractatus*] Madrid: Consejo Superior de Investigaciones Científicas, 1954, 2 vols., pp. 1–456 and 457–766; [*Enchiridion*] Madrid: Consejo Superior de Investigaciones Científicas, 1957, 810 pp. [*Gregorianum* 40 (1959) 155–56.]

Aloys Grillmeier's notable essay on the antecedents of Chalcedon.[2] For although Fr Xiberta distinguishes three levels of dogmatic and, further, three levels of theological explicitness in treating the hypostatic union (pp. 61–272), his viewpoint is anticipatory, illuminating earlier modes of thought by grasping them through later and clearer concepts, rather than generating the later concepts by attempting the delicate task of recreating earlier and somewhat elusive mental structures and situations.

Substantially, then, the treatment is in a scholastic *ordo doctrinae*, and, while throughout it is on a very generous scale, the five hundred pages devoted to the incarnation, the properties of the sacred humanity, and the mysteries of our Lord's earthly life seem to give an air of abruptness to sixty pages on the redemption, fifty on the permanent offices of the Savior, and thirty on the end of the Incarnation.

On its speculative side, the work endeavors to steer systematically a middle course between the positivism of repeating what has been said and, on the other hand, theoretical efforts that commonly end in what are considered by many to be merely philosophic disputes. The results, I think, are illuminating. For, in the last analysis, the author's thought is underpinned, not by a systematic structure of terms and relations that possess a meaning and, as it were, a life of their own, but rather by common notions whose connotation and implications have to be gathered from the context and hardly lead beyond it. Thus, we are told (p. 167) that the Incarnation means a real influence of the Word on the assumed humanity, that this influence occurs in the order of ontological constitution, that aptly it is conceived as the exercise of a dominion, and that the dominion is strictly ontological, pure, total.

Theologians will find Father Xiberta's work a rich source of information, a sustained example of well-balanced theological judgment, and, perhaps, a prolonged presentation of the question, What exactly is the nature of theological inquiry?

---

2   [Aloys Grillmeier, 'Die theologische und sprachliche Vorbereitung der christologischen Formel von Chalkedon,' in *Das Konzil von Chalkedon: Geschichte und Gegenwart*, ed. Aloys Grillmeier and Heinrich Bacht (Würzburg: Echter-Verlag, 1951, 1954) 5–202. Grillmeier's book *Christ in Christian Tradition: From the Apostolic Age to Chalcedon (451)*, trans. J.S. Bowden (New York: Sheed and Ward, 1965, and London: A.R. Mowbray & Co., 1965) is a thorough revision of this earlier article.]

53

Review of William Oliver Martin,
The Order and Integration of Knowledge and *Metaphysics and Ideology*[1]

The lecture on *Metaphysics and Ideology* sets as alternatives a reasoned meta-physics and a positivistic ideology. It is largely dependent on the book, *The Order and Integration of Knowledge*, which combines a traditional Scholasticism of a predominantly logical type with a determination to effect the logical adjustments believed necessary to take contemporary science into account and thereby restrain merely ideological abuses.

Such adjustments involve distinctions between (1) the order of being and the order of knowledge, (2) autonomous and synthetic (derivative) sciences, (3) phenomenological, mathematical, ontological, and synthetic contexts, and (4) in place of the familiar relations of subordination and subalternation, the triad of 'constitutive of,' 'regulative of,' and 'instrumental to.'

The use to which these distinctions are put may best be indicated by commenting briefly on a question. In a section in which Dr Martin took issue with M. Jacques Maritain and George P. Klubertanz, s.j., he wrote (p. 304):

> In terms of formal objects there is a difference between (1) gen-eral metaphysics: being *qua* being; (2) cosmology: being *qua* mobile (in general); (3) experimental science: mobile *qua* mobile

1 [*Order*] Ann Arbor: University of Michigan Press, 1957, 355 pp. [*Metaphysics*] Milwaukee: Marquette University Press, 1959, 87 pp. [*Gregorianum* 41 (1960) 171–73.]

(in detail); (4) the philosophy of nature: mobile (in detail) being.
Facts of sense experience are instrumental to, but not constitutive
of, (1) and (2); are wholly constitutive of (3); and are partly constitutive of (4). The (1) and (2) are regulative of (3), but partly constitutive of (4).

Here Dr Martin's position seems to be that (1) cosmology is general and
thereby independent of the results of experimental science, (2) philosophy of nature is detailed, takes into account the findings of experimental
science, and so varies with them, and (3) experimental science, while it
yields knowledge of the real, still has no professional competence on metaphysical or cosmological issues and, so far from dictating to metaphysicians
or cosmologists, should on the contrary be guided by them.

Such a position, however, is not in terms of the assigned formal objects.[2]
Being *qua* mobile and mobile *qua* mobile do not differ; both mean mobile
being *qua* mobile; for the only being that can be considered *qua* mobile is
mobile being; and the only mobile on which one can experiment is the
existent mobile. It remains that there is a difference between the two for
Dr Martin, but this difference lies between ontological and phenomenological contexts, where 'phenomenology' is to be understood, not in
Edmund Husserl's or Max Scheler's sense, but in the sense in which contemporary science refuses to discuss metaphysical issues.

Again, experimental science is not one but many. How, one may ask, can
many sciences have a single formal object? The answer seems to be that the
many sciences have a common, experimental method; the use of that
method places the pronouncements of these sciences in a common, phenomenological context; and it is the phenomenological context that effectively is meant by the formal object, mobile *qua* mobile.

Again, 'in general' and 'in detail' do not differentiate formal objects;
they denote different degrees of actuation of the same science. But Dr
Martin's real point seems to be that a developing science cannot be a regulative science; the philosophy of nature develops and therefore it cannot
regulate; still, there has to be some science that regulates experimental science, and so cosmology has to be detached from the philosophy of nature.

2   Elsewhere (p. 124) Dr Martin assigns cosmology the object 'mobile *qua*
being.' On p. 304, cosmology is said to deal with *being* (his italics) insofar as it
is mobile, while philosophy of nature knows 'the mobile (in some detail) insofar as it (in such detail) has being.'

At this point, of course, there arise questions of fact. Are there any sciences that do not develop? Is the regulation of one science by another a matter of omniscience instructing ignorance, or is it a matter of the interrelations of two levels in the process of learning? On the latter view, a developing science could also be regulative, though it would have to be circumspect when it came to laying down rules.

I have not attempted to follow Dr Martin over the whole range of knowledge, but perhaps enough has been said to indicate the problem with which he deals and the problem raised by his book. The problem with which he deals is real: when one speaks, with the ancients, of science as certain knowledge of things by their causes and, again, with the moderns, of science as the most probable knowledge that has been reached through observation and experiment, one is not employing the name 'science' univocally. It is this lack of univocity that makes real the problem of constructing a unitary view that includes both traditional metaphysics and contemporary science, and Dr Martin's array of distinctions has the merit of being relevant to this task. At the same time, I have the feeling that Dr Martin's predominantly logical approach is unfortunate: it involves a high degree of abstraction that concentrates attention on the timeless features of the issue and tends to neglect science *in fieri qua in fieri*; and this oversight leads to the attempt to fit things into categories in which they do not fit accurately.

54

Book Notice of *In Opera Sancti Thomae Aquinatis Index seu Tabula Aurea Eximii Doctoris* F. Petri De Bergomo. Editio Fototypica[1]

This is a quite clear and legible photo reprint of Peter of Bergomo's (ob. 1482) *Tabula Aurea* from the Paris or Vivès edition (1880) of the works of St Thomas. There have been restored Peter's marginal indications of opposed or variant statements and of the divisions he followed in arranging numerous references under a single key work. The reprint is to serve as the analytic index for a forthcoming edition of the *Summa theologiae*, which in a single volume is to give the Leonine text and doubts about it, the Ottawa edition's source references, rather full indications of parallel passages and of Peter of Bergomo's opposite passages, and select bibliographies.[2]

1 Alba-Rome: Editiones Paulinae, 1960, 1250 pp. [*Gregorianum* 44 (1963) 371–72.]
2 [Lonergan is referring to *Sancti Thomae de Aquino Summa Theologiae* (Alba-Rome: Editiones Paulinae, 1962). The editors wish to thank Rev. Richard Liddy for confirming this.]

55

Book Notice of Ignacio Escribano-Alberca, *Die Gewinnung theologischer Normen aus der Geschichte der Religion bei E. Troeltsch*[1]

Ernst Troeltsch (1865–1923) was a man of vast erudition and keen theoretical interests. Dilthey had seen a need of doing for history and human science what Immanuel Kant's *Critique* had done for natural science; and, as Anders Nygren and Rudolf Otto, so Troeltsch was engaged in the subsidiary task of determining a religious a priori. This he conceived as the goal that was becoming clear and distinct through history, but he was unable to master the problem of relativism, shifted from theology to philosophy, and in his last years was engaged in affairs of state, when Karl Barth appeared and a new chapter began. So Troeltsch marks the end of an era, and today he stands as a resourceful compendium of problems that have acquired new complications without reaching satisfying solutions.

Fr Escribano devotes the first part of his work to Troeltsch's background and his more general positions on history and religion and, in the second part, sets forth his *Religionsphilosophie* in its suppositions, its basic categories, and its implications for Christianity. The study is thorough and detailed but suffers, perhaps, from a certain eagerness to show that Troeltsch's enterprise was not viable.

---

1 Münchener Theologische Studien, II, 21, Munich: Max Hueber, 1961, xvi + 200 pp. [*Gregorianum* 44 (1963) 369–70.]

56

Review of Jean-Marie Levasseur, *Le lieu théologique, 'histoire.' Contribution à une ontologie et introduction à une méthodologie*[1]

In Melchior Cano's *De locis theologicis*, the tenth and last of the 'places' was history. But since the sixteenth century there have occurred two notable developments: there has emerged historical consciousness; and the content of the notion, and reality, of science has shifted from the abstract, universal, necessary, and immutable towards the concrete, ordered, intelligible, and dynamic. Following these developments with a notable lag, theology has been becoming conscious of its own historicity, and it has been giving more and more attention to the historical aspect of its sources and of its secondary objects. But a still further lag must be noted before we come to the theoretical treatment of the new issues in theology.

The interest, then, of Fr Levasseur's work is considerable. Inasmuch as he asks about history, he is concerned with the theoretical treatment of the new issues in theology. Inasmuch as he is concerned to relate history, in its modern sense, to Melchior Cano's *De locis*, he has taken upon himself one of the acutest forms of the problem of relating the new to the old.

His approach is from the old. Cano sought an integration of medieval Scholasticism and of the humanism of his own day by turning to Aristotle's *Topics* and Cicero's views on rhetoric. He conceived theology as a set of arguments proving Christian truth and refuting contrary error. His notion of method was a list of the 'places' where the arguments were to be found and an accompanying list of the values (*de fide*, certain, probable, etc.) to

---

1 Trois-Rivières: Éditions du Bien Public, 1960, 231 pp. [*Gregorianum* 44 (1963) 370–71.]

be associated with the 'places.' In the first part of his work, Fr Levasseur is concerned to grasp Cano's views clearly and exactly, to fill them out with the help of Fr Gardeil,[1] and to add to the multiple classifications a few modest refinements of his own. In the second part, the taste for clarity and exactitude remains in full vigor. In a Thomistic dress of secondary and primary material objects and of formal object, there is set forth a notion of history unknown to ancient and medieval thinkers and, to boot, a similarly unknown department of science. There then is executed the task of relating such history to Cano's 'places,' of fitting it into the complex classifications of the first part. The work closes with the observation that, when one comes to think of it, history is the *lieu des lieux*: all of Cano's 'places' in one way or another are interdependent and interpenetrate; but history does so in a massive fashion. If the author does not go on to conclude that a full recognition of the significance of history involves a revision of Cano's views on theology, his readers may suspect that that is so.

---

1 [Ambroise Gardeil, *La notion du Lieu théologique: Extrait de la Revue des Sciences Philosophiques et Théologiques* (Paris: J. Gabalda, [1908?]).]

57

Review of Edmond Barbotin,
Jean Trouillard, Roger Verneaux,
Dominique Dubarle, Stanislas Breton,
*La crise de la raison dans la pensée
contemporaine*[1]

The first three writers are brief but pointed witnesses to the crisis. From a phenomenological context Edmond Barbotin asks whether the rational is the enemy of the reasonable, whether the person, so essentially singular, can develop through access to a universal that seems either to ignore or to deny the singular (p. 26). From a Neoplatonist context Jean Trouillard argues for the 'One' that is, indeed, the negation of reason's multiplicity but thereby the negation of the negativity inherent in reason. Roger Verneaux speaks from a traditional context but only to conclude that the principle of sufficient reason is not a principle: it is not self-evident but false; what is self-evident is its negation; the alleged principle is merely a rationalist postulate that is to be abandoned along with rationalism (p. 38).

Dominique Dubarle envisages the issue historically in terms of the constitutions that human reason has given itself. In rapid but penetrating sketches of successive views that reason has held of reason, he tells us what *logos* was for the ancient Greeks, what *ratio* meant to Latin thought, what it became in medieval syntheses that enlightened reason by faith and, when the enlightenment of reason was sought by omitting faith, the rupture that arose not only with the medieval but also with the ancient view of reason. For modern man 'reason' is secularist self-constituting subjectivity that leaves to 'understanding' the theoretic and practical organization of the real as objectivity (pp. 80–82). Among Catholics, however, the ancient view

---

1 Recherches de Philosophie, v, Bruges: Desclée de Brouwer, 1960, 215 pp.
[*Gregorianum* 44 (1963) 372–73.]

is still alive, and even apart from religious concern one of the goals of contemporary spiritual renewal may be defined as an effective reconciliation of ancient tradition and modern discovery. For the crisis of reason in contemporary thought is simply the fact that reason has not yet given itself an adequate constitution, that its self-education remains incomplete, that as yet a fully determinate model, an explicit set of standards, an up-to-date codification does not exist (p. 113).

Stanislas Breton sets forth the changes that have occurred in mathematics, logic, and natural science. These changes, he insists, are neither the result of this or that discovery nor the work of this or that school. Rather they are the crumbling of an *ancien régime*, the outcome of a many-sided and complex historical process, in which events and discoveries occurring independently and in different fields have led opposed schools of thought and different climates of opinion to analogous conclusions. For while the conclusions differ with the schools and climates, still they agree in their opposition to the idea of necessity. Once enshrined in Euclid's *Elements*, Aristotle's *Posterior Analytics*, Laplace's hypothetical demon, and most philosophies, once the self-evident and necessary essence of science, necessity has become a marginal idea.

There has been a concomitant change in philosophy. There is a lack of interest in the possible and the a priori, a distrust of the universal, a devaluation of the impersonal. Philosophy has ceased to be the work of solitary thinkers deducing the world, and it has become the common task to be promoted by personal contact and dialogue, and to be achieved not by proof but by persuasion. *Erklären* has been left to the scientists; *verstehen* has become the heritage of philosophers, and its basic requirement is an openness to all the surprises that reality offers. So fixed systems give way to manifolds of intentional horizons which are to be, not justified but described; description goes back to genesis and motivation, but its aim is not criticism but comprehension; there slips away the *zoon logikon* whose mind corresponds to things and whose things imitate the Idea; there emerges the community of self-constituting spirits aware of a responsibility for what they make of themselves.

So too *La crise de la raison dans la pensée contemporaine* is a collaborative effort. Its aim is not to work out the systematic solution of the issues it raises, but to portray persuasively the situation within which our thinking in fact occurs. There is, of course, no heroic *epokhe* precluding any suggestion of what is to be done, but the suggestions that are made do not fall within a discernible pattern. It would be hard to reconcile Verneaux and

Breton, Trouillard and Dubarle. Still, there is a single direction to Barbotin's, Dubarle's, and Breton's papers, and one must be grateful to all of them for raising issues that in theology are very urgent. Modern scriptural, conciliar, patristic, medieval studies are 'science' not in the ancient Greek but in the modern sense of the term; and the dogmatic theologian has the task, if not of arranging for their baptism, at least of finding himself at home with them.

58

Review of Jean-Louis Maier,
Les missions divines selon saint Augustin[1]

In 1958 in this series (Paradosis, XII), G. Aeby published an extremely useful work, *Les missions divines de saint Justin à Origène.*[2] It now has its complement in J.L. Maier's study, since the first half of it is devoted to St Augustine's Greek and Latin predecessors from the beginning of the Arian heresy.

Maier found his way prepared by Altaner's investigations of Augustine's Greek sources,[3] by Courcelle's *Recherches,*[4] and by work done on the chronology of Augustine's writings.[5] But he gives us a review of this work and uses it to set forth the problems and the development of the doctrine of the Old Testament theophanies and of visible and invisible missions of the Son and of the Holy Spirit.

Though the solutions today seem simple and obvious, the problems then were real enough. It was the Arian heresy that made plain the distinction between divine missions and divine processions; that clear distinction made

---

1 Paradosis, XVI, Fribourg, Switzerland: Éditions Universitaires, 1960, 224 pp. [*Gregorianum* 44 (1963) 371.]
2 [Gervais Aeby, *Les missions divines de saint Justin à Origène* (Fribourg, Switzerland: Éditions universitaires, 1958).]
3 [See the list of Altaner's writings on pp. vii–viii of the bibliography of Maier's book.]
4 [Maier lists on p. viii of his bibliography Pierre Paul Courcelle's book *Recherches sur les Confessions de Saint Augustin* (Paris: E. de Boccard, 1950), where Courcelle himself provides a list of his own writings on pp. 263–64.]
5 [Among the writings listed in Maier's bibliography on pp. vii–ix of his book, Lonergan may have had particularly in mind the article by Seraphinus M. Zarb, 'Chronologia operum Sancti Augustini,' *Angelicum* 11 (1934) 78–91.]

it possible to clarify separately problems incidental to the missions and problems incidental to the processions; finally, the solutions of these problems made possible the astonishment of the many, since Pétau,[6] who seem incapable of conceiving the ante-Nicene situation in which the solutions had not been worked out and the distinctions had not been drawn effectively. As G. Aeby, so J.L. Maier, and no doubt the director of the series, O. Perler, are to be thanked for getting away from the abstruse processions and for treating the missions, which are much more amenable to straightforward historical techniques.

6 [Denis Pétau (Dionysius Petavius), Jesuit historian and theologian (1583–1652).]

59

Review of Herman M. Diepen,
La théologie de l'Emmanuel: Les lignes maîtresses d'une christologie[1]

For St Cyril of Alexandria, the Word assumed human flesh animated by an intellective soul. Both the common patristic expression, *assumptus homo,* and Aristotelian philosophy can be invoked in favor of the conclusion that the Word assumed a man. But a man is a person; the Word is a person; and the assumption of a person by a person is Nestorian doctrine. Cyril certainly was not a Nestorian; nor can patristic use of the expression *assumptus homo* countervail patristic rejection of Nestorianism. However, there remains Aristotle to be reckoned with, and the series of theological opinions on the nature of the hypostatic union, evolved from the twelfth century to our own day, represent so many not too conscious attempts to come to terms with Aristotle.

The Scotist minimal departure from Aristotle is too close to Nestorianism for Dom Diepen's taste. At the same time, he finds exorbitant the more radical departures illustrated by Capreolus, Cajetan, Billot. Accordingly, he opts for a certain *souplesse* (p. 113) in the application of metaphysical principles, so that somehow there is one *esse* in Christ and somehow two.

Dom Diepen, besides the hypostatic union, also discusses the consciousness of Christ. Consciousness is conceived as a perceiving; Christ perceives his acts as dependent on someone; that 'someone' is known by the beatific vision (p. 190). This, of course, is quite logical; if consciousness is perceiving, there is no psychological subject, not only in Christ, but not even in us:

---

1 Bruges: Desclée de Brouwer, 1960, 321 pp. [*Gregorianum* 45 (1964) 860.]

there are only objects. But logic alone is not enough. Where there is no psychological subject, there is no one that suffers *vera carnis passione.*

There is much that is acute in Dom Diepen's book and not a little erudition. But the climate is controversy. The method omits the now customary distinction between the successive contexts and levels in which a doctrine is discussed and developed. The style reflects the intensity of the author's commitment and too easily slips into rhetoric.[2]

2 [For Lonergan's assessment of Diepen's earlier articles on Christology, see *The Ontological and Psychological Constitution of Christ* (above p. 215, n. 3) pp. 69–73, 279–81.]

60

Book Notice of Michael Schmaus, *Katholische Dogmatik,* Band II, Teil 2: *Gott der Erlöser*[1]

When an enormous work reaches its sixth edition, the reviewer has only to acknowledge a landmark.

In the present volume Msgr Schmaus includes Christology within soteriology, and soteriology within God's redemptive decree. This gives three parts: (1) God's redemptive decree, (2) the incarnate Son of God, and (3) the work of Christ. It follows that the order of thought and exposition neatly coincides with the time series of the *Heilsgeschichte,* so that Msgr Schmaus can begin with Adam and Eve, draw on the Old Testament to set forth God's redemptive decree and the messianic promise, delineate the humanity of Christ from the New Testament and add Christological doctrines, along with sections on Our Lady's virginity and the Immaculate Conception, to treat finally Christ's mediation, priesthood, sacrifice, victory, vicarious satisfaction, descent into hell, rising from the dead, ascent into heaven, sending of the Spirit, and his roles as revealer, king, and shepherd, along with the remaining mariological doctrines.

This detailed panorama is prefaced with a brief note on some of the author's methodological views. He finds a distinction between scripture and tradition necessary, for he can prove some dogmas from tradition but not from scripture. Moreover, he finds contemporary theology in a crisis, and expresses acute dismay over the threat to *Glaubensfreude* occasioned by unnamed theologians who, it is stated, in their articles and studies begin by clearing away previous theological thought and proceed to erect a new structure.

1 6th ed., Munich: Max Hueber, 1963, xii + 562 pp. [*Gregorianum* 45 (1964) 859.]

PART FIVE

Later Shorter Papers, Responses, Reviews

61

Philosophic Difference and Personal Development[1]

In Europe at the present time, there is a widespread disaffection for St Thomas and not a little favor for the apparently more timely doctrines of personalists, phenomenologists, and existentialists. In America, while Thomism holds a secure position among Catholic philosophers, it does happen that those who, after a course in Scholastic philosophy, have gone on to other specialized fields, at times exhibiting a marked hostility to the philosophy in which earlier they had been educated.

It would seem difficult to disassociate this phenomenon with problems of personal intellectual development. A new higher viewpoint in the natural sciences ordinarily involves no revision of the subject's image and concept of himself, and so scientific advance easily wins universal and permanent acceptance. But a higher viewpoint in philosophy not only log-

---

1 [*The New Scholasticism* 32 (1958) 97. This piece was later published in the *Lonergan Studies Newsletter* 14 (March 1993) 8–9, preceded by the following note of Frederick E. Crowe, editor: 'Synopsis, published in *The New Scholasticism* (1958) 97, of a paper meant for the annual meeting of the American Catholic Philosophical Association, Detroit, April 9, 1958. But this paper was never presented (and perhaps never written); instead Lonergan wrote "*Insight*: Preface to a Discussion." The fragment has a special interest in view of the forthcoming *Topics in Education*, where philosophic differences are treated at length.' *Topics in Education* was published in 1993, volume 10 in Collected Works of Bernard Lonergan, ed. Robert M. Doran and Frederick E. Crowe (Toronto: University of Toronto Press). '*Insight*: Preface to a Discussion' can be found in *Collection* (see above, p. 13, n. 1) 142–52.]

ically entails such a revision but also cannot be grasped with a 'real apprehension' unless the revision actually becomes effective in the subject's mental attitudes. So the philosophic schools are many, and each suffers its periods of decline and revival.

It was to foster such a 'real apprehension' of one's own intelligence and reasonableness and to bring out its intimate connection with the fundamental differences of the philosophies that the present writer labored in his recent work *Insight*.

62A

De Argumento Theologico ex Sacra Scriptura[1]

Ponitur exemplum, quod deinde analysi subicitur, ut denique quaeratur utrum typicum sit.

1   Ponitur Exemplum

E. Gutwenger, *Bewusstsein und Wissen Christi*, Innsbruck 1960:[2]

I, 3; pp. 47–55: Die Ichaussagen Christi in den Evangelien.

I, 4; pp. 55–68: Das Ich in der psychologischen Erfahrung.

I, 5; pp. 68–78: Die menschliche Icherfahrung Christi.

Quae tria capita unum constituunt argumentum: primo, statuitur praemissa minor, nempe, haec et haec a Christo homine esse dicta (I, 3); deinde, modo generali statuitur praemissa maior, quemadmodum nempe in genere

---

1 [Notes for a lecture at a seminar of professors from the Gregorian University and the Biblical Institute, Rome: Gregorian University, 1962, 4 pp. Much of the material covered in these notes is more fully expressed in 'The Method of Theology,' Institute given at Regis College, Toronto, 9–20 July 1962, lecture 7, §§ 6–7, pp. 190–209 of the typescript (ed. Robert M. Doran) in the library of the Lonergan Research Institute. The typescript will eventually be published in vol. 22 in Collected Works of Bernard Lonergan, *Early Works in Theological Method I*. The lectures are available in audio form on compact discs produced by Greg Lauzon.

   There follows an English translation of the document by Michael Shields, S.J., who gratefully acknowledges the assistance of the late Theodore Zuydwijk, S.J., for the translations of the quotations in German.]

2 [Engelbert Gutwenger, S.J., *Bewusstsein und Wissen Christi, Eine dogmatische Studie* (Innsbruck: Verlag Felizian Rauch, 1960).]

procedendum sit ex dictis in experientiam psychologicam ipsius dicentis (1, 4); tertio, concluditur in conscientia Christi humana non solum dari centrum actuum humanorum sed etiam ipsum divinum Verbum ex parte subiecti esse praesens (1, 5).

Ad minorem stabiliendam citantur (pp. 50-55): Io 14.10, 11, 20, 23, 31; 15.26; 16.28; 17.21; Mt 12.50; 15.13; 18.10; Mc 8.38; 14.61, 62; Lc 22.70; Mt 20.28; Io 13.31; Mt 16.16; Io 13.13, 31; 8.12; 10.7, 10, 11; Mt 5.20, 21–32, 21–43; 11.29; Mc 14.36; Io 13.34; 14.31; 17.4; Mt 15.24; 5.17; 9.13; 10.34; 8.22; 10.38; 11.28-30; 10.32, 33, 40; 19.21.

Modus procedendi antea (p. 47 s.) explicatus est: 'Es ist dabei nicht beabsichtigt die einzelnen Aussprüche Iesu auch nach modernen methoden zu exegetisieren. Die Erwartung also, dass die Sätze Iesu formgeschichtlich oder themengeschichtlich behandelt werden oder dass gar die genera litteraria der einzelnen Perikopen, in die sie eingefügt sind, untersucht werden, kann sich nicht erfüllen. Der Dogmatiker bekennt sich sowohl zur Inspiration der Schrift als auch zu der Tatsache, dass die Evangelien geschichtliche Informationen vermitteln wollen. Ob Jesus in jedem Fall den genauen Wortlaut sprach, der in den evangelischen Berichten niedergelegt ist, oder ob die Worte Jesu von den Evangelisten chronologisch richtig untergebracht sind, diese Fragen und Antworten verschlagen nicht viel für unser Thema, solange darüber ein Einverständnis herrscht, dass Jesus in dem von den Evangelisten überlieferten Sinn gesprochen hat. Eine Exegese, die jeden Wort Jesu mit Hilfe moderner exegetischer Methoden nachgehen wollte, würde den Rahmen dieser Arbeit sprengen und ein eigenes Werk erfordern. Es muss darum, was die nähere Deutung der einzelnen von Jesus gesprochenen Sätze betrifft, auf die bewährten Kommentare und Einzeluntersuchungen der Exegeten verwiesen werden. Hier kommt es lediglich darauf an, festzustellen, was Christus meinte, wenn er in seinen Aussagen das Wörtlein "Ich" verwendete' (p. 47 s).

Et iterum, postquam principium selectionis explicaverat (pp. 48-50), addidit: 'Im folgenden soll nun ein schematischer, durchaus nicht alles umfassender Überblick über die Personalprädikationen Christi geboten werden. Das Material, das sich anführen lässt, ist derart überwältigend, dass kein berichtigter Zweifel gegen die Tatsache vorbringen lässt, dass mit dem Gebrauch des Wörtleins "Ich" in den Selbstaussagen Christi nur eines bezwecht ist, nämlich die Person Christi zu bezeichnen' (p. 50).

Circa praemissam maiorem et conclusionem, sufficit notare: *praesupponi* contextum dogmaticum a conciliis Nicaeno, Chalcedonensi, Constantinopolitano III haustum, contextum theologicum uti Christum hominem visione Dei immediata gavisum esse durante vita sua mortali, opinionem theologicam Tiphanum caeteris theologis melius unionem hypostaticam concepisse; *exponi* differentiam inter experientiam psychologicam 'tu' et 'ego'; *concludi* ad mutationem quandam sententiae P. Galtier,[3] nempe, propter rationem scripturisticam dicendum esse in conscientia Christi humana includi Verbum divinum.

2 . Argumenti Analysis

Logice: si haec et haec in scripturis leguntur, tale est subiectum psychologi-cum in Christo homine; atqui ...; ergo ...

Methodologice: (1) *quaestio* minime exsurgit immediate ex ipsis datis biblicis, imo vix intelligitur nisi praecognoscitur contextus quidam valde elaboratus et complicatus, dogmaticus, theologicus, ontologicus, psycho-logicus; (2) *solutiones possibiles* hoc contextu determinantur, scilicet, Verbum divinum Christo homini mediis finitis (a) aut est praesens aut non praesens et (b) si praesens est, tunc aut tantum per modum obiecti aut etiam ex parte subiecti; (3) *actualis solutio* ex scripturis habetur per modum experimenti, scilicet, quaeritur verificatio eorum quae ex solutionibus pos-sibilibus consequerentur; si ex scripturis non constaret Christum hominem 'ego' dixisse, vel si non constaret Christum eo sensu 'ego' dixisse qui ad personam propriam significandam adhibetur (e.g., 'ego sitio' forte non est nisi spontanea manifestatio status psychosomatici), tunc P. Gutwenger argumentum scripturisticum non haberet; si autem casus contrarius verifi-catur, adest argumentum.

Critice: quaenam est possibilitas, quodnam fundamentum, transeundi e contextu in contextum alium? Videtur transcendentia veri. Quia enim verum formale habet rationem inconditionati, absoluti, determinato cuidam contextui non alligatur sed servatis servandis in alios contextus transponi potest. Ita medicus patientem interrogat ut responsa patientis in categorias medicas transponat; iudex testes interrogat, non ut tragoediam quandam humanam affective participet, sed ut verba testium in categorias iuridicas transponat.

---

3 [Paul Galtier, *L'unité du Christ: être – personne – conscience* (Paris: G. Bauchesne, 1939).]

3   **Utrum Typicum Sit Allatum Exemplum**

Sensus quaestionis: quo usque exemplum illustret modum procedendi tradi-
tionalem inter dogmaticos receptum. Utrum Patres, Scholastici, theologi
dogmatici post Melchiorem Cano [1509–1560] (a) quaestiones e contextu
post-biblica hauserint, (b) per contextum hunc posteriorem definiverint,
(c) per locae scripturis undique selecta solverint.

   De themate et contextu: notiones forte utiles ad discussionem.

   In thema assumuntur scripturae exercite vel signate, et

(a) ut usus linguae, unde studia philologica,

(b) ut expressio, *Ausdruck*, unde hermeneutica romantica,

(c) ut occursus, unde existentialis mutatio legentis, conversio,

(d) ut fons multiplicis occursus, traditionis, doctrinae, systematis,

(e) ut eventus, ut de eventibus, unde historia bibliae et biblica,

(f) ut obscurae, male intellectae, unde labor exegeticus,

(g) ut verbum Dei, cui contradicere est nefas, unde dogmata.

   Contextus variis modis et gradibus contexitur:

(a) contextus dogmatico-theologicus non solum intelligitur sed inde a
medio aevo systematice explicatur et a modernis historice derivatur;

(b) contextus vitae humanae inter vivendum intelligitur (*existenziell*) sed a
philosopho phaenomenologice explicatur (*existenzial*);

(c) contextus paulinus a S. Paulo ut a contexente (*pensée pensante*) intellige-
batur sed ab eo non est explicatus;

(d) contextus paulinus ab exegeta ut contexendus (*pensée pensée*) intelligitur, sed disputari potest quo usque explicationem admittat (cogita categorias ex Heidegger apud Bultmann, vel ex Aristotele apud Thomistas, vel
Peinador, *Sacra Pagina*, 1, 168: '... las mismas categorías biblicas. Por
ejemplo ... las imáneges de "pueblo o reino de Dios," "Cuerpo místico de
Cristo," ...').

62B

The Theological Argument from Sacred Scripture[1]

An example is presented, which is then analyzed to find out whether it serves as a type or model.

1 The Example

E. Gutwenger, *Bewusstsein and Wissen Christi*, Innsbruck, 1960:[2]

1, 3; pp. 47–55: 'I' spoken by Christ in the Gospels.

1, 4; pp. 55–68: 'I' in one's psychological experience.

1, 5; pp. 68–78: Christ's human experience of 'I.'

These three sections comprise one argument: first, the minor premise is stated, namely, that Christ as man made various statements (1, 3); then the major premise is stated in general terms, that is, how one must proceed in general from a person's words to the psychological experience of the speaker (1, 4); third, the conclusion is drawn that in Christ's human consciousness there is not only a center of human acts but also the divine Word himself is present to himself as subject (1, 5).

---

1 [See above, page 247, n. 1. Translator's interpolations are in brackets.]

2 [See above, page 247, n. 2. Lonergan addresses Gutwenger's actual position at greater length in *De Verbo incarnato* (Rome: Gregorian University Press, 1964) theses 10 and 12. (This work will be published as vol. 8 in Collected Works of Bernard Lonergan, with Latin and English facing pages.) In the present paper it is Gutwenger's procedure or mode of argumentation that is investigated.]

In substantiation of the minor premise he quotes (pp. 50–55): John 14.10, 11, 20, 23, 31; 15.26; 16.28; 17.21; Matthew 12.50; 15.13; 18.10; Mark 8.38; 14.61, 62; Luke 22.70; Matthew 20.28; John 13.31; Matthew 16.16; John 13.13, 31; 8.12; 10.7, 10, 11; Matthew 5.20, 21–32, 21–43; 11.29; Mark 14.36; John 13.34; 14.31; 17.4; Matthew 15.24; 5.17; 9.13; 10.34; 8.22; 10.38; 11.28–30; 10.32, 33, 40; 19.21.

His way of proceeding was explained earlier: 'It does not intend to provide an exegesis of the individual sayings of Jesus according to modern methods. Hence it should not be expected that the statements of Jesus will be dealt with according to form-critical or thematic analysis, or that even the literary genres of the pericopes in which they are contained will be examined. The dogmatic theologian acknowledges the inspiration of scripture as well as the fact that the gospels intend to convey historical information. Whether Jesus in each case uttered word for word what was found in the gospel narratives, or whether his words were reported by the evangelists in a chronologically correct order, these questions and answers do not contribute much to our thesis as long as it is agreed that Jesus did speak in the sense which the evangelists have handed down. An exegesis of each and every word of Jesus according to modern methods would exceed the limits of this study and would require a separate undertaking. Hence, for any further meaning of the sayings of Jesus, the reader should consult the existing commentaries and investigations of the exegetes. Here we are concerned only with ascertaining what Christ intended when in his utterances he used the pronoun "I"' (pp. 47–48).

Again, having explained his principle of selection (pp. 48–50), he added: 'What follows will now be a schematic overview of Christ's personal statements, an overview which cannot be all-inclusive. The material at our disposal is so overwhelming as to leave no reasonable doubt about the fact that in the use of the word "I" in Christ's statements about himself only one thing was intended, namely, to indicate the person of Christ' (p. 50).

As to his major premise and conclusion, it will suffice to note the following points: (1) that the dogmatic context is *presupposed*[3] from the councils of Nicea, Chalcedon, and Constantinople III, the theological context that Christ as man enjoyed the immediate vision of God throughout his whole mortal life, and the theological opinion that Tiphanus had a better conception of the hypostatic union than other theologians, are all presupposed; (2) that the difference between the psychological experience of 'I'

3   [Italics here and to follow are emphases by Lonergan.]

and 'thou' is *expounded*; and (3) that the *conclusion* leads to a certain modification of Galtier's opinion,[4] namely, that on scriptural grounds it must be said that the divine Word is included within Christ's human consciousness.

2   Analysis of the Argument

Logically: If certain statements are found in Scripture, then the psychological subject in the man Christ is such; but ...; therefore ...

Methodologically: (1) the *question* does not at all arise immediately from the biblical data, and indeed is hardly intelligible without a prior knowledge of a very elaborate and complex context that is at once dogmatic, theological, ontological, and psychological; (2) *possible solutions* are determined by this context, that is, that the divine Word (a) is either present or not present to Christ as man by finite means, and (b) if present, then he is so either only as an object or also as subject; (3) the *actual solution* is arrived at from Scripture by way of experiment, that is, one seeks verification of what would follow from possible solutions; if it were not clear from the scriptures that Christ the man said 'I,' or if it were not clear that he used the word 'I' in the sense of referring to his own person (e.g., 'I thirst' is perhaps only a spontaneous manifestation of a certain psychosomatic state), then Fr Gutwenger would have no scriptural argument; but if the opposite is established as true, then he does have an argument.

Critically: wherein lies the possibility, what is the basis, for going from one context to another? It seems to be the transcendence of truth. For since formal truth is essentially unconditioned, absolute, it is not tied to a determinate context, but can be transposed to another context essentially intact. Thus a physician when questioning a patient transposes the patient's answers to medical categories; and a judge interrogates witnesses, not to

---

4 [Galtier, *L'unité du Christ: être – personne – conscience.* Lonergan expands in 'The Method of Theology,' p. 191 of typescript: 'Galtier held that the hypostatic union was in the ontological order, and simply in the ontological order, and therefore that there was nothing psychological about it. There was to be no consciousness of the divine ego in the human experience of Christ. If the person is something simply ontological, not a datum of consciousness, then there is no conscious experience of the ego in Christ's human consciousness. Gutwenger agrees with Galtier on the metaphysical analysis of the hypostatic union. But from his reading of scripture and the fact that Christ said "I" and "I" has to mean the person, there must have been some consciousness, apprehension, awareness of the person in Christ's humanity. That roughly is his line of thought.']

become affectively involved in some human drama, but in order to transpose the words of the witnesses to juridical categories.

3   Is This Example a Model?

Meaning of the question: to what extent does this example illustrate the traditional way of proceeding by dogmatic theologians? Did the Fathers, the
Scholastics, and the dogmatic theologians after Melchior Cano [1509–
1560] (a) take their questions out of a post-biblical context, (b) define the
questions in terms of this later context, and (c) solve them by means of
texts selected from all parts of the bible?

Theme and context: notions useful for discussion.

Scriptures are thematized performatively or thematically:

(a) as word-usage, giving rise to philological studies,

(b) as an expression, *Ausdruck*, giving rise to Romantic hermeneutics,[5]

---

5 [From 'The Method of Theology' 201–204: 'It [scripture] can be taken as an
expression, an *Ausdruck*. In that case one is interested in the precise nature or
way in which the book arose. One is concerned with the mentality, the affec-
tivity, the imagination, the feeling, the style of a writer and considering it as a
manifestation of him.

'... there ... is the radical difference between thematizing a text as true and
thereby grounding the possibility of a transference from one context to another, from one world to another and, on the other hand, the procedure of
Romantic hermeneutics.

Romantic hermeneutics attempts to eliminate difference of context. The
ideal interpreter by a process of empathy (*Einfühlung*) enters into the affectiv-
ity, the mode of imagination, the way of understanding, the way of feeling, the
way of writing, of the author. By that intimacy with the author he reaches the
point where he can explain just why the author expressed himself in this particular passage in this precise way. He will be able to say that the author might
have put it this way and might have put it that way and might have put it some
third way; but at the same time he will give the reasons why he chose this particular way because this was precisely what he wanted to convey. That ideal of
interpretation, of hermeneutics, aims at eliminating any difference of context
between the interpreter and the text he is interpreting. One enters into
another's mentality. The ideal interpreter from the viewpoint of Romantic
hermeneutics understands the text better than the author himself did. The
author is not able to give you the reasons why he used precisely those words;
he uses them but he is not able to do all this literary analysis that an expert at
that sort of thing can do. In Romantic hermeneutics one takes on the whole
viewpoint and mentality and mode of expression of the author and comes to
understand perfectly just why he wrote what he wrote in the way in which he
wrote it.']

(c) as an encounter, giving rise to an existential change in the reader, a conversion,

(d) as source of multiple encounters, of tradition, of doctrine, of a system,

(e) as an event or concerning events, giving rise to the history of the bible and biblical history,

(f) as puzzling or poorly understood passages, giving rise to the work of exegesis,

(g) as the word of God, which may not be contradicted, giving rise to dogmas.

Contexts are formed in various ways and various steps:

(a) the dogmatic-theological context is not only understood but also from medieval times has been explained systematically and derived by modern historians;

(b) the context of human life is understood in the actual living (*existenziell*) but is explained phenomenologically by philosophers (*existenzial*);

(c) the Pauline context was understood by St Paul as the framer of the context (*pensée pensante*) but was not explained by him;

(d) the Pauline context is understood by an exegete as the context to be framed (*pensée pensée*), but there may be disagreement as to what extent it admits of explanation (think of Bultmann's categories taken from Heidegger, or Thomistic categories taken from Aristotle, or Peinador, *Sacra Pagina*, 1, 168–69: '... the same biblical categories. For example, ... the images of "the People or Kingdom of God," "the Mystical Body of Christ," ...).'[6]

---

6   [Lonergan is referring to Máximo Peinador, 'La integración de la exégesis en la teología,' in *Sacra Pagina*, ed. J. Coppens, A. Descamps, and É. Massaux, vol. 1 (Gembloux: J. Duculot, 1959) 158–79.]

63

Luis de Molina[1]

MOLINA, LUIS DE (1535–1600), Spanish Jesuit theologian who worked out an original theory of the relationship between divine foreknowledge and human free will, was born into the lower nobility of Spain at Cuenca, Castile, in September, 1535. He became a Jesuit at Coimbra (1553), studied philosophy and theology there (1554–62) and at Evora (1562–63), taught philosophy at Coimbra (1563–67) and theology at Evora (1568–83), spent his last years writing, and died in Madrid on October 12, 1600. His works include his celebrated *Concordia liberi arbitrii cum gratiae donis* (1588–89), *Commentaria in primam partem divi Thomae* (1592), and *De justitia et jure*, six volumes (1593–1609).

Molinism has been a bone of contention between Dominicans (as Thomists) and Jesuits for over three centuries. Molina in his *Concordia* aimed at a unified and coherent conception of divine justice and mercy, foreknowledge and providence, predestination and reprobation, efficacious and sufficient grace, and human freedom. His originality lay in a reformulation of traditional views on divine knowledge to stress the component (called *scientia media*) regarding human choices that not only could but also would occur. The strength of his theory lies in its basic simplicity

---

1 [*Encyclopaedia Britannica*, 14th edition, 1965, pp. 667–68]

and coherence, its weakness in the possibility that the shift of attention to hypothetical future choices transposes issues without solving them.[2]

2 [The entry ends with '*See* MOLINISM.' Then a bibliography is added: 'Critical edition of *concordia* by J. Rabeneck (1953); letters and excerpts ed. by F. Stegmüller, *Geschichte des Molinismus,* vol. 1 (1935); *see also* J. Rabeneck, "De vita et scriptis Ludovici Molina," *Archivum historicum societatis Iesu,* 19:75–145 (1950); F. Stegmüller, *Zur Literaturgeschichte der Philosophie und Theologie an den Universitäten Evora und Coimbra in XVI. Jahrhundert* (1931).' The entry is signed '(B. J. F. L.).']

64

Existential Crisis[1]

It has been found, I am told, that existential philosophy has exerted an unfortunate influence on student behavior, and I have been asked to offer some brief elucidation of the matter.

First, then, an existential philosophy is not some abstract account of the universe, some materialism, idealism, rationalism. It is concerned with the concrete business of human living, not indeed with human living as physical, chemical, biological process, but with its sensitive, intellectual, rational, volitional, emotional components. It is concerned, then, with man not only as alive but also as awake. It does not aim at some recondite, scientific account of man's waking state. Rather it dwells upon the phenomena of everyday existence and experience. It does not stop short with phenomenological description but goes right on to value judgments. It will contrast, for example, unauthentic with authentic human existence. The unauthentic man is the drifter that thinks, says, does what everyone else is thinking, saying, and doing, and the others too are doing just that. On the other hand, authentic existence begins when one finds out for oneself that one has to decide for oneself just what one intends to make of oneself. Such authentic existence is precarious; it lasts just as long as one faces up to that challenge, but it lasts no longer.

To attain authentic human existence calls for illumination and motivation. It calls for illumination: one has to have reached some understanding

1 [A lecture given at Loyola College, Montreal, 3 November 1968. This was a time of considerable student unrest on university campuses, and Loyola College was no exception.]

of man, of human living, of one's social, cultural, historical situation, of the real possibilities, opportunities, necessities presented to one in that situation. It calls for motivation: to be authentically human is not just knowing; one has to deliberate, evaluate, decide, commit oneself; without motivation there is no commitment; and without commitment one just drifts.

By authentic human existence, then, is meant the goal that is referred to when we speak of people growing up, finding themselves, settling down, maturing. It is a goal to be attained by the individual in his own self-discovery, his self-determination, his own shaping of his life. But however personal and intimate, it does not occur in isolation. It also is a response to other persons, a response molded by a home, a response filled out by the schools that enable him to inherit his social and cultural tradition, a response deepened by religious example, instruction, experience. It is a response achieved when he loves, when he is pulled, transported, beyond himself, by the intimate love of the family circle, by the civic love dedicated to group welfare and to the welfare of mankind, by the love of God to which St Paul referred when he spoke of God's love flooding our hearts through the Spirit of God being given to us (Romans 5.5).

So much for authentic human existence. But my title is 'Existential Crisis,' and this, I think, arises in two manners. There is the crisis that arises from a conflict between the individual's need to exist authentically and the objective situation in which he finds himself. Then the situation is found so absurd that the project of being authentically human seems hopeless; then there is much to encourage hatred, loathing, defiance, and little to awaken love. When such a crisis is common experience, as in Germany in the catastrophic aftermath of the First World War, in France during the occupation, in Italy after the Second World War, existential philosophies emerge and flourish. They overflow the banks of academic philosophy, excite widespread interest, collect devoted followers, penetrate literature and the arts, are discussed in cafés, and give rise to new schools of psychiatry.

But there is another type of existential crisis. Canada and the United States have not been starved by a blockade; their cities have not been bombed; their territory has not been occupied by hostile troops. There, there occurs existential crisis, but it is confined to youth, and it creates a generation gap. To a greater or less extent youth suspects the authenticity of their elders, refuses to accept their way of life, is determined to reshape things in some quite different, if unspecified, manner. Why they should do so, is a very large and difficult question. To a great extent one's view will depend on one's estimate of youthful attitudes and behavior. Insofar as one finds them manifestations of broad experience, penetrating intelligence, well-informed and balanced judgment, and maturely conscious responsibility, then one is led to look for the root trouble in the grave evils that afflict our society as a whole. On the other hand, insofar as one finds current youthful attitudes and behavior manifesting a lack of experience, a rather superficial exercise of intelligence, hasty and poorly informed judgment, and no little measure of irresponsibility, then one will be inclined to place the problem, less in our society as a whole, and more in its educational procedures. In the former case, one will blame the morals of older people, the way our political institutions work, the tendencies of our economic organization, our wars, our poverty, our slums. In the latter case, one will be asking whether there has been too much permissiveness in the home, too much experimentation in the school, too much demythologizing in the pulpit, too much of the mass media supplying information and entertainment in the style and manner best calculated to reap a nice big profit.

But whatever its origins, existential crisis consists in a conflict between one's need to live one's own life and, on the other hand, the objective situation in which it is lived. Where that conflict occurs, there there is a market for existential philosophy. The effect of the philosophy will be to objectify the crisis, to clarify its contours, to work out its implications, to indicate lines of resolution. But different existential philosophies will do so in quite different manners. Kierkegaard was a deeply concerned Christian, and Nietzsche was a militant atheist. Gabriel Marcel is an ardent Catholic, Karl Jaspers, though not a Christian, is deeply concerned with religious values, Martin Heidegger is an agnostic with a Stoic twist, Jean-Paul Sartre is a successful writer, a brilliant phenomenologist, and an outrageously destructive dialectician.

Of these, it would be Sartre that would exert a sinister influence, and he would do so both on a popular level by his literary studies, his novels, and his plays, and, as well, on a theoretical level, by his philosophy. He affirms human freedom. He insists that man must be committed. He himself played a noble role in the French underground resistance to the Nazis. But he finds the universe absurd. For him nature is *de trop*, pointless, nauseating. Other people are hell: *l'enfer c'est l'autre*. God does not exist: indeed the concept of God is pronounced a contradiction in terms. The very structure of man's being destines man to failure: the *pour soi* wants to be *en soi*, and that just cannot occur. So Sartre depicts loving ending up as masochism, sexual desire as sadism, self-expression in the wanton gestures and deeds of the anti-hero.

Now a practical question was put to me, and it took the form, 'What can a counselor do when a student has come under existentialist influence and is considering the use of drugs? Can it be thàt there is very little that a counselor can do?'

First, then, the problem is of the type envisaged by logotherapy.[2] The apprehension of meaning and the response to values are constitutive of human living. Things can go wrong on the higher humanistic and philosophic levels of apprehension and response.

Secondly, even if the counselor were an excellent philosopher, I think it doubtful that much would be accomplished by pointing out the basic errors in Sartre's system. For these errors lie in cognitional theory; cognitional theory is so difficult and disputed because it is infested with cognitional myth; and, until it is broken, nothing appears more obvious, evident, certain, indubitable than a myth.

Thirdly, if the student is capable of philosophic reading, the counselor could recommend a broader approach to the issues. Directly on Sartre there is an excellent Harper Torchbook by Wilfred Desan entitled *Tragic Finale*.[3] On the main existentialists there are two further Harper Torchbooks, F.H. Heinemann's *Existentialism and the Modern Predicament*[4] and H.J. Blackham's *Six Existentialist Thinkers*.[5] There also is James Collins's book, *The Existentialists*, published by Regnery, Chicago, 1952.[6] In all of these there are further bibliographies.

Fourthly, if existentialist influence has been mainly literary, the counselor would have the problem of drawing up profiles of the different types of student he has been trying to help and then seeking to interest professors of literature in the task of finding and recommending remedial reading.

Fifthly, the influence of sinister existentialist writing is not the whole trouble. It is only a contributing factor. Behind existentialist writing there

2   [Logotherapy is a form of therapy oriented to the discovery of meaning. Its founder was Viktor E. Frankl (1905–77), a neurologist and psychiatrist whose book *Man's Search for Meaning*, first published in 1946, chronicles his experiences as a concentration-camp inmate at Auschwitz and Dachau (1942–45) and describes his psychotherapeutic method of finding a reason to live even in circumstances as tragic as these.]

3   [Wilfred Desan, *The Tragic Finale: An Essay on the Philosophy of Jean-Paul Sartre*, rev. ed. (New York: Harper & Row, 1960).]

4   [Frederick H. Heinemann, *Existentialism and the Modern Predicament* (New York: Harper & Row, 1958).]

5   [Harold J. Blackham, *Six Existentialist Thinkers* (New York: Harper & Row, 1959).]

6   [James Collins, *The Existentialists: A Critical Study* (Chicago: Regnery, 1952).]

is the existentialist crisis, and for this reason young people do not have to read European philosophers before being tempted to take drugs.

The function, then, of the remedial reading is to remove an extraneous factor that has been blocking the efforts of the counselor. But once that barrier is removed, the counselor will have to call upon his own special training and skills to bring to light the underlying existential crisis.

Sixthly, the problems of existential crisis cannot be solved by counselors alone. I suggested above that they arise either from the ills of our society, or from the defects of our educational process, or, more probably, from both. These issues are very large and complex, and this is not the occasion to ventilate them. But I should like to affirm in closing not merely that academic vice-presidents and deans and professors should be very concerned with them and with possible remedies but also that student unrest, student disenchantment with the whole system, forces the matter on their attention.

65

Bernard Lonergan Responds (1)[1]

I have been asked to respond and, obviously, I must. Not all papers, however, call for the same type of response. There are those that admit no more than an expression of my admiration and my gratitude. Bishop Butler has taken the heuristic structure set forth in chapter 20 of *Insight*, and filled it out in the light of his first-hand knowledge of the Second Vatican Council.[2] Quentin Quesnell is an impressive New Testament scholar;[3] but he is also at home in the intricacies of a theory of interpretation, and he is concerned to vindicate both biblical and dogmatic theology.[4] Frederick Crowe envisages a similar problem from an opposite angle; patiently and gently he cuts through much loose thinking to come up with a point I find

---

1 [On 31 March – 3 April 1970, 'Ongoing Collaboration: The International Lonergan Congress' was held at Saint Leo College, Saint Leo, Florida. As the name of the Congress indicates, scholars gathered from around the world to present papers on, and to discuss, the writings of Bernard Lonergan to that date. After the congress, a first volume of twelve papers was published, *Foundations of Theology: Papers from the International Lonergan Congress, 1970*, ed. Philip McShane (Dublin: Gill and Macmillan, and Notre Dame: University of Notre Dame Press, 1971). At the end of the volume (pp. 223–34), Lonergan responds to the papers.

Here, Lonergan's own footnotes are without brackets. Additional notes by the current editors are in brackets.]

2 [B.C. Butler, 'Lonergan and Ecclesiology,' in *Foundations of Theology* 1–21.]

3 See his *The Mind of Mark*, Analecta Biblica 38 (Rome: Pontifical Biblical Institute, 1969).

4 [Quentin Quesnell, 'Theological Method on the Scripture as Source,' in *Foundations of Theology* 162–93.]

highly illuminating, namely, that the mind revealed by a text may not be something coherent and tightly knit but may prove to be a conglomerate of items of great variety with representatives of every shade of difference from fleeting impressions up to well-formed and clearly formulated convictions.[5] Heinrich Ott has given us a delicately nuanced yet firmly fleshed account of the manner in which his theological reflection unfolds,[6] while Alois Grillmeier has drawn on the history of law, specifically of imported legal systems, to illustrate the problems that confront ecumenism as a result of centuries of diverging traditions.[7] To such work there manifestly is no finishing touch I could add.

In a number of papers, however, questions are raised regarding my views on the method of theology. On that topic I have a book in process. Some ten chapters have been completed of which one on 'Functional Specialties in Theology' has been published.[8] While I cannot make available here the 350 pages of typescript that have not been published, some answer, I feel, should be given to such questions as the following: Does theology begin from truths or from data? Is it to be conceived on the analogy of natural science? What is meant by religious conversion? Must not theological method contain a specifically theological principle? Is it dogmatic or critical? Is the method envisaged theologically neutral? Is it specifically theological?

First, then, Fr Crowe has noted that formerly I placed the starting point of theology in truths while now I place it in data.[9] This raises a complex issue that cannot be treated fully at once. But I would note that behind the shift there is a greatly enlarged notion of theology: if one accepts the notion of functional specialties, then there pertain to theology investigations that otherwise have to be conceived as auxiliary disciplines, e.g., textual criticism of scriptural, patristic, medieval manuscripts. A further point is that, as long as one remains within the Aristotelian orbit, one conceives theology in terms of its material and formal objects and, indeed, of its *formale quod* and *formale quo*.[10] On the other hand, when one adopts a strictly

---

5 [Frederick E. Crowe, 'Dogma versus the Self-Correcting Process of Learning,' ibid. 22–40.]
6 [Heinrich Ott, 'Questioning, Presentiment and Intuition in the Theological Thought-Process,' ibid. 141–60.]
7 [Alois Grillmeier, 'The Reception of Church Councils,' ibid. 102–14.]
8 See *Gregorianum* 50 (1969) 485–505. [This article later became chapter 5 of *Method in Theology.*]
9 [See Crowe, 'Dogma versus the Self-Correcting Process of Learning' 24.]
10 See Yves Congar, *A History of Theology*, trans. Hunter Guthrie (Garden City, NY: Doubleday, 1968) 230–35.

methodological viewpoint, the emphasis shifts from objects to operations and operators. In terms of functional specialties, theology is an eightfold set of interdependent normative patterns of recurrent and related operations with progressive and cumulative results. Where formerly a discipline was specifically theological because it dealt with revealed truths, now it is authentically theological because the theologian has been converted intellectually, morally, and religiously.

Next, does the shift from truths to data imply, as Professor Gilkey believes, that I am conceiving theology on the analogy of natural science?[11] By no means! P and Q are analogous if they are partly the same and partly different. To conceive Q on the analogy of P is to have only a partial knowledge of Q. Hence, the Scholastic attempt to conceive of theology on the analogy of the science set forth in Aristotle's *Posterior Analytics* was most unsatisfactory, and my concern with method is precisely to remedy the defects inherent in any approach by way of analogy.

However, to avoid analogy is not an easy matter. Over and above familiarity with the history of theology and with its current problems, there are two main steps. The first is an exploration of mathematics, natural science, common sense, and philosophy to uncover the basic and invariant structure of all human cognitional activity and so to reach a transcendental method, i.e., a method that is the condition of the possibility (not of the actuality) of all the special methods proper to each of the special fields of human inquiry. Such a method will be relevant to theology, for theologians always have had minds and always have used them. It will not be, however, the whole of theological method, for to it there must be added the specifically theological principle that differentiates theology from other fields.

Professor Gilkey also has philosophic and theological objections against the method I have proposed. The theological objection will have to wait until I have mentioned Fr Curran's paper on conversion. The philosophic objection is that there is a profound discrepancy between the very modern notion of intelligibility in the third chapter of *Insight* and, on the other hand, the retrograde, Greek notion that emerges in chapter 19, in which a tolerance for mere matters of fact is attributed to obscurantism. Now I grant that my third chapter presents an ideal of science quite different from that presented in Aristotle's *Posterior Analytics*. I deny that it offers any grounds for a Kantian or positivist assertion that the only valid human

---

11 [Langdon Gilkey, 'Empirical Science and Theological Knowing,' in *Foundations of Theology* 76–101. See esp. p. 77.]

knowledge is knowledge of this world. And, while the term 'intelligible' is used in different senses in *Insight*, the primary meaning is always the same: the intelligible is the content of an act of understanding. Understanding, of course, occurs in many ways. There is the understanding that occurs in mathematics, the understanding that occurs in natural science, the understanding that occurs in the exercise of common sense, the mathematical, scientific, and commonsense understanding that is sought in the first eight chapters of *Insight*, the philosophic type of understanding that emerges in chapter 11 when an act of understanding is reached that is not open to revision, the understanding developed in the process of encirclement and confinement that yields a metaphysics of proportionate being, and there is the final demand for understanding that in chapter 19 joins Professor Gilkey in rejecting the contingency, relativism, and transience of the contemporary secularist outlook.[12]

Fr Curran has taken Christian conversion as his topic.[13] Later I shall have something to say on the distinction and the relations of intellectual, moral, and religious conversion. For the moment I am concerned with religious conversion. What I mean by it I have set forth in Thomist categories in a series of articles on *Gratia operans*.[14] In those categories, by religious conversion I understand the gift of habitual grace as operative. It may be prepared by actual graces as operative, and it is to be perfected by still further actual graces as operative; but it is the central event. While the Thomist notion is basically metaphysical – an absolutely supernatural entitative habit radicated in the essence of the soul with the operative habits of faith, hope, and charity resulting in the potencies of the soul – still this notion was evolved to satisfy scriptural and patristic doctrines and to resolve religious problems. Specifically, it had to do with the contrasts between nature and grace, reason and faith, human affection and agape, a good name on earth and merit in God's eyes, moral impotence and a capacity to love God above all.

12 See Langdon Gilkey, *Naming the Whirlwind* (Indianapolis and New York: Bobbs-Merrill, 1969) 40–57.

13 [Charles E. Curran, 'Christian Conversion in the Writings of Bernard Lonergan,' in *Foundations of Theology* 41–59.]

14 *Theological Studies* 2 (1941) 289–324; 3 (1942) 69–88; 375–402; 533–78. The articles were later edited by J. Patout Burns in *Grace and Freedom: Operative Grace in the Thought of St. Thomas Aquinas* (London: Darton, Longman & Todd, and New York: Herder and Herder, 1970) [and subsequently included as Part One in *Grace and Freedom: Operative Grace in the Thought of St Thomas Aquinas*, vol. 1 in Collected Works of Bernard Lonergan.]

Now both the transcendental and the methodological turn require that the realities of the subject be primary and basic while metaphysical concepts become secondary and derivative. Accordingly, instead of speaking of habitual grace, I speak of conversion, of a transformation of the subject that is radical, dynamic, and, in principle, permanent. That such a transformation occurs and what are its properties can be worked out from the scriptures, patristic writings, ascetical and mystical writers, and one's own experience of the spiritual life; and one can reach such results with the same assurance as one can establish from the same sources the existence of habitual grace.

To religious conversion, then, I would ascribe as a minimum two notes: first, it is a change in one's antecedent willingness; one becomes antecedently willing to do the good that previously one was unwilling to do; secondly, the free and full acceptance of this change constitutes the existential decision that contemporary moral theologians name one's fundamental option, one's basic religious commitment. While this decision may lead to a change of ecclesiastical allegiance, it need do no more than make one a better member of the religion or non-religion one has inherited. Again, as a change in the subject, it can be detected within the data of consciousness; but this does not mean that the data are labelled 'religious conversion' or 'fundamental option'; nor does it mean that one is freed from temptations or from aridity in prayer or that one is not inclined to have a poor opinion of oneself. Finally, the fact of conversion appears much more in its effects than in itself; and when it becomes noticeable in itself, then, in Fr Rahner's phrase, it is with a content but without an object. *Nihil amatum nisi praecognitum* is true of human love, but it is not true of God's love that floods our hearts through the Holy Spirit given to us.[15]

Enough has been said for it now to be possible to meet Professor Gilkey's demand for a specific theological principle. That principle is religious conversion, but it must be explained (1) in what sense conversion is a principle, (2) how this principle produces its effects, (3) what is its point of insertion, (4) how it is objectified, and (5) why such a principle should be invoked instead of divine revelation, the inspiration of scripture, the authority of the church, the agreement of patristic and theological writers, the *sensus fidelium.*

---

15 See Romans 5.5; Karl Rahner, *The Dynamic Element in the Church* (Montreal: Palm Publishers, 1964) 132–39; Olivier Rabut, *L'Expérience religieuse fondamentale* (Tournai: Casterman, 1969) esp. p. 168; William Johnston, *The Mysticism of the Cloud of Unknowning* (New York, Rome, Paris, Tournai: Desclée, 1967).

First, then, a principle is what is first in an ordered set, *primum in aliquo ordine*. If the ordered set consists in propositions, then a principle in the set will be the premises from which the rest of the propositions may be deduced. If the ordered set consists not in propositions but in real causes and real effects, then the principle consists in the causes. Now the theological principle is religious conversion itself. It is not knowledge of religious conversion, awareness of religious conversion, interpretation of the psychological phenomena of conversion, propositions concerning conversion. It is simply the reality of the transformation named conversion, and it is that reality whether or not its subject has the foggiest notion of what it is or whether it has occurred.

Secondly, how does the principle produce its effects? It does so spontaneously. Conversion results in a transvaluation of values, in a new efficacy in one's response to values, in a new openness to belief, in a new outlook upon mankind and upon the universe. Specifically, it does not import into theological method any special rules for research into religious matters, the interpretation of religious documents, the history of religious events and movements. On the contrary, especially in the first four functional specialties – research, interpretation, history, dialectic – the same methodical precepts are to be acceptable to believers and agnostics alike.

Thirdly, though believers and agnostics follow the same methods, they will not attain the same results. For in interpreting texts and in resolving historical problems, one's results are a function, not only of the data and the procedures, but also of the whole previous development of one's understanding. To aim at eliminating that previous development would result in a second childhood. All that can be done is to purge it of its biases, to remove its blind spots, to enlarge its horizons. Nor is that to be achieved by some simple masterstroke, but only by unremitting efforts to be attentive, to advert to one's failures to understand and to strive to overcome them, to be more exact in one's judgments, to be ever more responsive to values, and, above all, to be ever able to learn from what others have learned.

Such is the general character of the interpretative and historical work. Carl Becker had no doubt that the historian's investigation and judgment were under the influence of the dominant ideas in the climate of opinion of his day.[16] H.-I. Marrou was willing to distinguish the historian from the

16 See *Detachment and the Writing of History, Essays and Letters of Carl L. Becker*, ed. Phil L. Snyder (Ithaca, NY: Cornell University Press, 1958) esp. p. 25. Also Charlotte Watkins Smith, *Carl Becker: On History & the Climate of Opinion* (Ithaca, NY: Cornell University Press, 1956).

history he writes but he denied that the history can be independent of the concrete man that the historian is.[17] While Becker and Marrou were struggling against a positivism that had captured historical thought at the end of the nineteenth century, H.-G. Gadamer traces similar thought back to the Enlightenment and to Cartesian methodic doubt. The task, for him, is not the elimination of all assumptions but the elimination of mistaken assumptions. The Enlightenment assumed that assumptions were to be eliminated. In fact, they are not the personal judgments of the individual but rather the historicity of his cultural being. It is only through that historical heritage that he can become equipped to understand his past history, and the greater that heritage the greater the development it demands of him if he is to understand it aright.[18]

What holds generally for interpretation and history also holds for the interpretation of religious documents and for accounts of religious history. The point was already made by St Paul. 'A man who is unspiritual refuses what belongs to the Spirit of God; it is folly to him; he cannot grasp it, because it needs to be judged in the light of the Spirit. A man gifted with the Spirit can judge the worth of everything, but is not himself subject to judgement by his fellow men' (1 Corinthians 2.14–15).

Fourthly, how is the theological principle 'conversion' objectified? Its spontaneous objectification is called by St Paul the harvest of the Spirit: love, joy, peace, patience, kindness, goodness, fidelity, gentleness, and self-control (Galatians 5.22). In mediating theology, in research, interpretation, history, dialectic, the discernment of the spiritual man brings to light what others disregard. Dialectic brings to light oppositions in appreciative and evaluative interpretation and history, in the history of movements, in determining the meaning of texts, and in the special research performed in the prosecution of the foregoing tasks. Foundations takes sides: it selects as its stand some coherent set out of the array of opposing positions; and insofar as it is guided by authentic conversion, its selection will be an implicit objectification of what conversion is. The explicit objectification, however,

---

17 Henri-Irénée Marrou, *The Meaning of History*, trans. Robert J. Olsen (Baltimore: Helicon, 1966). See also his 'Comment comprendre le métier d'historien,' in *L'histoire et ses méthodes*, Encyclopédie de la Pléiade 11 (Paris: Gallimard, 1961) 1465–1540.

18 Hans-Georg Gadamer, *Wahrheit und Methode* (Tübingen: J.C.B. Mohr, 1960) 254–55, 260–61. The whole section, 250–90, is relevant. [In English, see *Truth and Method*, 2nd rev. ed., trans. Joel Weinsheimer and Donald G. Marshall (New York: Crossroad, 1989, with the corresponding section at pp. 265–307.]

occurs in doctrines, in systematics, and in communications, in accord with the several purposes of these specialties.[19]

Fifthly, why is the theological principle placed in religious conversion and not in divine revelation, the inspiration of scripture, the authority of the church, the consensus of patristic and theological writers, the *sensus fidelium*, or the like?

The reason for the shift is functional specialization. If there are eight functional specialties, if they are ordered, not chronologically for they are interdependent, but by presupposition and complementation, if foundations is fifth in the order and doctrines is sixth, then manifestly the foundations do not consist in some of the doctrines. But the existence of a divine revelation, the inspiration of scripture, the authority of the church, the significance of the patristic and theological teaching are all doctrines. Therefore, none of them pertain to foundations.

Now this does not imply that divine revelation, inspired scripture, ecclesiastical pronouncements, patristic and theological writings are not sources for theology. They remain sources, but they are considered in a series of different manners. In the first instance, they are data for general and special research. In the second instance, each item is acknowledged to possess a meaning, and this meaning is determined by an exegete. In the third instance, the many items of meaning come together in an ongoing process, history. In the fourth instance, the history is acknowledged to manifest the values and disvalues brought about by persons, and the conflicts brought to light are catalogued and compared. In the fifth instance, a decision is taken with respect to the conflicts. Only in the sixth instance, do we come to the truths contained in the sources.

Next, if the foregoing tasks are to be performed properly, there are three main requirements. The first is that one's idea of interpretation and of critical history must not be distorted either by the abundant supply of mistaken and misleading theories of knowledge or by the widespread and abominable practice of those that are convinced that an academic discipline must be this or that because of the analogy of some other academic discipline. The second is that one must find a methodical way of handling the problem of divergent value judgements. The third is the insertion of a

---

19 May I note here that the specialty 'foundations' provides not the total foundation of theology, for that includes method in theology, but simply the foundation for doctrines, systematics, communications, inasmuch as these make explicit a personal or collective stand on disputed issues.

theological principle. Just how all this is to be done, I have explained in some 200 pages of unpublished typescript. More cannot be said now.

The next question is Fr Tracy's[20] and, as well, it bears on a point made by Professor Davis.[21] Is, then, the functional specialty 'foundations' dogmatic or critical?

From what has already been said, it is clear that foundations does not consist in the enumeration and affirmation of some or all dogmas, for dogmas are doctrines, and doctrines are the concern of the sixth specialty, doctrines. On the other hand, since foundations founds doctrines, systematics, and communications, it follows that foundations will lead to the acceptance of doctrines and so of dogmas.

The question may mean, however, is foundations merely assumed or asserted and in that case dogmatic or, on the other hand, does foundations itself rest on earlier grounds that are critically evaluated?

Foundations, then, consists in a decision that selects one horizon and rejects others. The horizons in question are determined by the conflicts revealed in dialectic. The choice of one and the rejection of the others are operations on the fourth level of intentional consciousness, the level of deliberation, evaluation, and decision, the level on which consciousness becomes conscience. Operations on this level are critically motivated when the deliberation has been sufficiently comprehensive and when the values chosen and the disvalues rejected really are values and disvalues respectively. But the sufficiently comprehensive deliberation is secured through the functional specialties of research, interpretation, history, and dialectic. The value judgments are correct when they occur in a duly enlightened and truly virtuous man and leave him with a good conscience. Due enlightenment and true virtue are the goals towards which intellectual and moral conversion move. Conscience, finally, is the key, and its use by humble men does not encourage dogmatism in the pejorative sense of that word.

Is this critical? On views I consider counterpositions it is not critical. On views I consider positions it is critical. On the counterpositions the object is out there now, the subject is in here now, the two are irreducible, objectivity is a matter of taking a good look, and value judgments are always merely subjective. On the positions, objects are what are intended in questions and known by answers, subjects do the questioning and answering,

---

20   [David Tracy, 'Lonergan's Foundational Theology: An Interpretation and a Critique,' in *Foundations of Theology* 197–222.]
21   [Charles Davis, 'Lonergan and the Teaching Church,' ibid. 60–75.]

objectivity is the fruit of authentic subjectivity, and subjectivity is authentic when it is self-transcending. Such self-transcendence is twofold: there is the cognitive self-transcendence that reaches a virtually unconditioned to pronounce on facts, possibilities, probabilities; there is the moral self-transcendence in which one becomes a principle of benevolence and beneficence by acknowledging and choosing what truly is good, really is worth while; and the criterion that one has done so is one's good conscience, provided one is duly enlightened on the issues and truly virtuous.

Such is the general scheme, but the method implements it. The implementation is a prolongation of the procedures in my book *Insight*, where positions and counterpositions were distinguished on knowledge, objectivity, and reality, and readers were invited and helped to attain a self-appropriation that would enable them to opt unhesitatingly for the positions and against the counterpositions. But in theology there has to be faced the further problem of value judgments. To evade that problem would eviscerate theology. To assert one's own values as the true ones would simply be dogmatism. There exists, however, a third way. One can allow all comers to participate in research, interpretation, history, and dialectic. One can encourage positions and counterpositions to come to light concretely and to manifest to all their suppositions and their consequences. One can expect some to mistake counterpositions for positions and, inversely, positions for counterpositions. One can hope that such mistakes will not be universal, that the positions will be duly represented, that they will reveal themselves as positions to men of good will. It is by this third way that the method would ground foundations, objectively, in the situation revealed by dialectic and, on the side of subjective development, in intellectual, moral, and religious conversion.

The second last question to be considered was raised by Professor Lindbeck, Is the method theologically neutral?[22] He concludes that it is. I should agree that it is, first, because theological sources initially have the status of data; secondly, because the methodologist leaves the theologians to determine which sources are relevant and how privileged each one is, and thirdly, because in general the methodologist leaves all theological questions to the theologians.

There is, however, a necessary exception. For the method to be a method

22 [George A. Lindbeck, 'Protestant Problems with Lonergan on Development of Dogma,' ibid. 115–23.]

in theology it must implement a specifically theological principle, and the principle selected has been religious conversion. About such conversion the methodologist has to make some theological statements, but his purpose is not to influence results to be obtained by the method but simply to explain how the method can be expected to reach any theological results whatever. Indeed, it is not the methodologist's views on conversion, any more than those of Aquinas or Luther or Calvin or some introspective psychologist, but conversion itself in its spontaneous consequences that exerts an influence on the results of research, interpretation, history, and dialectic.

In the second phase of mediated theology, however, there are to be set up not only general categories regarding man and his world but also specifically theological categories. These radiate out from the initial theological category of conversion to the community of the converted, to its traditions, to its origins, to its destiny, to its God. Such categories, be it noted, as presented in foundations are regarded simply as models. They are not descriptions of reality or hypotheses about reality but simply explanatory sets of interconnected terms that it will be useful to have available when the time comes in doctrines, systematics, communications to describe realities or to form hypotheses about them.

When it comes to doctrines, one can at present expect divergences to become manifest. But the method does possess a strong measure of theological neutrality. It provides an operative framework within which different communions can do much in common, acknowledge differences, work backwards to their roots, define issues with clarity, and, where they still disagree, regard each other with genuine mutual respect.

While, then, I think the method possesses considerable theological neutrality, it is not methodically neutral, and it is not philosophically neutral. It cannot be methodically neutral, for if one proposes a method, one means what one says and not something else. It is not philosophically neutral, for it evaporates into thin air when rather firm positions on cognitional and moral operations, on their objectivity, and on the corresponding reality either are not grasped or are abandoned.

This absence of methodical and philosophical neutrality may delay acceptance of the method. But a too rapid acceptance would risk being superficial, and a superficial acceptance would betray the method with superficial performance. What is to be hoped for is the open-eyed and fully deliberate acceptance that brings forth solid fruits and thereby initiates a movement.

The final question is Fr Rahner's, who has asked whether the account of method in the article on functional specialties is specifically theological.[23] Clearly, functional specialties as such are not specifically theological. Indeed, the eight specialties we have listed would be relevant to any human studies that investigated a cultural past to guide its future. Again, since the sources to be subjected to research are not specified, they could be the sacred books and traditions of any religion. Finally, while there is a theological principle assigned, still it is not placed in authoritative pronouncements but in the religious conversion that turns men to transcendent mystery; and while I believe such a turn always to be God's gift of grace, still it becomes specifically a Christian conversion when the gift of the Spirit within us is intersubjective with the revelation of the Father in Christ Jesus.

Three observations are, perhaps, in order. The incompleteness of the chapter on functional specialties only shows that one is not trying to say in one chapter what one hopes to convey in a dozen. Secondly, in our day of ecumenism, of openness with non-Christian religions, of dialogue with atheists, there is not a little advantage in a theological method that with slight adjustments can be adapted to related yet quite different investigations. Thirdly, to advert now to some points raised by Fr Curran, I should urge that religious conversion, moral conversion, and intellectual conversion are three quite different things. In an order of exposition I would prefer to explain first intellectual, then moral, then religious conversion. In the order of occurrence I would expect religious commonly but not necessarily to precede moral, and both religious and moral to precede intellectual. Intellectual conversion, I think, is very rare.

To conclude, writing this paper has helped me clarify my own thinking, and so it may be of use to others. I fear, however, that the answers I have given will at crucial points only raise further and more complicated questions. But to attempt to anticipate them here would only raise still further issues, and so I must be content if I somehow manage to meet most points in the rounded whole of my overdue book.

May I take this occasion to thank the organizers of the meeting at St Leo's, to thank all that participated, and in particular to thank those that contributed to the present volume.

23   [Karl Rahner, 'Some Critical Thoughts on "Functional Specialties in Theology,"' ibid. 194–96.]

66

Bernard Lonergan Responds (2)[1]

I must begin by thanking the contributors whose work is enlightening without calling for any reply. Then I shall attempt a partial answer to the questions Bernard Tyrrell raised at the end of his paper. Finally, I shall discuss three pairs of papers: Garrett Barden and David Rasmussen are concerned with myth; Schubert Ogden and Robert Johann are concerned with experience; Emerich Coreth and William Richardson are concerned with being.

First, then, two former students, Matthew Lamb and Frederick Lawrence, have related my thought to that of Wilhelm Dilthey and Hans-Georg Gadamer respectively to give us the benefit of their years of study in German-speaking universities.[2] Joseph Flanagan has done a pertinent piece of work by contrasting my methodical approach to knowledge and language with a purely logical or conceptualist approach.[3] Patrick Heelan has

---

1 [The response of Bernard Lonergan to eleven more papers given at the International Lonergan Congress at Saint Leo's College (see above, p. 263, n. 1). These papers constitute volume 2 of the Congress, *Language Truth and Meaning*, ed. Philip McShane (Dublin: Gill and Macmillan, and Notre Dame: University of Notre Dame Press, 1972). At the end of the volume (pp. 306–12), Lonergan responds to the papers.

  Here, Lonergan's own footnotes are without brackets. Additional notes by the current editors are in brackets.]

2 [Matthew Lamb, 'William Dilthey's Critique of Historical Reason and Bernard Lonergan's Meta-methodology,' in *Language Truth and Meaning* 115–66, and Frederick Lawrence, 'Self-Knowledge in History in Gadamer and Lonergan,' ibid. 167–217.]

3 [Joseph Flanagan, 'Knowing and Language in the Thought of Bernard Lonergan,' ibid. 49–78.]

employed the tools of linguistic analysis to offer a coherent account of a recalcitrant aspect of quantum theory and, at the same time, to point to other areas where similar problems arise.[4]

Next, Bernard Tyrrell ends his paper[5] by asking for a comparison between Karl Rahner's views and my own on four topics: the independence of philosophy as science; Christian philosophy; God as meaning and God as mystery; and the philosophy of God. I shall indicate my own opinion on these topics without venturing to pronounce on Karl Rahner's.

With regard to philosophy as science, I must distinguish. Philosophy is not science in any rationalist sense; it is not the work of some pure reason or some speculative intellect; it is not a set of self-evident and necessary truths from which follow necessary conclusions; it is not some precisely defined and permanent system of eternal verities; and so it does not enjoy the independence that would be claimed by any rationalist stand. At the same time, philosophy is not science in the sense that the natural sciences are sciences. Their immediate goal is not truth but an ever fuller understanding of phenomena. Their advance is an ever greater approximation to truth. But such approximations are ever subject to radical revisions that, as it were, change the whole aspect of things. For me, then, philosophy occupies an intermediate position. It is primarily concerned with the three questions, What am I doing when I am knowing? Why is doing that knowing? What do I know when I do it? The answer to the first question is derived from the data of consciousness. The answer to the second is derived from the answer to the first. The answer to the third is derived from the answers to the first and the second. The answer to the first question is a cognitional theory. The answer to the second is an epistemology. The answer to the third is a metaphysics.

It will be noted that we have inverted the Aristotelian procedure. Aristotle's basic terms and relations are metaphysical. His physical concepts add further determinations to his metaphysical concepts, and his psychological concepts add still further determinations. On the contrary, our basic terms and relations refer to elements in cognitional experience. From the analysis of cognitional activity there is derived an epistemology. From the analysis and the epistemology there is derived a metaphysics.

4   [Patrick A. Heelan, 'The Logic of Framework Transpositions,' ibid. 93–114.]
5   [Bernard Tyrrell, 'The New Context of the Philosophy of God in Lonergan and Rahner,' ibid. 284–305.]

Such a metaphysics is, in a sense, empirical. It contains nothing that does not find a corresponding and grounding element in cognitional activity. Again, it is in a sense critical, for any alleged aspect of metaphysics that does not possess a corresponding and grounding element in cognitional activity is to be eliminated.

Philosophy, in the primary meaning we have been outlining, is an ongoing process. It will always be possible to learn more about cognitional activity, and, consequently, further refinements in epistemology and metaphysics are also possible. On the other hand, philosophy in this sense is not subject to the radical revisions to which the natural sciences are subject. For the conditions of the possibility of a revision have to be admitted by any reviser and, when they are, they are found to coincide with the already proposed cognitional theory.

There remains the question of the independence of such a philosophy. In the first place, then, it is not independent of conscience, of man's ability to deliberate on what truly is good, to evaluate how good it is, to decide accordingly. On the contrary, the whole of philosophic investigation has been guided and ruled by a deliberate and conscientious pursuit of truth. Indeed, it is through total dependence on such guidance that philosophy attains what is meant by its independence.

I have been speaking of philosophy in what I believe to be its primary concern. But that primary concern is only a beginning. It provides a basic tool that has very many applications. It provides a nucleus to which further elements from other sources can be added. So there arises philosophy with a roving commission. If its various applications and the sundry additions are arranged in some order, philosophy becomes defined not by a fixed but by a moving viewpoint.

The significant order, I find, is reached by conceiving a horizon as a line of ongoing development, by conceiving a conversion as the repudiation of a less adequate and the acceptance of a more adequate horizon, and by distinguishing intellectual, moral, and religious conversion. By intellectual conversion I understand the elimination of blindspots with regard to human cognitional activity, its objectivity, and the reality it knows. It is the goal of what I have already called the primary concern of philosophy. By moral conversion I understand the shift of motivation from satisfactions to values. Such a conversion is the ground of ethical philosophy. For just as philosophy in its primary concern is guided and grounded by a conscientious pursuit of truth, so ethical philosophy is guided and grounded by a conscientious pursuit of value. By religious conversion, finally, I understand God's gift and man's acceptance of God's love (Romans 5.5; 8.38–39).

Now from a rationalist or deductivist viewpoint it may seem of great importance to determine just what is presupposed and just what is implied by any of the meanings attributed to the word 'philosophy.' But I believe such importance to be greatly reduced, if not to vanish, when the rationalist or deductivist viewpoint is rejected, when procedures are, not from premises to conclusions, but from data through understanding to judgments and decisions, when significant decisions are the highly personal and indeed existential matter of conversion, and when conversions are not logical consequences of previous positions but rather notable rejections of previous positions.

So with regard to Christian philosophy my views are rather humdrum. There is no philosophy that sets up an exigence for God's gift of his love, or that constitutes a sufficient preparation for that gift. There is a philosophy that is open to the acceptance of Christian doctrine, that stands in harmony with it, and that, if rejected, leads to a rejection of Christian doctrine.

With regard to God as mystery and God as meaning, I think the simplest answer is to refer to Aquinas's five ways of proving the existence of God. The article concludes with the statement that what has been proved to exist is what everyone means by God. But what is this meaning known by everyone? Is it that everyone in some fashion or other does prove the existence of God? Or is it that God gives sufficient grace to everyone, that the one sufficient grace is the gift of charity without which nothing else is of avail (1 Corinthians 13), that that gift orientates one to what is transcendent in lovableness, that that orientation can occur without any corresponding apprehension, that it can be, in Rahner's phrase, a content without a known object, that such a content is an orientation to the unknown, to mystery? Such an orientation to mystery, in my opinion, is a main source of man's search for God. As Pascal quoted in his *Pensées*: 'You would not be seeking for me unless you had already found me.'[6]

Finally, by a philosophy of God I would understand knowledge of God achieved by man as man. It is a nice theoretical issue that does not arise when thought becomes existential and personal. Then discourse on religion takes many forms of which the fullest is theological.

6 [See Blaise Pascal, *Pensées*, trans. with intro. A.J. Krailsheimer (Harmondsworth, Middlesex: Penguin Books Ltd., 1966) 314. Lonergan's own note at this point reads, 'Blaise Pascal, *Pensées*, VII, 553.']

I think that the papers by David Rasmussen[7] and Garrett Barden[8] are complementary. The intention of truth in myth, which is Barden's topic, is concerned with the object that a hermeneutic of recollection, desired by Rasmussen, would uncover. At the same time, Barden's account of a contemporary student's advance from mythic to critical consciousness is a case in which deserting the myth constitutes a liberation. My own contention in *Insight* that as metaphysics advances myth recedes is not to be taken out of context.[9] For Professor Rasmussen a myth is a symbolic narrative. In *Insight* there are two kinds of symbolic narratives: mysteries and myths.[10] I did not contend that as metaphysics advances, mysteries recede, and so I see no difficulty in finding room in my position for symbolic consciousness or for a hermeneutic of recollection.

At least from my viewpoint, the papers by Robert Johann[11] and by Schubert Ogden[12] are also complementary. The former relates me to John Dewey, the latter to Alfred North Whitehead, and both question my use of the word 'experience.' I employ it, not in the sense intended when one speaks of men of experience, but in the sense of a distinct type of cognitional activity which, however, does not normally occur without the occurrence of other types. Now I do not think that distinction presupposes separation, but it will be more helpful to avoid abstract argument and to draw attention to Professor Johann's claim that what I call an ongoing, self-correcting process of learning is just what Dewey means by experience. If Professor Ogden were to discover that Whitehead meant something similar when he took his stand on experience, the distance that separates us would in some measure be reduced.

Professor Johann proposes that I should borrow something from John Dewey's pragmatism. He finds a basis for this view in my own recognition of the subordination of experiencing, understanding, and judging to the fourth-level operations of deliberating on what truly is good, evaluating how good it is, and deciding what to do about it. Now this does imply that a moral

---

7 [David M. Rasmussen, 'From Problematics to Hermeneutics: Lonergan and Ricoeur,' in *Language Truth and Meaning* 236–71.]
8 [Garrett Barden, 'The Intention of Truth in Mythic Consciousness,' ibid. 4–32.]
9 [See Lonergan, *Insight* 566–67. For the context, see the entire discussion, pp. 554–72, under the heading 'Metaphysics, Mystery, and Myth.']
10 [Ibid.]
11 [Robert O. Johann, 'Lonergan and Dewey on Judgement,' in *Language Truth and Meaning* 79–92.]
12 [Schubert M. Ogden, 'Lonergan and the Subjectivist Principle,' ibid. 218–35.]

decision should lie at the root of cognitional enterprise. But it is a further point to claim that the grounds for a sound moral decision have been set forth by Dewey's pragmatism. If it is pragmatism to hold that men individually are responsible for their own lives and collectively they are responsible for the world in which they live, I have no hesitation about agreeing.

At the same time, I cannot regret the way I wrote *Insight*. My purpose was not a study of human life but a study of human understanding. My strategy was a moving viewpoint that gradually moved from simpler to more complicated types of understanding. My goal was to prepare the way for working out a method for theology.

Professor Ogden finds that I use the traditional term 'unrestricted understanding' without deriving it from my cognitional theory. I suggest that the derivation at least is indicated by the statement: '... such a procedure [from restricted to unrestricted understanding] not only is possible but also imperative. For the pure desire [to know] excludes not only the total obscurantism which arbitrarily brushes aside every intelligent and reasonable question, but also the partial obscurantism which arbitrarily brushes aside this or that part of the range of intelligent and reasonable questions that admit determinate answers.'[13]

I cannot directly discuss Professor Ogden's argument about possibility and actuality, for his precise meaning most probably has roots with which I am not familiar. In my own terms, however, I would distinguish possibility as something conceptual and potency as something real. Further I would distinguish active and passive potency. I would grant that potency and act are relevant categories for the whole of reality, that all finite beings are constituted by really distinct passive potency and act, and that God is constituted by really identical act and active potency. I do not conceive God as the actuation either of the totality of passive potency or of some notable part of passive potency. I conceive him as simply act, as identical with unrestricted active potency, and so as the ground of the possibility of all passive potency. Finally, I see no difficulty in an unrestricted act of understanding grasping that certain *possibilia* are not *compossibilia*.

However much Emerich Coreth and William Richardson differ from each other, they make a similar complaint about my position.[14] I recognise

---

13 Lonergan, *Insight* 644 [page 667 in the Collected Works edition].
14 [Emerich Coreth, 'Immediacy and the Mediation of Being: An Attempt to Answer Bernard Lonergan,' in *Language Truth and Meaning* 33–48, and William J. Richardson, 'Being for Lonergan: A Heideggerean View,' ibid. 272–83.]

a notion of being, a concept of being, theories of being, knowledge of being, and the idea of being. But I do not show proper concern for the Aristotelian topic of being as being. I speak of being not in terms of being but only in terms of the cognitional activities by which being is known or to be known. I analyze finite being into central and conjugate potencies, forms, and acts, but the meaning of these elements is reached not by profound metaphysical intuition or reflection but simply by their isomorphism with the structure of cognitional activity. If I am asked about the being of beings, the ontological difference, I take refuge in the adequate real distinction between central act and, on the other hand, central potency and form, or alternatively in the inadequate real distinction between central act and the subsistent being it actuates. If I am pressed to say what is the sense, the meaning, the intelligibility, of being as being, I am content to reply that to understand being is to understand everything about everything, that such understanding is unrestricted, and that unrestricted understanding pertains only to God. In brief, I hold that different beings have different essences, that only one being has being itself (*ipsum esse*) as its essence, and that to understand that being as being is to understand that essence.

The display of medieval metaphysics in these last paragraphs may lead the reader to suspect that really I do take over traditional concepts that have no place in my own explicit thinking. The fact is that my aim is *vetera novis augere et perficere*. Nor is my procedure haphazard. Basically it is a matter of deriving basic terms and relations from the data of consciousness, of accepting traditional metaphysics in the sense that is isomorphic with these basic terms and relations, and of rejecting traditional metaphysics in any sense that is not the to-be-known of human cognitional activity. Nor is this procedure gratuitous. It is the one way of systematically avoiding the verbalism to which the Aristotelian 'as such' is open and even prone.[15]

15 [In *Insight* (386) Lonergan assigns a 'general meaning for the phrase "being as being"' that accords with his position on being and his procedure in discussing being.]

67

Bernard Lonergan Responds (3)[1]

I must begin by thanking Giovanni Sala for presenting his masterful account of Kant largely in my terms[2] and, no less, William Ryan for his penetrating comparison of Husserl's and my own cognitional theory.[3] Xavier Monasterio extends this comparison by relating my work to that of Husserl particularly and of phenomenologists generally,[4] but I must enter a protest in favour of my philosophy teachers. They did not tell me all that

---

1   [Papers for a third volume of the International Lonergan Congress at Saint
    Leo's College (see above, p. 263, n. 1) were collected and prepared but it was
    decided not to proceed with publication. Clearly, Lonergan had access to the
    papers, and he comments here on fifteen of them. The titles of the papers are
    given here at the appropriate places, and mention is made when publication
    elsewhere is known to the editors. The typescripts of the papers can be found
    in the library of the Lonergan Research Institute, Toronto.]
2   [Giovanni Sala, 'The Notion of the A Priori in Kant's *Critique of Pure Reason* and
    Lonergan's *Insight.*' See Sala's published article 'The A Priori in Human Knowl-
    edge: Kant's *Critique of Pure Reason* and Lonergan's *Insight,*' *The Thomist* 40
    (1976) 179–221; subsequently published as chapter 1 in Giovanni B. Sala,
    Lonergan and Kant: Five Essays on Human Knowledge, trans. Joseph Spoerl,
    ed. Robert M. Doran (Toronto: University of Toronto Press, 1994) 1–32.]
3   [William F.J. Ryan, 'Intentionality in Edmund Husserl and Bernard Lonergan:
    The Perspectives of Intuition-Constitution and Affirmation.' See Ryan's paper
    'Intentionality in Edmund Husserl and Bernard Lonergan,' *International Philo-
    sophical Quarterly* 13 (1973) 173–90.]
4   [Xavier Ortiz Monasterio, 'Lonergan and Phenomenology' (16 pp.).]

I later discovered, but I doubt that I would have discovered very much had they not been such honest men.[5]

Vincent Potter has drawn a parallel between my position on causality and that of Charles Peirce.[6] He is correct in his surmise that I did not get my idea from Peirce. I got it from Aristotle's refutation of determinism, and my account of that may be read in an article published thirty years ago and, more recently, in book form under the title *Grace and Freedom*.[7]

Miss Anscombe's thought runs in the same direction.[8] For her causality is one thing and necessity another, so that it is not true to say that, posited the cause, the effect follows necessarily. In fact, the days of the necessary laws of physics and even of the iron laws of economics have been over for some forty years. Any universal law is abstract. It holds only under the proviso that other things are equal. Whether other things are equal is a matter of statistics, while the law itself has the intelligibility not of necessity but of verifiable possibility.

In chapter 8 of *Insight* I extended emergent probability to propose a theory of explanatory genera and species. Philip McShane, to whom we all are grateful for editing these volumes, has gone to work verifying that theory, and has found that biophysics and biochemistry, while they account for

5   [Lonergan is here responding to a comment in Monasterio's paper (p. 9, note 11) in which Lonergan is reported to have said that 'one of the reasons that had prompted him to enterprise his philosophical research had been the discovery that many of his professors of philosophy did not seem to have the slightest idea of what they were talking about.']

6   [Vincent Potter, 'Lonergan and Peirce on "Objective Chance": A Preliminary Sketch.' See Potter's later article 'Objective Chance: Lonergan and Peirce on Scientific Generalization,' *Method: Journal of Lonergan Studies* 12 (1994) 91–107.]

7   [Lonergan refers to *Grace and Freedom* (see above, p. 198, n. 3 and p. 266, n. 14). The pages of the 1971 edition to which he refers (77, 108, 113) correspond in the Collected Works edition, respectively, to pp. 79–80, 109–11, and 115.]

8   [G.E.M. Anscombe, 'On Causality,' an early, abridged version of a lecture later delivered in the University of Cambridge on 6 May 1971. The lecture was published, first, as *Causality and Determination: An Inaugural Lecture* (London: Cambridge University Press, 1971) and subsequently included under the title 'Causality and Determination' in *Metaphysics and the Philosophy of Mind*, vol. 2 in the Collected Philosophical Papers of G.E.M. Anscombe (Minneapolis: University of Minnesota Press, 1981) 133–47.]

much that goes on in a cell, do so only by bits and pieces that constitute no more than a coincidental manifold.[9]

Thomas Owens would raise the question whether my philosophy allows for intersubjective encounter.[10] I did not treat the matter in *Insight*. I do in my forthcoming book *Method in Theology*, where the first section of the third chapter draws on Max Scheler on intersubjectivity and the second section illustrates intersubjective meaning by outlining the phenomenology of a smile. Nor does my position offer any resistance to such an addition, for the position admits everything that can be experienced, understood, affirmed. Indeed, both the paper of Eric O'Connor[11] and the one by Cathleen M. Going[12] reveal not a little sympathy for *Insight* yet manage to be very much at home with the intersubjective dimensions of communication.

Timothy Fallon has extended my notions of horizon and conversion into a theory of collaboration.[13] Carl Bauer has found my philosophy of science relevant to a re-education of the re-educators concerned with leadership-group dynamics and organizational behavior.[14] Bernard McGinn has put together what is good and what is insufficient in my earlier remarks on history;[15] and I feel I can hope that chapters seven to ten of *Method in Theology* will remedy some of the deficiencies.

9   [Philip McShane, 'Image and Emergence: Towards an Adequate *Weltanschauung*,' published in McShane, *Plants and Pianos: Two Essays in Advanced Methodology* (Dublin: Milltown Institute of Theology and Philosophy, 1971) 12–56; published later in *The Shaping of the Foundations: Being at Home in the Transcendental Method* (Washington, DC: University Press of America, 1976) 6–45.]
10   [Thomas Owens, 'Does Lonergan's Philosophy Allow for Intersubjective Encounter?' (15 pp.).]
11   [R. Eric O'Connor, 'Towards an Articulation in Education of Transcendental Method,' subsequently published in the July 1973 issue of *The International Congress of University Adult Education Journal*, and in *Curiosity at the Center of One's Life: Statements and Questions of R. Eric O'Connor* (Montreal: Thomas More Institute Papers 84, 1987) 91–101.]
12   [Cathleen M. Going, 'Persons: A Study in Communications' (12 pp.).]
13   [Timothy P. Fallon, s.j., 'Horizon, Conversion and Collaboration' (17 pp.).]
14   [Carl E. Bauer, 'Bernard J.F. Lonergan's Philosophy of Science and Empirical Studies of Leadership-Group Dynamics and Organizational Behavior' (14 pp.).]
15   [Bernard McGinn, 'Bernard Lonergan and the Crisis in Historical Knowledge' (23 pp.). See McGinn's later article 'Critical History and Contemporary Catholic Theology: Some Reflections,' *Criterion* 20/1 (1981) 18–25, in which some of the paragraphs from this paper reappear.]

Rocco Cacopardo finds the first eighteen chapters of *Insight* highly acceptable but finds the last two unpalatable.[16] The root of our difference, I think, lies in the meaning we assign to the complete intelligibility of being. For me it is the exclusion of all obscurantism: at no point is it legitimate to brush aside arbitrarily any intelligent and reasonable question. To him it appears to be the arrogance of supposing that there are no questions that we cannot answer.

Both Donald Johnson[17] and Michael Novak[18] complain that I am not with it. The former would have me align myself more with Marx and Freud and Norman Brown. The latter would want me to think with Marx and Sartre. Neither seems to be aware that I am a child of the depression of the thirties and that I have an as yet unpublished paper on economic analysis as the premise for moral precepts.[19] I agree with Marx inasmuch as I find intrinsic to the developing economy a surplus. I disagree inasmuch as I have no doubt that it is a blunder to conceive this surplus as surplus value; it is to be understood and conceived, not in terms of marginal analysis, but in terms of macroeconomics. Again, I agree with Marx inasmuch as he finds the fact of surplus a source for moral indignation, but I disagree with him on his interpretation of the fact of surplus and on the moral conclusions he draws. Further, I agree with Marx inasmuch as he wants philosophers not only to know but also to make history, but I feel he made a very incomplete rejection of the mistaken efforts of Fichte, Schelling, and Hegel to restore the hegemony of speculative reason that had been attacked by Kant. After all, Marx is only a left-wing Hegelian. He does not really belong to the company of a Kierkegaard who took his stand on faith,

16 [Rocco Cacopardo, 'The Relevance of Lonergan for the Social Sciences' (29 pp.). This title, it seems, is not the author's own; it does not appear anywhere in the typescript.]

17 [Donald H. Johnson, 'Rational Evolution or Apocalyptic Vision: A Critique of Lonergan from the Standpoint of Norman O. Brown' (22 pp.).]

18 [Michael Novak, 'The Political Theology of Bernard Lonergan' (40 pp.).]

19 ['An Essay in Circulation Analysis,' dated 1944, which became part 3 of *For a New Political Economy*, vol. 21 in Collected Works of Bernard Lonergan, ed. with intro. Philip J. McShane (Toronto: University of Toronto Press, 1998), pp. 231–318. Lonergan returned to the manuscript in the late 1970s, and the results of that work are found in *Macroeconomic Dynamics: An Essay in Circulation Analysis*, vol. 15 in Collected Works of Bernard Lonergan, ed. Frederick G. Lawrence, Patrick H. Byrne, and Charles C. Hefling, Jr (Toronto: University of Toronto Press, 1999).]

of a Newman who took his stand on conscience, of a Dilthey concerned with a *Lebensphilosophie*, of a Blondel who wanted a philosophy of action, of the personalists and many existentialists of the present century, and of Paul Ricoeur's still unfinished *philosophie de la volonté*. With such men I am more easily in sympathy than with Jean-Paul Sartre or Norman Brown.

68

Foreword to David Tracy, *The Achievement of Bernard Lonergan*[1]

The attention accorded theologians in the latter part of the twentieth century is due, I think, less to themselves than to their times. For theology is a function not only of revelation and faith but also of culture, so that cultural change entails theological change. For over a century theologians have gradually been adapting their thought to the shift from the classicist culture, dominant up to the French Revolution, to the empirical and historical mindedness that constitutes its modern successor. During this long period there has been effected gradually an enormous change of climate. It crystallized, burst into the open, and startled the world at Vatican II. Earlier contributors to the movement made their mistakes and were denounced. Later contributors, despite their mistakes, not only are acclaimed but even have books written about them.

For twenty-five years I was a professor of theology, first in Montreal, then in Toronto, and, finally, for twelve years in Rome. I turned out the usual notes and handbooks, contributed to periodicals and wrote a long book on methods generally to underpin an as yet unfinished book on method in theology.[2] Insofar as I have been alert to what has been going forward in Catholic thought, perforce I have had my modest part in the contemporary process of renewal. But if I have lived to see the day when laborers in the theological vineyard are not without honor, I must bear witness that later fruits were made possible only by earlier planting, and watering, and God-given growth.

1 [New York: Herder and Herder, 1970, pp. xi–xii.]
2 [Lonergan is referring, of course, to *Insight* and *Method in Theology*.]

In the pages that follow, Professor Tracy is offering an introduction to my thought. He believed an introduction was needed because my work has been highly specialized, because it occurred outside the framework of the American university, and because the vastly increased audience for theological discourse implies a demand for information on what had been going forward in the past.

For his task Professor Tracy is notably qualified. He has read my books, followed the various courses I gave when he was a student in Rome, studied my notes and unpublished papers, and wrote his doctoral dissertation on the development of my thought on theological method up to 1965.[3] In our many conversations he has let me experience Schleiermacher's paradox, namely, that an intelligent interpreter will know the process of a writer's development better than the writer himself.

---

3 [David William Tracy, 'The Development of the Notion of Theological Methodology in the Works of Bernard J. Lonergan, s.j.,' Dissertation ad lauream in Facultate Theologica, Rome: Pontificae Universitatis Gregorianae, 1969.]

69

Foreword to Maria Shrady, *Moments of Insight: The Emergence of Great Ideas in the Lives of Creative Men*[1]

Ordinarily insights are a dime a dozen. They may make observation intelligent, speech witty, work efficient. But they also may be mistaken, relevant indeed to things as they are imagined, but irrelevant to things as they are.

Great insights do not differ from ordinary ones in any intrinsic manner. Their greatness is due to the fact that they occur at the culminating point of a long series of commonly unnoticed insights. What slowly, and perhaps secretly, has been going forward suddenly or in a brief and intense period comes fully into view. At times the moments of insight set forth in this book are moments of truth or moments of goodness as well. But perhaps the emphasis lies elsewhere. It is on change, discovery, intelligence. These are prerequisites of truth and goodness without necessarily attaining them.

The author has gone far and wide in her striking selection of creative moments. I liked the easy way in which quotations are introduced and informally annotated and the challenge to one's wits set by the non-chronological order of presentation. Many will find the book fascinating. It is good reading, a broad document on a notable feature of the human mind, a repository of great moments in great lives.

---

1 [New York: Harper & Row, 1972, p. vii.]

70

Foreword to Bernard Tyrrell,
Bernard Lonergan's Philosophy of God[1]

Students of man's mental operations fall into three classes. There are behaviorists, phenomenologists, and traditionalists. The behaviorists feel that human psychology is to be studied in the same manner as animal psychology, and, since they have no access to the immediate data of animal psychology, they rule out attention to the immediate data of human psychology. Phenomenologists, the more closely they follow Edmund Husserl, begin by bracketing external reality to concentrate all the more fully and freely on the content of our immanent, intentional operations. Traditionalists, finally, employ a faculty psychology: they advert to the immediate data of consciousness; but they go beyond the data to posit nonconscious faculties or potencies whence the conscious operations proceed.

These three classes provide no more than an initial orientation. They do not preclude subdivisions, overlaps, transitions. One may speak of 'intellect' or 'will' in accordance with common English usage and without any commitment to a faculty psychology. At the opposite pole, one may be a thoroughgoing Aristotelian and use the words to denote potencies because one wants a unified science with a metaphysics as the principle of unification and with the unification made effective by conceiving physical and psychological terms and relations as further determinations of metaphysical terms and relations.

My own writings are an instance of transition. I had been educated in the Aristotelian-Thomist tradition, and I had published two monographs

1 [Notre Dame: University of Notre Dame Press, 1974, pp. ix–x.]

on the thought of Aquinas.[2] My book *Insight* expressed a cognitional theory which, so far from depending on a metaphysics, presented a metaphysics derived from cognitional theory. Hence, though I used the English words 'intellect' and 'will,' my cognitional theory was an intentionality analysis and not properly a faculty psychology.

It remains that intentionality analysis has ulterior implications. They were not adverted to in *Insight*. They came to the fore in subsequent incidental papers and more fully in my *Method in Theology*. Where faculty psychology leans to a priority of intellect over will, intentionality analysis has to conceive questions and answers for deliberation as sublating questions and answers both for reflection and for intelligence. There follows a fuller and happier apprehension of the human person and, in particular, of the human person's approach to God.

In this later view chapter 19 of *Insight* appears incongruous. It approaches the question of God in the old manner of the Aristotelian-Thomist tradition and not in the new manner made possible by intentionality analysis. The point was amply and vigorously made in the Lonergan Congress of Easter Week, 1970.[3] In the present volume Fr Tyrrell, who had so much to do with the Lonergan Congress, gives full and professional treatment to the issues.

2 [The monographs first appeared in *Theological Studies*, 1941–42 and 1946–49. Later they were published in book form: *Verbum: Word and Idea in Aquinas*, ed. David B. Burrell (Notre Dame: University of Notre Dame Press, 1967, and London: Darton, Longman & Todd, 1968); *Grace and Freedom: Operative Grace in the Thought of St. Thomas Aquinas*, ed. J. Patout Burns (New York: Herder and Herder, and London: Darton, Longman & Todd, 1971). *Grace and Freedom* is now vol. 1 and *Verbum* vol. 2 in Collected Works of Bernard Lonergan; see above, p. 266, n. 14, and p. 5, n. 7.]

3 [Papers presented at the Congress have been edited by Philip McShane and published by Gill and Macmillan, Dublin, and by University of Notre Dame Press, Notre Dame, *Foundations of Theology*, 1971; *Language Truth and Meaning*, 1972. See above, p. 263, n. 1, and p. 275, n. 1.]

71

Foreword to Matthew L. Lamb, *History, Method, and Theology: A Dialectical Comparison of Wilhelm Dilthey's Critique of Historical Reason and Bernard Lonergan's Meta-Methodology*[1]

In this study Professor Matthew Lamb fits together Wilhelm Dilthey's concern with history, the political theology of Professor Johann B. Metz, and my work in method. It is this conjunction, I feel, that most calls for elucidation. For it rests not, as one might expect, on some genetic dependence, but on an overarching and somewhat complex dialectic. And it is this dialectic that both constitutes the unity of the study and informs the interpretation of the authors under examination.

Now dialectic denotes both conflict and movement. In this case the relevant conflict is between the promise of the Enlightenment and its fulfillment. There was promised that liberation of man under the rule of emancipated reason. But the implementation of that rule was entrusted to modern science; and modern science put its faith far less in the immanent reasonableness of the human spirit, far more in the embodiment of reason in experimental results and mathematical hardheadedness. So extrinsic a criterion and so abstruse a control, it can be argued, have done more for the mechanization than for the liberation of human life.

No less than conflict dialectic implies movement, and the relevant movement has been supplied by the ongoing development of modern science. For in the main, it was Newton's achievement that the eighteenth-century Enlightenment celebrated as the inauguration of a new

---

1 [Missoula, MT: Scholars Press, 1978, pp. ix–xii.]

era. But later achievements have kept shifting the meaning and enlarging the horizon of scientific endeavor. Even scientists have been slow to adapt their conceptions of science to real advances of their field. One can hardly be surprised if an even greater lag is discerned in adapting the ideals and norms of the new era to the ever changing embodiments of scientific reason.

One such change and enlargement was seen by Wilhelm Dilthey in the work of the German Historical School. For its technique was not correlation of measurements, and the coherence of its narratives was not secured by borrowing mathematical syntheses. If Kant's *Critique of Pure Reason* could supply the theoretical foundations that Hume had denied to Euclidean geometry and Newtonian mechanics, there still was needed a supplementary critique of historical reason. Where Kant had grounded an *Erklären* of things, Dilthey sought a *Verstehen* of concrete human living. For concrete human living was the very stuff of history, and with that stuff one became familiar only through a heightening of one's own conscious feeling, knowing, doing.

What Dilthey undertook and carried forward, he did not complete. At the turn of the century positivist views were still dominant in accounts of historical method. Even Dilthey's great follower, Ernst Troeltsch, was unable to break with historical relativism. Still, Dilthey's quest for foundations lived on in Husserl's transcendental phenomenology, while Dilthey's technique of a *Besinnung* that interprets not *Erfahrung* so much as *Erlebnis* continues in the various forms of hermeneutic phenomenology.

Meanwhile, however, the very notion of modern science was being transformed. The success of Einstein's special theory of relativity transposed the invariants of physics from the Euclidean image of space to the realm of empirical laws and theoretical principles. The investigation of the subatomic order led to ultimates that could be envisaged exclusively neither as wave nor as particle. Heisenberg's principle of indeterminacy ran counter to the universal determinism that had been vindicated by Laplace when he established the periodicity of the planetary system. The extension of the relevance of statistical theory from thermodynamics to quantum theory invited a further extension that introduced schedules of probabilities to replace Darwin's chance variations and his survival of the fittest. Finally, these revolutions in the natural sciences found an echo in rebellions against positivist domination in historical studies. In Germany there was Heussi's *Die Krisis des Historismus*; in France Henri-Irénée Marrou's *De la connaissance historique*; in England R.G. Collingwood's *Idea of History*; and even before these three, in the United States the penetrating essays of Carl Becker.[2]

The twentieth-century development of the notion of 'modern' science not only has cast a retrospective light on Dilthey's work, but also contributed to the ferment that in Roman Catholic circles prepared the way for the Second Vatican Council. So Lamb finds in my work an instance in which an awareness of contemporary mathematics and science led to a revision of traditional interpretations of Aquinas and of Aristotle. It brought to light, as well, a generalized empirical method that covers the learning process of common sense, the procedures of empirical science, the ways of historical scholarship, and the philosophic grounding of the objectivity of human knowledge. This grounding is placed in authentic subjectivity. It challenges the once seductive implementation of reason through experimental science. It invites thoughtful men and women to the self-understanding and self-appropriation that can follow from a heightened awareness of their own powers of attention, their own intelligence, their own reasonableness, their own conscientiousness. It founds a methodology that not only accounts for the diversity of specializations but also stresses the historicity of their past development and promotes their future interaction and collaboration.

It is the intrinsically practical aspect of my work on method that enables Lamb to relate it to the work of Johann B. Metz. For the latter's political theology has wide-ranging academic implications. Its specific difference seems to be twofold. Where other theology tended to center its attention on its justifying past, political theology would add concern with man's future. Where other theology in its medieval phase ambitioned the role of queen of the sciences and, more recently, has been content to stress the significance of religion for man's inner life, political theology assumes an interdisciplinary role and seeks an interdisciplinary setting. Indeed, its proper *Sitz im Leben* would be found in the projected Theological Research Center at the interdisciplinary University of Bielefeld, and with that project Metz himself is actively concerned.

Now with such a vision the dialectic of the Enlightenment moves to a new plane. For an interdisciplinary university carries on the aspirations for

2   [In *Method in Theology*, Lonergan refers to the following: Karl Heussi, *Die Krisis des Historismus* (Tübingen: Mohr, 1932), Henri-Irénée Marrou, *The Meaning of History* (Baltimore and Dublin: Helicon, 1966, an English translation of *De la connaissance historique*), R.G. Collingwood, *The Idea of History* (Oxford: Clarendon, 1946), and Carl Becker, *Detachment and the Writing of History* (Ithaca, NY: Cornell University Press, 1958).]

unity and comprehensiveness of the eighteenth-century *Encyclopédie*. At the same time the notion of science, inspired by Galilei, Descartes, Newton, is sublated by the advances of Einstein, Heisenberg, Darwin. The natural sciences are complemented by human studies. A future-oriented theology adds a corrective to a utilitarianism that denied limits to utility, and so set our activities, our policies, our institutions on the fatal course of exponential growth.

In endeavoring to communicate what I consider the overarching idea informing Lamb's study, I had to simplify the dialectic of the Enlightenment by taking as a base line the subsequent unfolding of natural science. In his own treatment of that dialectic, Lamb had to attend to a far larger scope of historical detail. In doing so he has displayed a great erudition. If his subject matter and style are at times difficult, the effort of drawing on his learning and of entering into his thought is highly rewarding.

72

Review of Frances Moore Lappé and
Joseph Collins (with Cary Fowler),
Food First: Beyond the Myth of Scarcity[1]

The authors' concern and intention had best be left in their own words:
'There is no such thing today as absolute scarcity. *Every country in the world
has the capacity to feed itself* ... Moreover we came to see that no society setting out to put Food First can tolerate the concentration of wealth and
power that characterizes most nations today. The heaviest constraint on
food production and distribution turns out to be the inequality generated
by our type of economic system – the system now being exported to the
underdeveloped countries as the supposed answer to their problems. We
are *not* saying merely that the solution lies in better distribution – getting
the food to the hungry instead of the well-fed. We are saying something
else: that food distribution only reflects the more fundamental issue of
who controls and who participates in the production process. Thus to
accept the challenge of Food First is to accept the challenge of confronting
the basic assumptions of our economic system' (7–8).

'Hungry people do and can and will feed themselves, if they are allowed
to do so. This qualifying phrase – "if they are allowed to do so" – is the
heart of our answer ... Instead of "How can we feed the world?" we now ask
an entirely different question: "What are we doing – and what is being
done in our name and with our money – to prevent people from feeding
themselves?" And "How should we work to remove those obstacles?"' (8)

1 Boston: Houghton Mifflin, 1977, 466 pp. [*Theological Studies* 39 (1978)
   198–99.]

The authors' procedure is not so much to expound what Colin Tudge has named *The Famine Business*[2] as to explode the myths that make that business plausible and so in the minds of most people respectable. Some forty-eight questions are presented as briefly as possible. Each has been raised over and over in the course of campaigning for Food First. Each is followed immediately by an answer that appeals to matters of fact; the facts are documented in thirty-one pages of footnotes; and the arguments are incisive.

Since myth tends to be a many-headed hydra, I cannot refer to each of the many issues raised, much less to the many points made on each issue. The best I can attempt is a few snippets that illustrate the style. Famines are not due to the population explosion: 'only about 44 percent of the earth's potentially arable land is under cultivation' (16). There is no general correlation between hunger and population: 'France has just about the same number of people for each cultivated acre as India. Taiwan, where most are adequately nourished, feeds twice as many people per acre as famine-endangered Bangladesh. And China, where starvation was eradicated in only twenty-five years, has twice as many people for each cropped acre as India' (17–18).

I warmly recommend this book and, as well, its associated Institute for Food and Development Policy. In particular, I would stress the word 'policy.' In a pluralistic society the human good may be greatly promoted by describing concrete evils and proposing concrete policies to remedy them. The reason for this is simple: one is appealing to the human conscience in its native and spontaneous working. On the other hand, an appeal to moral absolutes is tied in with ethical and/or theological systems. Such a system can be, of course, an accurate reflection on conscience and a helpful objectification. But reflection on conscience is no easier than reflection on insight. As there are many theories of human intelligence, so too there are many ethical systems. It is in this fashion that appeals to moral absolutes too easily lead to disputes, divisions, disharmony, ineffectiveness.

2   [Colin Tudge, *The Famine Business* (London: Faber and Faber, 1977).]

73

A Response to Fr Dych[1]

In the eleventh volume of his *Theological Investigations* Fr Rahner published a 47-page paper setting forth his 'Reflections on Methodology in Theology.' He began by expressing his embarrassment when asked to treat this topic for, while over the years he had touched upon methodological aspects of particular questions, he had never attempted to tackle the issue in its full range.[2] I think one has to accept some such view of Rahner's work. Dr Anne Carr of the University of Chicago Divinity School did a doctoral dissertation on Fr Rahner's views on method and found it necessary to reach them by inference from his writings on more particular topics.[3] And Fr Dych, to whose address I am to offer an appendage, reviewed Dr Carr's work favorably in *Theological Studies*.[4] But if Fr Rahner has not tackled the problem of method in a general fashion, he has given us an extremely penetrating account of the difficulties of that task at the present time. The work of a contemporary theologian, he has said, has to find a niche in the midst of an uncontrollable pluralism of theologies. This pluralism emerges out of an

---

1 [William J. Kelly, ed., *Theology and Discovery: Essays in Honor of Karl Rahner, S.J.* (Milwaukee: Marquette University Press, 1980) 54–57. Lonergan's response is to Dych's paper 'Method in Theology According to Karl Rahner,' ibid. 39–53.]
2 Karl Rahner, 'Reflections on Methodology in Theology,' *Theological Investigations* 11, trans. and ed. David Bourke (London: Darton, Longman & Todd, and New York: Seabury Press, 1974) 68–114.
3 [Anne Carr, *The Theological Method of Karl Rahner* (Missoula, MT: Scholars Press, 1977).]
4 [*Theological Studies* 39 (1978) 181–83.]

ongoing and incalculable development of human thought. His task can hardly be the contribution of a collaborator working on a common site on which a single building is being erected according to a settled plan that is known to all. On the contrary, he finds himself an alien, alone, isolated. He may work on the basis of a world of ideas, from certain premises, with certain philosophical preconceptions as his tools. But he can hardly fail to be aware that all such suppositions are subject to historical conditions and to the limitations of particular epochs. Yet such awareness does not make him capable of eliminating these limitations. For the first time in the history of theological thought, theology not only is conditioned by history but also is aware of being unable to overcome this conditioning.[5]

Such sentiments are not peculiar to Fr Rahner. Well before Vatican II, while I was teaching at the Gregorian, Fr Eduard Dhanis, who held a succession of high offices at the Gregorian and in the Roman Congregations, expressed to me his firm conviction that, while Catholic theologians agreed on the dogmas of the church, they agreed on little else. Finally, while Vatican II brought many blessings, it remains that Fr Rahner's paper on methodology in theology was begun in 1969 and that Fr Dhanis's contention that theologians were unanimous in their acceptance of the dogmas of faith only with difficulty can any longer be maintained.

It remains that Fr Rahner himself has very clear ideas on a particular method. He names it indirect method. He has given us a large sample of it in his *Foundations of Christian Faith*. It is a method that can be backed by appeals to the rules for the discernment of spirits for the second week of St Ignatius's *Spiritual Exercises*, to Newman's *Grammar of Assent*, to Polanyi's tacit knowledge, to articles by Eric Voegelin, and to my own account of 'Natural Right and Historical Mindedness.'[6]

---

5 Rahner, 'Reflections on Methodology in Theology' 74.
6 Ibid. 76–84. See also Karl Rahner, *Foundations of Christian Faith*, trans. and ed. William Dych (New York: Seabury Press, 1978) 8–9, 316–17; Eric Voegelin, 'Reason: The Classic Experience,' *The Southern Review* 10 (1974) 237–64; Eric Voegelin, 'The Gospel and Culture,' in *Jesus and Man's Hope*, ed. D.G. Miller and D.Y. Hadidian (Pittsburgh: Pittsburgh Theological Seminary, 1971) 59–101; Bernard Lonergan, 'Natural Right and Historical Mindedness,' *Proceedings: American Catholic Philosophical Association* 51 (1977) 132–43 [later published in *A Third Collection: Papers by Bernard J.F. Lonergan, S.J.*, ed. Frederick E. Crowe, s.j. (Mahwah, NJ: Paulist Press, and London: Geoffrey Chapman, 1985) 169–83.].

Nor is his contribution limited to such an indirect method. For if one understands by method, not something like 'The New Method Laundry'[7] or a book of recipes for a cook, but rather a framework for collaboration in creativity and, more particularly, a normative pattern of related and repeated operations with ongoing and cumulative results, then I believe one will find ways to control the present uncontrollable pluralism of theologies, one will cease to work alien, alone, isolated, one will become aware of a common site with an edifice to be erected, not in accord with a static blueprint, but under the leadership of an emergent probability that yields results proportionate to human diligence and intelligence. In brief, I should say that Fr Rahner has laid down the conditions and expounded the need for a radical development in theological method. Such insight into the needs of contemporary theology are, to my mind, a remarkable confirmation of the widely held view that Fr Rahner has been among the foremost doctrinal theologians of his age.

It remains that my own concern has been less with developing doctrines than with discovering how one develops them with method. A first point, of course, is that 'method' means different things in different historical contexts. Perhaps the most celebrated was Descartes's proposal that we begin from indubitable truth and proceed by deduction, even to the point of deducing the conservation of momentum from the immutability of God. In contrast, Hans-Georg Gadamer's great work on *Wahrheit und Methode, Truth and Method*,[8] has been understood to take 'method' in a Cartesian sense and to contend that the search for truth was what counted while 'method' was an obstacle.

My own thought on method began in England where I studied philosophy. H.W.B. Joseph's *Introduction to Logic*[9] not only grounded one thoroughly in the Aristotelian syllogism but also offered an instructive introduction to scientific procedures, an account that was broadened by some knowledge of the calculus and of the logical inadequacy of Euclid's argumentation. Then Newman's *Grammar of Assent* charmed me with its convincing account that common sense does not develop in accord with

---

7 [See Bernard Lonergan, *Method in Theology* 5–6: '… method is often conceived as a set of rules that, even when followed blindly by anyone, none the less yield satisfactory results. I should grant that method, so conceived, is possible when the same result is produced over and over, as in the assembly line or "The New Method Laundry." But it will not do, if progressive and cumulative results are expected.']

8 [See above, p. 269, n. 18.]

9 [See above, p. 10, n. 19.]

the rules of syllogism. From Newman I went to Plato and from Plato to Augustine's early dialogues at Cassiacum. I studied theology in Rome where among my companions was an Athenian who had studied philosophy at Louvain, was at home with Maréchal, and taught me what was meant by the statement that human knowledge was discursive, not a matter of taking a look with the eyes of the mind, but of asking questions and coming to know when one chanced upon satisfactory answers.[10] Doctoral work on Aquinas's development of the concept of actual grace and on the dependence of concepts on understanding helped me towards a rounded view.

So by 1949 I began to work out my notion of method as a Generalized Empirical Method. A first stage was the book *Insight*, which found common features in mathematics, physics, common sense, and philosophy, and later, with help from Hans-Georg Gadamer, in interpretation and history.

I recount these strange *faits divers* because they throw some light on my perhaps stranger opinions. I list them with some attempt at order.

First, metaphysics is first in itself but it is not first for us. What is first for us on a reflective level is our own conscious and intentional activities. Such reflection must not presuppose metaphysics, else the metaphysics will not be critical, and so it does not speak of potencies and habits, however implicit, but only of conscious and intentional events and their experienced interrelations.

Second, as Vernon Gregson has remarked,[11] such reflection is like a therapy. Just as Carl Rogers's client-centered therapy aims at having the client discover in himself the feelings he cannot name or identify, so reflection on one's interior operations is a matter of coming to name, recognize, and identify operations that recur continuously but commonly are thought to be very mysterious. Insights are a dime a dozen, most of them are inadequate when taken singly, but far too many people are certain either that they do not exist or at least are excessively obscure.

Third, the omission of talk about potencies and habits and concentration on events and their experienced relations pulls thought out of the realm of faculty psychology into that of intentionality analysis. That yields a psychology of data, questions, and answers, with the questions on the three

---

10 [The Athenian was a fellow Jesuit whose name was Stefanos Stefanu. See Bernard Lonergan '*Insight* Revisited,' in *A Second Collection*, 265.]

11 [Vernon Gregson, *Lonergan, Spirituality, and the Meeting of Religions* (Lanham, MD: University Press of America, 1985) 10–15.]

levels of questions for intelligence, questions for sufficient reason for factual judgments, and questions for evaluation and decision.

Fourth, this makes the precedence of intellect on will like the precedence of sense on intellect. It makes it just what normally happens. It does not exclude divine operation directly on the fourth level. As St Paul instructed the Romans: God's love has flooded our inmost hearts by the Holy Spirit he has given us [Romans 5.5]. Such flooding hardly can be due to some intellectual apprehension in this life, especially since the mystics are given to celebrating their cloud of unknowing.

Fifth, at this point Generalized Empirical Method becomes theological. The transition may be illustrated by the words of our Lord to St Peter, 'Blessed art thou, Simon Bar Jonah, for flesh and blood has not revealed this to thee but my Father who is in heaven' (Matthew 16.17), words that Eric Voegelin contrasts with the words to the other disciples, 'Tell no man that I am the Christ' (see Matthew 16.20). The two, Voegelin contrasts as *revelation*, the Father to Peter, and *information*, the words of the disciples to every Tom, Dick and Harry. A similar doctrine is to be had from John 6.44–45, and John 12.32. Besides the inner gift of the spirit, there is the sensible spectacle of Christ on the cross. With those steps we are already into Christian theology.

74

Foreword to Michael C. O'Callaghan, *Unity in Theology: Lonergan's Framework for Theology in Its New Context*[1]

The problem is familiar. Traditional theology knew many divisions and subdivisions. But the success of the German Historical School has added a new dimension to all of them, to emphasize their separateness, and to make unity less a problem for highly specialized professors than for disoriented students.

Such in brief is the new context of theology. But this book also offers a new context for Lonergan's framework. The old context was the cognitional theory presented in *Insight*. The new context comes out of the German theological milieu where contemporary theologians unify their work in different manners: Pannenberg stresses theology's scientific character; Rahner its churchly role; Metz the timeliness of its summons. Each of the three emphasizes a necessary quality. Each treats the same material object in a different manner. But together they offer not one theology but three overlapping theologies. The problem of unity remains.

In this fashion Dr O'Callaghan keeps the issue not only purely theological but also contemporary and concrete. His work was done at Tübingen, and his numerous, extensive, and apposite quotations from influential German theologians reveal an enviable mastery of the current situation. His anticipation of objections brings to light his searching exploration of opposed viewpoints. His treatment of them is both inconspicuous and persuasive. Finally, while his work is specialist, still it solidly if only implicitly recalls specialists from totalitarian ambitions.

---

1 [Lanham, MD: University Press of America, 1980, p. xiii.]

Appendix: Correspondence on Lonergan's Review of Dietrich von Hildebrand, *Marriage*[1]

[1 / 30 May 1942]

The Editor
The Canadian Register

Dietrich v. Hildebrand may be confusing in his definition of what is the primary end of marriage, as Rev. Bernard Lonergan, s.j., suggests in his review of the former's book on 'Marriage,' but I think he may be in a little better company than where Father Lonergan has placed him.

For even the official pronouncements of the church are confusing – if not contradictory. In Canon Law we are told that the primary end of marriage is the procreation and education of children. But in the Roman Catechism, issued by the Council of Trent, it is said that man and woman should be joined together in Holy Matrimony, first of all, for companionship and mutual assistance in bearing more easily the discomforts of life and the infirmities of old age, and secondly, for the procreation and education of children.

---

1   [Lonergan's review of von Hildebrand's book *Marriage* (see above, pp. 153–56) sparked a brief exchange of letters in *The Canadian Register*, 30 May 1942, p. 9; 6 June 1942, p. 9; 13 June 1942, p. 10; 20 June 1942, p. 9. The correspondence is included here because of the relevance of the issues to Lonergan's 'Finality, Love, Marriage,' published in 1943 in *Theological Studies*, and now available as chapter 2 in *Collection*. See the editorial notes on this piece, ibid. esp. 258–59.]

In 'Casti Connubii' the late Holy Father affirms that what the Roman Catechism teaches on marriage is true. And yet Canon Law is quite specific on the point.

Would Father Lonergan care to clarify the situation?

BACHELOR

[2 / 6 June 1942]

The Editor
The Canadian Register

To an anonymous correspondent it appears that my review of Dr von Hildebrand's book on 'Marriage' was too severe because Canon Law, the Roman Catechism, and the Encyclical 'Casti Connubii' are confusing if not contradictory on the primary end of marriage.

First, then, the alleged opposition between the documents in question is fictitious. When Canon Law states that the primary end of marriage is the proper rearing of children, it refers (a) to marriage in the strict sense of the term and (b) to an objective finality that exists whether anyone ever thinks of it or not. The passage alleged from the Encyclical explicitly is speaking of marriage in what it terms a broad sense. The passage alleged from the Roman Catechism cannot be shown to be dealing with the objective ends of marriage or with their hierarchy; on the contrary, it can be argued very solidly that it is dealing with the intentions or motives of prospective husbands or wives; see II, VIII, 13 and 14.

Second, Dr von Hildebrand is in full agreement with Canon Law on the primary end of marriage, nor can your correspondent fairly say that I implied or suggested the contrary. Accordingly his appeal to the Encyclical and to the Roman Catechism seems beside the point.

BERNARD LONERGAN, S.J.

[3 / 13 June 1942]

The Editor
The Canadian Register

I am very grateful to Father Lonergan for his reply to my letter and query on Marriage. However, I am afraid it is not quite satisfactory.

In his letter he says that it can be very strongly argued that the Roman Catechism deals only with motives or intentions. That may be, but to what avail? In 'Casti Connubii' the late Holy Father says: 'The mutual inward molding of husband and wife, this determined effort to perfect each other, can in a very real sense, as the Roman Catechism teaches, be said to be the chief reason and purpose of matrimony, provided matrimony be looked at not in the restricted sense as instituted for the proper conception and education of the child, but more widely as a blending of life as a whole and the mutual interchange and sharing thereof.' It is quite evident from the foregoing that the late Holy Father quite definitely considered that the Roman Catechism dealt with objective ends, and not merely motives or intentions.

Also, from the foregoing, it would seem quite correct to say that if Marriage is considered from the viewpoint of 'a way of life,' then mutual aid and assistance is the primary end. And secondly, that if Marriage is considered in the restricted sense, then procreation is the primary end.

In other words, the apparent contradiction between Canon Law and the Roman Catechism can perhaps be explained by the fact that Marriage has two equal aspects, each of which has its own ends.

Incidentally, I hope Father Lonergan has no objection to my remaining anonymous, if not a

BACHELOR

[4 / 20 June 1942]

The Editor
The Canadian Register

I am extremely grateful to your correspondent on Marriage, still anonymous if now doubtfully a bachelor, for his at least tacit concession of the two points made in my previous letter. His second letter does not attempt to deny that his first letter had nothing to do either with Dr Hildebrand's book or my review. Further, so far from finding that the Roman Catechism, Canon Law, and the Encyclical 'Casti Connubii' are confusing if not contradictory, he now agrees that the Encyclical drew a distinction, and on this basis he proceeds to do a bit of theological speculation on his own.

This speculation stands or falls with its fundamental assertion that the Holy Father evidently was speaking of the objective ends of marriage in a passage quoted from the Encyclical. I object to the word 'evidently.' If the Holy Father was evidently speaking of the objective ends of marriage, he could and would have used the term 'end,' 'finis,' which is found in all philosophic, theological, and juridical treatises as well as in Canon Law. In point of fact, the Holy Father avoided the term 'end' and spoke of 'reason and purpose,' 'ratio et causa.' Further, he indicated a parallel to his statement, the Roman Catechism, where one does not find 'finis' but only 'causa.' The meaning of 'causa' in the Catechism is illustrated by the wealth, station, and good looks of the prospective bride, and on this ground seems to mean not objective end but motive or intention. Accordingly, since what your correspondent affirms to be evident is, in fact, not evident, and since the rest of his position stands on that affirmation, I may perhaps consider myself absolved from discussion of his other assertions.

Now your correspondent will not find this any more satisfactory than my previous letter. What he wants is a treatise on the whole problem of the end of marriage. What he does not seem to realize is that such a treatise would require at least two or three years' work and, when it was written, would not be accepted for publication in *The Canadian Register.*

BERNARD J.F. LONERGAN

Lexicon of Latin and Greek Words and Phrases

---

actu: actually, in act

Amor procedens: proceeding Love

an sit? is it? is it so?

beatitudo perfecta est soli Deo naturalis: perfect beatitude is natural to God alone

bonum est diffusivum sui: the good is diffusive of itself

cui convenit secundum suam substantiam movere seipsam, vel agere se quocumque modo ad operationem: to which it is proper by reason of its substance to move itself or to activate itself in whatever way to its operation

de quibusdam aliis: about some other things

dictum de omni: predicated of every instance

disciplina arcani: discipline of secrecy (withholding the mystery of faith from some)

ens ut sic: being as such

epieikeia: fairness, reasonableness [in adjustments to strict justice]

exigetive de ratione subjecti: demanded by reason of the subject

Fecisti nos ad te, Domine: You have made us for yourself, Lord

finis ultimus: ultimate end

fontana Deitas: overflowing Godhead ['communicating the Infinite Good to Son and Spirit and finite good to creatures']

formale quo: formal [object] by which

formale quod: formal [object] which

haecceitas: thisness

homo assumptus: an assumed human being

ideo Filius quia Verbum: therefore [he is] Son precisely because [he is] the Word

index onomasticus: index of names

in fieri qua in fieri: in becoming as in becoming

in puris naturalibus: in the state of pure nature

intelligentia fidei: the understanding of the faith

libertas errandi: liberty to err

lumen gloriae: the light of glory

medium sub quo: the medium under which

modus tollendo ponens: mode of affirming by denying; literally, mode which by taking away affirms [The example Lonergan gives on p. 37 is 'He is either a knave or a fool; he is not a knave; therefore he is a fool.']

nihil amatum nisi praecognitum: nothing is loved unless first it is known

nihil in intellectu nisi prius fuerit in sensu: there is nothing in the intellect unless it was first in sense

nihil in natura frustra: nothing in nature is in vain

ordo doctrinae: the order of teaching

per partes proportionales/aliquotas: *partes proportionales* are parts that diminish in size according to a ratio (eg., 1:2); *partes aliquotae* are parts of a determinate quantity.

per speciem alienam: through the species of something else

petitio principii: begging the question

potentia obedientialis activa: active obediential potency

quae utilitas in sanguine meo?: what is the use of my [shedding] blood?

quidquid movetur, ab alio movetur: whatever is moved is moved by another

quod se intelligit, dicitur se movere: what understands itself is said to move itself

ratio essendi: the reason/cause of being

ratio ratiocinandi: the reason/cause of reasoning

reductio ad impossibile: reduction to the impossible

secundum dici: [real relations] entailed in the being of something [as, e g , to be created]

secundum esse: [real relations] whose being is to be a relation [as, e.g., 'Son']

sensibile per accidens: sensible by accident (that is, not *per se* but in and through what is sensible *per se*)

sensibile per se: sensible *per se*

sensibilis demonstratio: sensible demonstration

sensibilis demonstratio seu resolutio facta ad sensum: sensible demonstration or resolution to sense

sensus fidelium: the common consent of the faithful

Socrates, dum sedet, necessario sedet: while Socrates is sitting, he is necessarily sitting

syllogismus expositorius: expository syllogism [above, p. 5, n. 8: 'one that admits of singular terms and premises or, in a more restricted sense, one in which the middle term is singular']

vera carnis passione: with the real suffering of the flesh

verbum spirans amorem: the word that spirates love

vetera novis augere et perficere: to augment and perfect the old with the new

via doctrinae: way of teaching

vis cogitativa: the cogitative faculty/sense [L: 'a sensitive potency ... which operates under the influence of intellect and prepares suitable phantasms']

zōon logikon: rational animal

Index